Guide to Tanzania

Guide to
Tanzania

Philip Briggs

BRADT PUBLICATIONS, UK
HUNTER PUBLISHING, USA

First published in 1993 by Bradt Publications, 41 Nortoft Rd, Chalfont St Peter, Bucks SL9 0LA, England.
Distributed in the USA by Hunter Publishing Inc., 300 Raritan Center Parkway, CN94, Edison, NJ 08810.
Distributed in Southern Africa by Media House Publications, PO Box 782395, Sandton 2146, South Africa.

British Library Cataloguing in Publication data

A catalogue record for this book is
available from the British Library

ISBN 094 698 3 99 2

Additional research by Laura Grant.
Cover photos: front, Tanzanian woman by Jack Grove; cheetah by James Davis (James Davis Travel Photography); back, Kilimanjaro by Rod Grant.
Maps by Hans van Well.
Typeset from the author's disc by Patti Taylor, London NW10 1JR.
Printed by the Guernsey Press, Channel Islands.

v

Acknowledgements

Thank you Laura Grant, once again, for keeping me company for the six months we spent in East Africa, for your valuable input and support throughout, and for keeping things in perspective when I didn't. Also on the home front, thanks to Beyers Bezuidenhout for your company, support, faith and, naturally, the endless flow of wine; and to my brother Ant, for providing me unasked with a one-man faxing and printing service.

In no particular order, I would like to thank Dr Alan Tye for putting us up in Amani; Denise Charlton for information on Rungwa and Tabora; Charlotte Uhlerbroek for info on Gombe Stream and Mahale and for writing to confirm ferry timetables; Sally-Anne for details on Gombe Stream; Msafiri Allan Shomari for the hospitality, dancing and endless supply of beer when we were stuck in Ikola; Terri, Oliver and Steven at Hoopoe Tours, and the two Williams, our guide and cook in the Serengeti; the staff of Impala Tours; Kelvin Moody for a variety of snippets around the country; Stef, who we kept crossing paths with around Arusha, for his highly welcome sense of the absurd; Louise at Kilwa for her company; Steven Bell, who wrote to Bradt Publications with information on Tanzania for Backpacker's Africa, much of which ended up in this guide; the manager of the Bandorini Hotel in Tanga for info on the Usambara; the manager of the Iringa Hotel for the serenade on guitar; the German missionary we met at Matema but never exchanged names with, for background info on the Mbeya region; Howard Geech of the Conservation Corporation and the person I spoke to on the phone at the Wilderness Leadership School (both in South Africa) for advice relating to the Creatures Great and Small section; Dr Jane Wilson, for her section on health; and David Else, who wrote the Zanzibar chapter.

Many other travellers passed on useful bits and pieces. And there must be hundreds of Tanzanians who helped us out in various ways: finding us a room when we arrived in town after dark, acting as spontaneous guides, doing their best to explain things to us despite our appalling Swahili and passing on bits of information we may otherwise have missed. Thank you all.

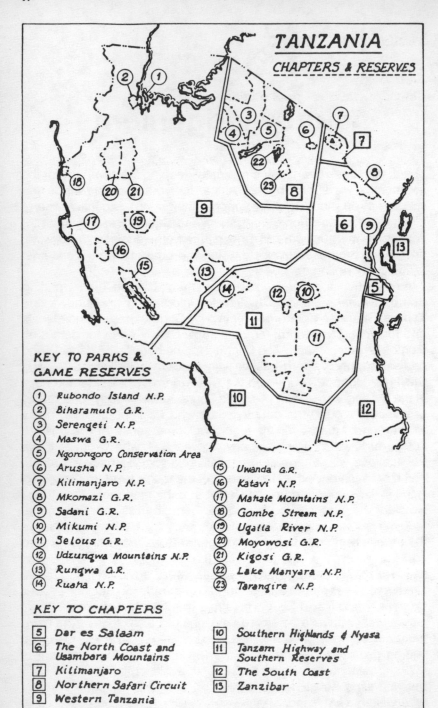

TANZANIA
CHAPTERS & RESERVES

KEY TO PARKS & GAME RESERVES

1. Rubondo Island N.P.
2. Biharamulo G.R.
3. Serengeti N.P.
4. Maswa G.R.
5. Ngorongoro Conservation Area
6. Arusha N.P.
7. Kilimanjaro N.P.
8. Mkomazi G.R.
9. Sadani G.R.
10. Mikumi N.P.
11. Selous G.R.
12. Udzungwa Mountains N.P.
13. Rungwa G.R.
14. Ruaha N.P.
15. Uwanda G.R.
16. Katavi N.P.
17. Mahale Mountains N.P.
18. Gombe Stream N.P.
19. Ugalla River N.P.
20. Moyowosi G.R.
21. Kigosi G.R.
22. Lake Manyara N.P.
23. Tarangire N.P.

KEY TO CHAPTERS

5. Dar es Salaam
6. The North Coast and Usambara Mountains
7. Kilimanjaro
8. Northern Safari Circuit
9. Western Tanzania
10. Southern Highlands & Nyasa
11. Tanzam Highway and Southern Reserves
12. The South Coast
13. Zanzibar

Table of Contents

MAPS *in this book*

adhere, more or less, to the following conventions:-

International Boundary

Provincial or Regional Boundary

National Park, Nature or Game Reserve
  (Entrance also shown)

Motorway, Major Highway
  (Plus Road Reference)

Other Major Road

Secondary Road

(METALLED) (ROUGH)

Track (may be seasonal)

Path, Bridleway or Trail

Railway & Railway Station

("NORMAL") (NARROW GAUGE)

Bridge; Embankment; Viaduct

Cutting; Tunnel

Cable Car or Chairlift

Power Cables; Pipeline

Bus Station; Taxi Rank

Airport or Airstrip

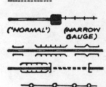

(INTERNATIONAL) (OTHER)

Coast or Shoreline

Lake; Seasonal Lake, Swamp or Marsh

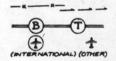

River; Seasonal River

Waterfall or Cataracts; Dam

River (Town Maps)

Canal; Lock

Wharf, Pier or Jetty; Marina or Docks

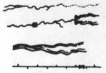

Ford; Ferry

Spring or Well-head

Travelling Distances - km [hrs] {days}

Recommended Route

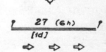

x

MAPS in this book

adhere, more or less, to the following conventions:-

Mountain, Peak, Hill or Volcanic Cone	▲ (or ∧)
Spot Height (m.) ; Contour Line (m.)	• 100 ; ---(100)--
Cliff or steep slope ; Ridge	⊥⊥⊥⊥ ; ⊥⊥⊥⊤⊤⊤⊤
Ravine ; Crater	;
Rocks ; Lava Flow ; Cave	; ; ∩
Cities, Towns, Villages (According to Size or Importance)	
Chapter Reference ; Map Key Reference	5 ; ⑬
Forest or Woodland ; Park or Garden	
Plantation or Farm ; Cemetery, Burial Gnd.	
Oilfield ; Factory or Industrial Area	
Market	MKT.
Post Office ; Telephone ; Bank	✉ ; T ; £$
Hospital, Medical Centre ; Official Building	✚ ; ⊠
Sports Centre or Stadium	⬭
Hotel, Hostel or Pension	H
Hut, Refuge or Lodge	⌂
Campsite	Ⴥ
Restaurant or Bar	Ⴘ
Educational or Cultural Establishment	
Ancient Monument or Historic Site	▽
Castle, Palace ; Religious Building	; ◆
Lighthouse ; Tower or Mast	; △
Other Buildings	

INTRODUCTION

It would be easy to reduce an introduction to Tanzania to a list of statistics: it contains Africa's highest mountain, most famous national park and largest game reserve, while along its borders lie the three largest lakes on the continent. It would be just as easy to reduce Tanzania to a list of evocative place names: Zanzibar, Kilimanjaro, Serengeti, Dar es Salaam, Ngorongoro Crater, Olduvai Gorge, Gombe Stream, Lake Victoria...

Put simply, Tanzania embodies the Africa you have always dreamed of: vast plains teeming with wild animals, rain forests alive with cackling birds and monkeys, Kilimanjaro's snow-capped peaks rising dramatically above the surrounding flat scrubland, colourful Maasai herding their cattle alongside herds of grazing wildebeest, and perfect palm-lined beaches lapped by the clear warm waters of the Indian Ocean stretching as far as the eye can see. Almost 25% of the country is given over to conservation, protecting an estimated 20% of Africa's large mammals.

You might expect a country that can be described in such superlative terms to be crawling with tourists, but in the 1980s Tanzania attracted a fraction of the tourism of countries like Kenya, South Africa and more recently Zimbabwe. This was for a variety of reasons: an underfunded and underdeveloped tourist infrastructure, a reputation for corruption and bureaucracy, persistent food and fuel shortages, poor roads and inefficient public transport, and a lack of exposure. This is changing, however, and what started off as a trickle of tourism in the late-1980s could soon become a flood. New hotels are being built, main roads have been re-surfaced, trains and ferries run on time, shortages are a thing of the past, and in our experience you couldn't hope to meet more agreeable officials anywhere.

For the average fly-in, fly-out tourist, Kilimanjaro, Zanzibar and the Serengeti are justification enough to visit Tanzania. For the adventurous traveller who is prepared to put up with basic accommodation and slow transport and who is prepared to learn a bit of KiSwahili, the national language, it is one of the most challenging, rewarding and fascinating countries in Africa. Virtually anywhere south of the Dar es Salaam-Mwanza railway line is miles from any beaten tourist track — except for Kigoma and Mbeya, both important junctions for overlanders, we spent two months in this part of Tanzania without seeing another traveller.

When you spend a long time in a country, your feelings towards it are determined as much by the people who live there as by the sights you see. My affection for Tanzania is greater than for any other African country I have visited. It is an oasis of peace and egalitarian values in a continent stoked-up with political and tribal tensions, and its social mood embodies all that I respect in African culture. I found Tanzanians to be polite and courteous, yet also warm and genuine, both amongst each other and in their dealings with foreigners.

Enjoy Tanzania. It's a wonderful country.

Notes

Swahili names

In KiSwahili, a member of a tribal group is given an m- prefix, the tribe itself gets a wa- prefix and the language gets a ki-prefix (for example, an Mgogo person is a member of the wagogo who speak kigogo). The wa- prefix is commonly but erratically used in English books; the m- and ki- prefixes are rarely used, except for in the case of KiSwahili. There are no apparent standards; in many books the Swahili are referred to as just the Swahili while non-Swahili tribes get the wa- prefix. I have decided to drop all these prefixes: it seems as illogical to refer to non-Swahili people by their KiSwahili name when you are writing in English as it would be to refer to the French by their English name in a German book. I have, however, referred to the Swahili language as KiSwahili on occasion.

Lake Nyasa/Malawi

Many readers may not realise that Lake Nyasa and Lake Malawi are one and the same. Nyasa was the colonial name for the lake, just as Nyasaland was the colonial name for what is now the country of Malawi. For historical reasons, the name Nyasa has been retained in Tanzania and it is used both officially and casually; if you ask a Tanzanian about Lake Malawi they will either look at you blankly or tell you to go to Malawi. Despite the initial confusion it may cause, for the purposes of this guide I have referred to the lake as Lake Nyasa.

Some words you might wonder about...

There are a few terms that crop up occasionally in the text which you might not know. Some are explained elsewhere, but this is as good a place as any to put them all together. *Koppie* (or *kopje*) is an Afrikaans word which in East Africa is used to refer to a small free-standing hill such as those which dot the Serengeti Plains. A *Hoteli* is a local restaurant. *Miombo* and *Acacia* are types of woodland; the first dominated by broad-leaved trees belonging to a variety of families, the second dominated by thorny, thin-leaved trees of the acacia family. The *Cichlids* are a family of colourful fish found in the Rift Valley lakes. A *banda* is a hut.

Planning an Itinerary

Tanzania's main tourist circuit centres around Zanzibar, Dar es Salaam, Kilimanjaro and the northern game reserves. If you only have two or three weeks in the country and plan on visiting Zanzibar, climbing Kilimanjaro and going on safari, you are unlikely to be able to fit much else in. If you have a few extra days, however, or don't want to climb Kilimanjaro, you could include just about anywhere covered in Chapter Six in your itinerary, or could think about climbing Mount Meru or visiting Pemba Island.

The itinerary below is fairly typical, and includes a five-day safari and three nights on Zanzibar. You would need an extra five or six days to climb Kilimanjaro.

Day 1	Dar es Salaam
Day 2	Catch a bus to Arusha
Day 3-4	Organise safari from Arusha, book train for day 10
Day 5-9	Safari; sleep night 9 in Arusha
Day 10	Overnight train to Dar es Salaam
Day 11-13	Zanzibar
Day 14	Return to Dar es Salaam
Day 15	Fly home

Beyond this, it is difficult to recommend any particular itinerary. Tanzania is a large, diverse country, transport there is slow, and people's tastes and interests differ. Unless you have a lot of time — six weeks at least — you are unlikely to be able to do more than concentrate on a couple of particular areas. Whatever you do, allocate your time reasonably generously; if you don't you are likely to spend most of your trip on public transport.

To give you some idea, if you wanted to visit Rubondo Island, you would be looking at a 10 to 14 day round trip from Dar es Salaam, and even Gombe Stream would be a week's round trip. The south coast could be explored comfortably over seven to 10 days, the Udzungwa Mountains would be a good four to five day trip, the southern highlands and Lake Nyasa would be good for anything over a week, and the Selous is normally visited on a four to five day safari.

Visitors who have a longer period of time could do one of a few loops: you could, for instance, catch a train to Mbeya, spend a few days exploring around Tukuyu, cross to Mtwara via Lake Nyasa and Songea and then work your way up the south coast. Another possibility from Mbeya is to work your way up to Mwanza via Lake Tanganyika taking in some of the western national parks on the way, then catch a bus across the Serengeti to Arusha and return to Dar es Salaam from there. For either of these trips, you would want around a month.

When it comes to really off-the-beaten-track hiking, the only limitations are your imagination. Even a small-scale map of Tanzania throws up plenty of alluring possibilities, some of which are mentioned under *Hiking* in Chapter Two.

Part one

2

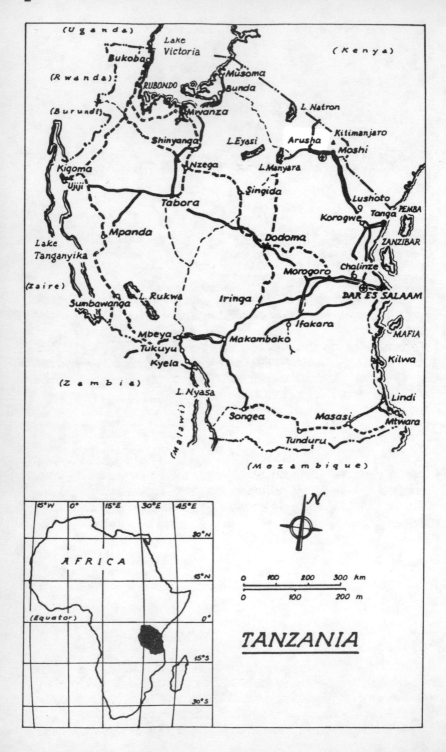

TANZANIA

Chapter One

Background information

FACTS AND FIGURES

Location

The United Republic of Tanzania was formed in 1964 when Tanganyika on the African mainland united with the offshore island state of Zanzibar.

Tanzania lies on the east African coast between 1° and 11°45' south, and 29°20' and 40°35' east. It is bordered by Kenya and Uganda to the north; Rwanda, Burundi and Zaire to the west, and Zambia, Malawi and Mozambique to the south.

Size

Tanzania covers an area of 945,166km². It is one of the largest countries in sub-Saharan Africa, larger than Kenya and Uganda combined. To put it in a European context, Tanzania is about 4½ times the size of Britain; in an American context, it's about 1½ times the size of Texas.

Capital

Dar es Salaam is the capital of Tanzania. Dodoma is projected to become the capital by the end of the century.

Population

The total population of Tanzania is about 26,365,000 (1989 estimate), of which roughly 600,000 live on Zanzibar. Apart from the towns the most densely-populated areas tend to be the highlands, especially those around Lake Nyasa and Kilimanjaro.

There are estimated to be 120 linguistic groups in Tanzania. None exceeds 10% of the country's total population. The most numerically significant groups are the Sukoma of Lake Victoria, the Hehe of Iringa, the Gogo of Dodoma, the Chagga of Kilimanjaro and the Nyamwezi of Tabora.

Government

The ruling party is Chama Cha Mapinduzi. Ali Hassan Mwinyi has been President since Nyerere retired in 1985. The Prime Minister is John Malacela. Until 1992 Tanzania was a one-party state, but other parties have now been legalised and a multi-party election is planned for 1995.

Major Towns

Dar es Salaam is far and away the largest town in Tanzania, with a population of around one million. Other important towns, in rough order of size, are Mwanza, Tanga, Arusha, Mbeya, Dodoma, Zanzibar Town, Mtwara, Moshi, Tabora, Kigoma, Songea, Lindi and Iringa.

Economy

After independence Tanzania became one of the most staunchly socialist countries in Africa, but since the mid-1980s there has been a swing to free market systems. Tanzania is considered to be one of the 25 poorest counties in the world, with a per capita GNP of US$285 (1985). Less than 10% of the workforce is in formal employment; most Tanzanians live a subsistence lifestyle. The country's major exports are coffee, cotton, cashew nuts, sisal, tobacco, tea and diamonds. Zanzibar and Pemba are important clove producers. Gold, tin and coal are also mined.

Languages

KiSwahili and English are the official languages. Little English is spoken outside of the larger towns, but KiSwahili is spoken by most Tanzanians.

Currency

The unit of currency is the Tanzanian Shilling (pronounced *Shillingi*), which is divided into 100 cents. The rate of exchange in July 1993 was around US$1.00 = Tsh 420.

Climate

Most of Tanzania has a tropical climate, but there are large regional variations. The coastal belt and the Lake Nyasa and Tanganyika areas are hot and humid, with little relief at night. The rest of the interior is hot and dry, cooling down significantly at night. Highlands such as Kilimanjaro, Ngorongoro and the various mountain ranges of eastern Tanzania are generally warm during the day and cold at night.

Tanzania is too near the equator to experience a recognisable summer and winter. The months between October and April are marginally hotter than May to September. In Dar es Salaam, for instance, the hottest month is March (average maximum 32°C; average minimum 23°C), and the coolest month is July (28°C; 18°C).

Virtually all of Tanzania's rain falls between November and May. The division of this period into short rains (November to December) and long rains (March to May) only applies to coastal areas and the extreme north around Arusha and Lake Victoria, where there is relatively little rainfall in January and February. Available figures suggest that rain falls fairly consistently between mid-November and mid-April in other parts of the country.

Geography

The bulk of East Africa is made up of a vast, flat plateau rising from a narrow coastal belt to an average height of about 1,500m. This plateau is broken dramatically by the 20 million year old Great Rift Valley, which cuts a trough up to 2,000m deep through the African continent from the Dead Sea to Mozambique.

The main branch of the Rift Valley bisects Tanzania. A western branch of the rift valley forms the Tanzania-Zaire border. Lakes Natron, Manyara, Eyasi and Nyasa-Malawi are all in the main rift, Lake Tanganyika lies in the western branch, and Lake Victoria lies on an elevated plateau between them.

East Africa's highest mountains are volcanic in origin, created by the same forces which caused the Rift Valley. Kilimanjaro is the most recent of these: it started to form about one million years ago, and was still growing as recently as 100,000 years ago. Mount Meru is older. Ngorongoro Crater is the collapsed caldera of a volcano that would once have been as high as Kilimanjaro is today. The only active volcano in Tanzania, Ol Doinyo Lengai, lies a short way north of Ngorongoro.

HISTORY

Tanzania's rich and fascinating history is also highly elusive. For a non-historian such as myself, unravelling it is a frustrating process. Specialist works often contradict each other to such an extent it is difficult to tell where fact ends and speculation begins, while broader or more popular accounts are riddled with obvious inaccuracies. This is partly because there are huge gaps in the known facts; partly because much of the available information is scattered in out-of-print or difficult-to-find books; partly because once an inaccuracy gets into print it becomes true, and spreads like a virus. For whatever reason, there is not, so far I am aware, one concise and reliable account of Tanzanian history that is readily-available to the layman.

I have tried to make the following account as comprehensive as possible while still keeping it readable. It is, to the best of my knowledge, as accurate as the known facts will allow, but at times I have had to decide for myself the most probable truth amongst a mass of contradictions, and I have speculated freely where speculation seems to be the order of the day. My goals are to stimulate the visitor's interest in Tanzanian history, and to give them easy access to information that would have enhanced our trip greatly.

Pre-history of the interior

It is widely agreed that the evolution and early history of humanity was played out on the savannas of East and southern Africa. The hominid (proto-human) evolutionary chain split from that of the pongoid apes (whose modern representatives include chimpanzee and gorilla) about 20 million years ago. Two hominid genera are recognised: *australopithecus* and *homo*. *Australopithecus* is unlikely to have been a direct ancestor of modern man; it lived contemporaneously with *homo* until about one million years ago.

A 1.75 million year old skull found by Mary Leakey at Olduvai Gorge in Tanzania in 1957 was the first to confirm man's great antiquity and Africa as the probable site of human evolution. Since then further skulls have been found at a number of sites in East Africa. The oldest known hominid skull, found in Namibia in 1991, is about 12 million years old.

The immediate ancestor of modern man, *homo erectus* first appeared about 1.5 million years ago. *Homo erectus* was the first hominid to surmount the barrier of the Sahara and spread into Europe and Asia, and is credited with the discovery of fire and the first use of stone tools and recognisable speech.

Although modern man, *homo sapiens*, has been around for at least half a million years, only in the last 10,000 years have the African races recognised today more-or-less taken their modern form. Up until about 1,000 BC, East Africa was exclusively populated by hunter-gatherers, similar in physiology, culture and language to the Khoisan (or bushmen) of southern Africa. Rock art accredited to the Khoisan is found throughout East Africa, most notably in the Kondoa-Irangi region of Tanzania near Lake Eyasi, home of the Hadza, the only remaining Tanzanian hunter-gatherers.

The pastoralist and agriculturalist lifestyles which emerged on the Nile Delta in about 5,000 BC had spread to various parts of sub-Saharan Africa by 2,000 BC, most notably to the Cushitic-speaking people of the Ethiopian highlands and the Bantu-speakers of West Africa. Cushitic-speakers first drifted into Tanzania in about 1,000 BC, closely followed by Bantu-speakers. Familiar with iron-age technology, these migrants would have soon dominated the local hunter-gatherers. By 1,000 AD, most of Tanzania was populated by Bantu-speakers, with Cushitic-speaking pockets in areas such as the Ngorongoro highlands.

There is no detailed information about the Tanzanian interior prior to 1500, and even after that details are sketchy. Except for the Lake Victoria region, which by then supported large authoritarian kingdoms similar to those in Uganda, much of the Tanzanian interior is too dry to support large concentrations of people. In most of Tanzania, an informal system of *ntemi* chiefs emerged. The *ntemi* system, though structured, seems to have been flexible and benevolent. The chiefs were served by a council and performed a role that was as much advisory as it was authoritarian. By the 19th Century there are estimated to have been more than 200 *ntemi* chiefs in western and central Tanzania, each with about 1,000 subjects.

The *ntemi* system was shattered when southern Tanzania was invaded by Ngoni exiles from what is now the Natal province of South Africa. In Natal, the leader of the small Zulu clan, Chaka, had melded a giant kingdom from the surrounding clans using revolutionary military tactics based on horseshoe formations and a short-stabbing spear. By 1830, his marauding troops had either killed, incorporated or driven away most of the other tribes in the region. The exiled tribes swept northwards, taking with them Chaka's methods, and they in turn wreaked havoc over much of southern Africa, slaughtering existing tribes in order to take their land.

The Ngoni entered southern Tanzania in about 1840. They attacked resident tribes, destroying communities and leaving survivors no option but to turn to banditry. Their tactics were observed and adopted by the more astute *ntemi* chiefs, who needed to protect themselves, but had to forge larger kingdoms to do so.

The situation was exacerbated by the growing presence of Arab slave traders. Tribes controlling the areas that caravan routes went through were able to extract taxes from the slavers and to find work with them as porters or organising slave raids. This situation was exploited by several chiefs, most notably Mirambo, who dominated the interior between about 1840 and 1880.

The coast to 1800

There have been links between the Tanzanian coast and the rest of the world for millennia, but only the barest sketch is possible of events before 1,000 AD.

The ancient Egyptians believed their ancestors came from a southerly land called Punt. In about 2,500 BC an explorer called Sahare sailed there. He returned laden with ivory, ebony, and myrrh, which suggests he landed somewhere on the East African coast. There is no suggestion that Egypt traded regularly with Punt, but they did visit it again. Interestingly, an engraving of the Queen of Punt, made after an expedition in 1493 BC, shows her to have distinctly Khoisan features.

The Phoenicians first explored the coast in about 600 BC. According to the 1st-Century *Periplus of the Ancient Sea* they traded with a town called Rhapta. This is thought to have been on the Tanzanian coast, at a major estuary such as that of the Pangani or Rufiji.

Bantu-speakers arrived at the coast about 2,000 years ago. It seems likely they had trade links with the Roman Empire: Rhapta gets a namecheck in Ptolemy's 4th-Century *Geography* and a few 4th-Century Roman coins have been found at the coast. The fact that the Romans knew of Kilimanjaro and the great lakes raises some interesting questions. One suggestion is that the coastal Bantu-speakers were running trade routes into the interior and that these collapsed at the same time as the Roman Empire, presumably because there was no longer anyone with whom they could trade. The idea is attractive and plausible, but the evidence seems rather flimsy. The Romans could simply have gleaned the information from Bantu-speakers who had arrived at the coast recently enough to have some knowledge of the interior.

Historians have a clearer picture of events on the coast from about 1,000 AD onwards. By this time, trade between the coast and the Persian Gulf was well-established. The earliest known Islamic buildings on the coast, on Manda Island off Kenya, have been dated to the 9th Century AD. Items sold to Arab ships included ivory, ebony and various spices, while a variety of Oriental and Arabic goods were imported for the use of wealthy traders.

The coastal trade was dominated by gold, almost certainly mined in the Great Zimbabwe region. It arrived at the coast at Sofala, in modern-day Mozambique, probably via the Zambezi Valley, and was then transported by local traders to Mogadishu, where it was sold to the Arabs. The common assumption that Swahili language and culture was a direct result of Arab traders mixing with local Bantu speakers is probably inaccurate. KiSwahili is a Bantu language. It spread along the coast in the 11th Century; most of the Arab words which have entered it did so *after* this. The driving force behind a common coastal language and culture was almost certainly internal trade between Sofala and Mogadishu.

More than 30 Swahili city-states were operating between the 13th and 15th Centuries, a large number of which were in modern-day Tanzania. This period is known as the Shirazi Era after the sultans who ruled these city-states, most of whom claimed descent from the Shiraz region of Persia. Each city-state had its own sultan; they rarely interfered in each other's business. The Islamic faith was widespread during this period, and many Arabic influences crept into coastal architecture. Cities were centred around a Great Mosque, normally constructed in rock and coral.

Many Arabs settled on the coast before and during the Shirazi Era. For a long time it has been assumed they controlled the trade, but this has been questioned in recent years. Contemporary descriptions of the city-states suggest they were predominantly populated by Africans. It is possible that African traders claimed Shirazi descent in order to boost their standing, both locally and with Shirazi ships.

In the mid-13th Century, probably due to improvements in Arab navigation and ship construction, the centre of the gold trade moved from Mogadishu to the small island of Kilwa. Kilwa represented the peak of the Shirazi period. It had a population of 10,000 and operated its own mint, the first in sub-Saharan Africa. The multi-domed mosque on Kilwa was the largest and most splendid on all the coast, while another building, now known as *Husuni Kubwa*, was a gargantuan palace, complete with audience courts, several ornate balconies, and even a swimming pool. Kilwa is discussed more fully in Chapter Twelve.

Although Kilwa had been superseded in importance by Mombasa by the end of the 15th Century, coastal trade was still booming. It came to an abrupt halt in 1505 when Mombasa was captured by the Portuguese and several other coastal towns, Kilwa included, were ransacked. Under Portuguese control the gold trade collapsed and the coast stagnated. In 1698, Fort Jesus, the Portuguese centre in Mombasa, was overthrown by Arabs from Oman. Rivalries between the Omani and the old Shirazi dynasties soon surfaced. In 1728, a group of Shirazi sultans went so far as to conspire with their old oppressors, the Portuguese, to overthrow Fort Jesus, but the Omani re-captured it a year later. For the next 100 years an uneasy peace gripped the coast, nominally under Omani rule but dominated in economic terms by the Shirazi Sultan of Mombasa.

Slavery and exploration in the 19th Century

The 19th Century was a period of rapid change in Tanzania, with stronger links established between the coast and the interior as well as between East Africa and Europe.

The decisive figure in the first half of the century was Seyyid Said, the Sultan of Muscat from 1804 to 1854. Britain had signed a treaty with Said's father, and in the wake of the Napoleonic wars did not want to see the coast fall into French hands. In 1827, Said's small but efficient navy captured Mombasa and effectively took control of the coast. It is debatable whether this would have happened without British support.

Said chose Zanzibar as his East African base because of its proximity to Bagamoyo, which had been the terminus of a caravan route to Lake Tanganyika since 1823. Said's commercial involvement with Zanzibar began in 1827 when he set up clove plantations with scant regard for the land claims of local inhabitants. By 1840, when he moved his capital from Muscat to Zanzibar, commerce on the island was dominated by Said and his fellow-Arabs.

The extent of the East African slave trade prior to 1827 is unclear. It certainly existed, but was never as important as the gold or ivory trade. The traditional centre of slave trading was West Africa, but trade there had recently been stopped by the British, leaving the way open for Said and his cronies. By 1839, over 40,000 slaves were being sold from Zanzibar annually. These came from two sources: the central caravan route between Bagamoyo and the Lake Tanganyika region, and a southern route between Kilwa Kivinje and Lake Nyasa.

The effects of the slave trade on the interior were numerous. The Nyamwezi of the Tabora region and the Yua of Nyasa became very powerful by serving as porters along the caravan routes and organising slave raids and ivory hunts. Weaker tribes were devastated. Villages were ransacked; the able-bodied men and women were taken away while the young and old were left to die. Hundreds of thousands of slaves were sold in the mid-19th Century, and no-one knows how many more died of disease or exhaustion between being captured and reaching the coast.

The slave trade was the driving force behind the second great expansion of KiSwahili. This became the lingua franca along caravan routes.

Europeans knew little about the African interior in 1850. The first Europeans to see Kilimanjaro (Rebmann, 1846) and Mount Kenya (Krapf, 1849) were ridiculed for their reports of snow on the equator. Arab traders must have had an intimate knowledge of parts of the interior, but no-one seems to have thought to ask them. In 1855, a German missionary, James Erhardt, produced a map of Africa based on third-hand Arab accounts. This showed a large slug-shaped lake in the heart of the continent. Known as the slug-map, it fanned interest in a mystery that had tickled geographers since Roman times — the source of the Nile.

The men most responsible for opening up the East African interior to Europeans were Richard Burton, John Speke and David Livingstone, and later Henry Stanley. In 1858, on a quest for the source of the Nile funded by the Royal Geographical Society, Burton and Speke were the first Europeans to see Lake Tanganyika. Later that year, while Burton recovered from fever in Tabora, Speke was the first European to set eyes on Lake Victoria. Speke returned to the northern shore of Victoria in 1863 and concluded that Ripon Falls (near to modern-day Jinja in Uganda) was the Nile's source. Burton, perhaps the most forceful and intelligent of all the 19th-Century explorers, ridiculed this conclusion. In 1864, on the eve of a public debate on the subject between the two men, Speke died of a self-inflicted gun wound. His death was described by the coroner as a shooting accident, but it seems likely he killed himself deliberately.

David Livingstone came from a poor Scots background. He left school at the age of 10, but educated himself to become a missionary. He arrived in the Cape in 1841 to work in the Kuruman Mission, but — overcome by the enormity of the task of converting Africa to Christianity — he decided he would be of greater service opening up the continent so that other missionaries could follow. Livingstone was the first European to cross the Kalahari Desert, the first to cross Africa from west to east and the first to see Victoria Falls. In the same year Speke and Burton saw Lakes Tanganyika and Victoria, Livingstone stumbled across Africa's third great lake, Nyasa.

Like most explorers of his time, Livingstone was obsessed by the Nile issue. Nevertheless, he had ample opportunity to witness the slave caravans at first hand. Sickened by what he saw — the human bondage, the destruction of entire villages, and the corpses abandoned by the traders — he became an outspoken critic of the trade. He believed the only way to curb it was to open up Africa to the three C's: Christianity, Commerce and Civilisation. Though not an imperialist by nature, Livingstone had seen enough of the famine and misery caused by the slavers and the Ngoni in the Nyasa area to believe the only solution was for Britain to colonise East Africa.

In 1867, Livingstone set off from Mikindani to spend the last six years of his life wandering between the great lakes making notes on the slave trade and trying to settle the Nile debate. He believed the source of the Nile to be Lake Benguela (in northern Zambia), from which the mighty Laualaba River flowed. In 1872, he was found at Ujiji by Henry Stanley, an American journalist and explorer. Stanley's alleged greeting, "Dr Livingstone, I presume", are probably the most famous words spoken in Africa. Livingstone died near Lake Benguela in 1873. His heart was removed and buried by his porters, who then carried his cured body over 1,500km to Bagamoyo.

Livingstone's quest to end the slave trade met with little success during his lifetime, but his death and highly emotional funeral at Westminster Abbey seem to have acted as a catalyst. Missions were built in his name all over the Nyasa region, while industrialists such as William Mackinnon and the Muir brothers invested in schemes to open Africa to commerce (which Livingstone had always believed was the key to putting the slavers out of business).

In the year Livingstone died, John Kirk was made the British Consul in Zanzibar. Kirk had travelled with Livingstone on his 1856-62 trip to Nyasa. Deeply affected by what he saw, he had since spent years on Zanzibar hoping to find a way to end the slave trade. In 1873, the British navy blockaded the island and Kirk offered Sultan Barghash full protection against foreign powers if he banned the slave trade. Barghash agreed. The slave market was closed and an Anglican Church built over it. The trade continued on the mainland for some years — 12,000 slaves were sold at Kilwa in 1875 — but that too was stopped.

The slave trade continued on a small scale well into the 20th Century and was only fully eradicated in 1918, four years after the British took control of Tanganyika. Within 10 years of Livingstone's death, however, the volume was a fraction of what it had been in the 1860s. Caravans reverted to ivory as their principal trade, while many of the coastal traders started up rubber and sugar plantations, which turned out to be just as lucrative as their former trade.

In 1875, Henry Stanley resolved the Nile issue. Lake Benguela was the source of a large river all right, but it was the Congo. Speke had been right all along.

The partitioning of East Africa

The so-called scramble for Africa was entered into with mixed motives, erratic enthusiasm and an almost total lack of premeditation by the powers involved. Britain already enjoyed a degree of influence on Zanzibar which amounted to informal colonialism and it was quite happy to maintain this mutually agreeable relationship. The government of the time, led by Lord Salisbury, was opposed to the taking of African colonies.

The scramble was initiated by two events. The first, the decision of King Leopold of Belgium to colonise the Congo Basin, had little direct bearing on events in Tanzania. The partitioning of East Africa was a direct result of an about-face by the German Premier, Bismarck, who had previously shown no enthusiasm for acquiring colonies. Germany probably only developed an interest in Africa in the hope of acquiring pawns to use in negotiations with Britain and France.

In 1884, a young German metaphysician called Carl Peters arrived inauspiciously in Zanzibar, then made his way to the mainland to sign a series of treaties with local chiefs. The authenticity of these treaties is questionable, but when Bismarck announced claims to a large area between the Pangani and Rufiji Rivers, it was enough to set the British government into a mild panic. Britain had plans to expand the Sultanate of Zanzibar, its informal colony, to include the fertile lands around Kilimanjaro. Worse, large parts of the area claimed by Germany was already part of the Sultanate. Not only was Britain morally bound to protect these, it also did not want to surrender control of Zanzibar's annual import-export turnover of two million pounds.

Despite pressure put on the British government by John Kirk, angry that his promises to Barghash would not be honoured, there was little option but to negotiate with Germany. A partition was agreed in 1886, identical to the modern border between Kenya and Tanzania. You may read that Kilimanjaro was part of the British territory before Queen Victoria gave it to her cousin, the Kaiser, as a birthday present. This amusing story was possibly dreamed up by a Victorian satirist to reflect the arbitrariness of the scramble. It is a complete fabrication.

In April 1888, the Sultan of Zanzibar unwillingly agreed to lease Germany the coastal strip south of the Umba River. Germany mandated this area to Carl Peters's German East Africa Company (GEAC), which placed agents at most coastal settlements north of Dar es Salaam. These agents demanded heavy taxes from traders and were encouraged to behave high-handedly in their dealings with locals.

The GEAC's honeymoon was short. Emil Zalewski, the Pangani agent, ordered the Sultan's representative, the Wali, to report to him. When the Wali refused, Zalewski had him arrested and sent away on a German warboat. In September 1888, an uprising against the GEAC was led by a sugar plantation owner called Abushiri Ibn Salim. Except at Dar es Salaam and Bagamoyo, both protected by German warboats, GEAC agents were either killed or driven away. A horde of 20,000 men gathered on the coast, including 6,000 Shambaa who refused to relinquish their right to claim tax from caravans passing the Usambara. In November, the mission at Dar es Salaam was attacked. Three priests were killed and the rest captured. The coast was in chaos until April 1889 when the Kaiser's troops invaded Abushiri's camp and forced him to surrender. The German government hanged Abushiri in Pangani; they withdrew the GEAC's mandate and banned Peters from ever setting foot in the area.

The 1886 agreement only created the single line of partition north of Kilimanjaro. By 1890, Germany had claimed an area north of Witu, including Lamu, and there was concern in Britain that they might try to claim the rich agricultural land around Lake Victoria, thereby surrounding Britain's territory. Undeterred by the debacle at Pangani (and with a nod and a wink from Bismarck), Carl Peters decided to force the issue. He slipped through Lamu and in May 1890, after a murderous jaunt across British territory, he signed a treaty with the King of Buganda entitling Germany to most of what is now southern Uganda. This time, however, Peters's plans were frustrated. Bismarck had resigned in March of the same year and his replacement, Von Kaprivi, wanted to maintain good relations with Salisbury's government. In any case, Henry Stanley had signed a similar treaty with the Buganda when he passed through the area in 1888 on his way from rescuing the Emin Pasha in Equatoria.

Germany had its eye on Heligoland, a small but strategic North Sea island that had been seized by Britain from Denmark in 1807. To some extent, German interest in Africa had always been related to the bargaining power it would give them in Europe. In 1890, Salisbury and Von Kaprivi knocked out an agreement which created the borders of Tanzania as they are today (with the exception of modern-day Burundi and Rwanda, German territory until after World War One). In exchange for an island less than 1km^2 in area, Salisbury was guaranteed protectorateship over Zanzibar and handed the German block north of Witu, and Germany relinquished any claims it might have had to what are today Uganda and Malawi.

German East Africa

The period of German rule was not a happy one. In 1891, Carl Peters was appointed governor. Peters had already proved himself an unsavoury and unsympathetic character: he boasted freely of enjoying killing Africans and — under the guise of the GEAC — his lack of diplomacy had already instigated one uprising.

The 1890s were plagued by a series of natural disasters. A rinderpest epidemic at the start of the decade was followed by an outbreak of smallpox and a destructive plague of locusts. A series of droughts brought famine and disease in their wake. Many previously-settled areas reverted to bush, causing the spread of tsetse fly and sleeping sickness. The population of Tanganyika is thought to have decreased significantly between 1890 and 1914.

It took Peters a decade to gain full control of the colony. The main area of conflict was in the vast central plateau where, led by Mkwawa, the Hehe had become the dominant tribe. In 1891, the Hehe ambushed a German battalion led by Emil Zalewski. They killed or wounded more than half Zalewski's men, and made off with his armoury. Mkwawa fortified his capital near Iringa, but it was razed by the Germans in 1894. Mkwawa was forced to resort to guerilla tactics, which he used with some success. In 1898, Mkwawa shot himself rather than face capture.

Germany was determined to make the colony self-sufficient. Sugar and rubber were well-established on parts of the coast; coffee was planted in the Kilimanjaro region, a major base for settlers, and cotton grew well around Lake Victoria. The colony's leading crop export, sisal, was grown throughout the rest of the country. In 1902, Peters decided that the southeast should be given over to cotton plantations. This was an ill-considered move: the soils were not right for the crop and the scheme was bound to cause great hardship.

The people of the southeast had suffered throughout the 19th Century and distrusted outsiders. They had been terrorised by the notoriously cruel Kilwa slavers and suffered regular raids by the Ngoni; the cotton scheme, which created back-breaking work for little financial return, was the final straw. In 1905, a prophet called Kinjikitile discovered a spring which spouted out magic water. He claimed that bullets fired at anyone who had been sprinkled with this water would have no effect. His messengers carried the water to people throughout the region; by August 1905 the entire southeast was ready to rise against the Germans.

The Maji-Maji (water-water) Rebellion began in Kinjikitile's village in the Mutumbi hills near Kilwa. The house of the German agent in Kibatu was burnt down, as was a nearby Asian trading centre. Troops from the regional headquarters at Kilwa captured and

hanged Kinjikitile, but the news of his magic water had already
spread. A group of missionaries led by the bishop of Dar es Salaam
was speared to death when they passed through the region, several
trading posts were burnt along with their occupants, and the entire
staff of the Ifakara garrison was killed.

The rebellion's first setback came when 1,000 warriors attacked
the Mahenge garrison. The commander had been warned of the
attack and a bank of machine guns awaited its arrival. Although
many warriors were killed, the garrison was pinned down until troops
from Iringa forced the rest to retreat. The Iringa troops then
continued to the Ngoni capital of Songea. The Ngoni were extremely
dubious about the water's power; when a few Ngoni were shot, the
rest fled.

The news of the water's ineffectiveness spread; the rebellion had
lost much of its momentum by mid-October when Count Gotzen and
200 German troops arrived in the area. Gotzen decided the only way
to flush out the ringleaders was to create a famine. Crops were burnt
indiscriminately. Within months most of the leaders had been
hanged. The ensuing famine virtually depopulated the area: over
250,000 people died of disease or starvation and the densely-
populated Mutumbi and Ungindo hills were reclaimed by miombo
woodland and wild animals. They now form part of the Selous Game
Reserve.

The Maji-Maji rebellion was the most important and tragic event
during German rule, but it did leave some good effects in its wake.
It was the first time a group of disparate tribes had dropped their
own disputes and united against European invaders. Many
Tanzanians feel the rebellion paved the way for the non-tribal
attitude of modern Tanzania and it certainly affected the strategies
used against colonial powers throughout Africa. More immediately,
the public outcry it caused forced Germany to rethink its approach
to its colonies.

Carl Peters was fired from the colonial service in 1906. He believed
his African mistress had slept with his manservant, so he had
flogged her close to death then hanged them both. His successor
introduced a series of laws protecting Africans from mistreatment. To
the disgust of the settler community, he created an incentive-based
scheme for African farmers. This made it worth their while to grow
cash crops and allowed the colony's exports to triple in the period
leading up to World War One.

When World War One broke out in Europe, East Africa rapidly
became involved. In the early stages of the war, German troops
entered southern Kenya to cut off the Uganda Railway. Britain
responded with an abortive attempt to capture Tanga. The balance
of power was roughly even until Jan Smuts led the Allied forces into

German territory in 1916. By January 1918, the Allies had captured most of German East Africa and the German commander, Von Lettow, retreated into Mozambique.

The war disrupted food production, and a serious famine ensued. This was particularly devastating in the Dodoma region. The country was taken over by the League of Nations. Ruanda-Urundi, now Rwanda and Burundi, was mandated to Belgium. The rest of the country was re-named Tanganyika and mandated to Britain.

Tanganyika

The period of British rule between the wars was largely uneventful. Tanganyika was never heavily settled by Europeans so the indigenous populace had more opportunity for self-reliance than it did in many colonies. Nevertheless, settlers were favoured in the agricultural field, as were Asians in commerce. The Land Ordinance Act of 1923 secured some land rights for Africans; otherwise they were repeatedly forced into grand but misconceived agricultural schemes. The most notorious of these, the Groundnut Scheme of 1947, was an attempt to convert the southeast of the country into a large-scale mechanised groundnut producer. The scheme failed through a complete lack of understanding of local conditions; it caused a great deal of hardship locally and cost British taxpayers millions of pounds.

On a political level, a system of indirect rule based around local government encouraged African leaders to focus on local rivalries rather than national issues. A low-key national movement called the TAA was formed in 1929, but it was as much a cultural as a political organisation.

Although it was not directly involved in World War Two, Tanganyika was profoundly affected by it. The country benefited economically. It saw no combat so food production continued as normal, while international food prices rocketed. Tanganyika's trade revenue increased sixfold between 1939 and 1949. World War Two was a major force in the rise of African Nationalism. Almost 100,000 Tanganyikans fought for the Allies. The exposure to other countries and cultures made it difficult for them to return home as second-class citizens. They had fought for non-racism and democracy in Europe, yet were victims of racist and non-democratic policies in their own country.

The dominant figure in post-war Tanganyikan/Tanzanian politics is Julius Nyerere. Schooled at a mission near Lake Victoria, he went on to university in Uganda and gained a masters degree in Edinburgh. After returning to Tanzania in 1952, Nyerere became involved in the TAA. This evolved into the more political and nationalist TANU in

1954. Nyerere became the president of TANU at the age of 32. By supporting rural Africans on grass root issues and advocating self-government as the answer to their grievances, TANU gained a strong national following.

By the mid-1950s Britain and the UN were looking at a way of moving Tanzania towards greater self-government, though over a far longer time-scale than TANU envisaged. The British governor, Sir Edward Twining, favoured a system of multi-racialism, which would give equal representation to whites, blacks and Asians. TANU agreed to an election along these lines, albeit with major reservations. Twining created his own "African" party, the UTC.

In the 1958 election there were three seats per constituency, one for each racial group. Electors could vote for all three seats, so in addition to putting forward candidates for the black seats TANU indicated their preferred candidates in the white and Asian seats. Candidates backed by TANU won 67% of the vote; the UTC did not win a single seat. Twining's successor, Sir Richard Turnball, rewarded TANU by scrapping multiracialism. In the democratic election of 1960, TANU won all but one seat. In May 1961, Tanganyika attained self government and Nyerere was made Prime Minister. Tanganyika attained full independence on 9 December 1961. Not one life had been taken in the process.

Britain granted Zanzibar full independence in December 1963. A month later the Arab government was toppled and in April 1964 the two countries combined to form Tanzania.

Tanzania

At the very core of Tanzania's post-independence achievements and failures lies the figure of Julius Nyerere, who ruled Tanzania until his retirement in 1985. In his own country, where he remains highly respected, Nyerere is called *Mwalimu* — the teacher. In the west, he is a controversial figure, often portrayed as a dangerous socialist who irreparably damaged his country. This image of Nyerere doesn't bear scrutiny. He made mistakes and was intolerant of criticism — at one point Tanzania is said to have had more political prisoners than South Africa — but he is also one of the few statesmen to have emerged from Africa, and has been a force for positive change both in his own country and in a wider African context.

In 1962, TANU came into power with little policy other than their attained goal of independence. Tanganyika was the poorest and least economically-developed country in East Africa, and one of the poorest in the world. Nyerere's first concerns were to better the lot of rural Africans and to prevent the creation of a money-grabbing elite. The country was made a one-party state, but had an election system which, by African standards, was relatively democratic. Tanzania pursued a policy of non-alignment, but the government's socialist policies and Nyerere's outspoken views alienated most western leaders. Close bonds were formed with socialist powers, most significantly China, who built the Tanzam Railway (completed in 1975).

Relations with Britain soured in 1965. Nyerere condemned the British government's tacit acceptance of UDI in Rhodesia. In return, Britain cut off all aid to Tanzania. Nyerere also gave considerable vocal support to disenfranchised Africans in South Africa, Mozambique and Angola. The ANC and Frelimo both operated from Tanzania in the 1960s.

Nyerere's international concerns were not confined to white-suprematism. In 1975, Tanzania pulled out of an OAU conference in Idi Amin's Uganda saying: 'The refusal to protest against African crimes against Africans is bad enough...but...by meeting in Kampala...the OAU are giving respectability to one of the most murderous regimes in Africa'. Tanzania gave refuge to several Ugandans, including the former president Milton Obote and the current president Yoweri Musveni. Amin occupied part of northwestern Tanzania in October 1978, and bombed Bukoba and Musoma. In 1979, Tanzania retaliated by invading Uganda and toppling Amin. This action was condemned by other African leaders, despite Amin having been the initial aggressor. Ousting Amin drained Tanzania's financial resources, but it received no financial compensation, neither from the west nor by from any other African country.

At the time of independence, most rural Tanzanians lived in scattered communities. This made it difficult for the government to provide such amenities as clinics and schools and to organise a productive agricultural scheme. In 1967, Nyerere embarked on a policy he called villagisation. Rural people were encouraged to form Ujamaa (familyhood) villages and collective farms. The scheme met with some small-scale success in the mid-70s, so in 1975 Nyerere decided to forcibly re-settle people who had not yet formed villages. By the end of the year 65% of rural Tanzanians lived in Ujamaa villages. In many areas, however, water supplies were inadequate to support a village. The resultant mess, exacerbated by one of Tanzania's regular droughts, ended further villagisation. Ujamaa is often considered to have been an unmitigated disaster. It did not achieve what it was meant to, but it did help the government improve education and health care. Most reliable sources claim it did little long-term damage to agricultural productivity.

By the late 1970s Tanzania's economy was a mess. There were several contributory factors: drought, Ujamaa, rising fuel prices, the border closure with Kenya, lack of foreign aid, bureaucracy and corruption in state-run institutions, and the cost of the Uganda episode. After his re-election in 1980 Nyerere announced he would retire at the end of that five-year term. In 1985 he was succeeded by Ali Hasan Mwinyi. Nyerere remained chairman of the CCM, the party formed when TANU merged with the Zanzibari ASP in 1975, until 1990.

Under President Mwinyi Tanzania has moved away from socialism. In June 1986, in alliance with the IMF, he implemented a three-year Economic Recovery Plan. This included freeing up the exchange rate and encouraging private enterprise. Since then Tanzania has achieved an annual growth rate of around 4% (in real terms). Many locals complain the only result they have seen is greater inflation. In 1990 attempts were made to rout corruption from the civil service, with surprisingly positive results. The first multi-party election is planned for 1995. As with independence, this transition has so far caused no bloodshed.

Into its fourth decade of independence, most of Africa still suffers from the tribal problems it had at the outset. Nyerere's great achievement is the tremendous sense of national unity he created; by making KiSwahili the national language, by banning tribal leaders, by forcing government officials to work away from the area in which they grew up, and by his own example.

Things look better for Tanzania now than they have at any time since independence. It remains one of the world's least-developed 25 countries, but most sources agree that the economic situation of the average Tanzanian has improved since independence, as have adult literacy rates and health care. Tanzania's remarkable political stability and its increasingly pragmatic economic policies are a positive base for future growth.

Tourism could play a big part in this. Until the closure of the Kenya border in the late-1970s, most of Tanzania's tourism came via Kenya, which profited from it more than Tanzania did. Tourism ground to a standstill during the early 1980s, but Tanzania is now developing a tourist infrastructure independently of an increasingly wobbly-looking Kenya.

When I first visited Tanzania in 1986, it looked to be beyond redemption. Ten years hence it could well be a beacon of hope, stability and relative prosperity in an increasingly turbulent continent.

Chapter Two

Natural History

INTRODUCTION

There are plenty of good reasons to visit Tanzania — its beautiful coastline, fascinating history and magnificent scenery — but for most tourists one attraction overwhelms all others. Tanzania is Africa's prime game-viewing country. Its national parks and game reserves, which include the famous Serengeti and Ngorongoro Crater, cover almost 25% of the country and protect an estimated 20% of Africa's large mammals.

All the national parks receive detailed coverage in the main part of the guide, as do any other conservation areas which are reasonably accessible. This chapter provides an overview of Tanzania's conservation areas and natural history, as well as descriptions of the more common large mammals.

CONSERVATION

The plight of the rhinoceros and elephant has made African conservation a household concern in the west. Despite this, few westerners have any grasp of the issues. What follows is certainly opinionated, and probably simplistic, but does attempt to clarify the root problem as I see it. You may well disagree...

We all romanticise Africa. An incredible amount of drivel was written about it during the colonial era, and this dominates our perception of the continent. The macho blustering of Hemingway and exaggerated accounts of the Great White Hunters vie in our heads with the nostalgic meandering of *Out of Africa*. For the west, Africa represents wildness and space, vast horizons and shimmering red sunsets; powerful images we do not want shattered by the realities of the late 20th Century.

It was, of course, European settlers who destroyed the Africa they mythologised. The vast herds which had existed alongside people for millennia were decimated during the colonial era. By the early 1960s, when most of Africa became independent, these herds were by and large restricted to conservation areas that had been set aside by the colonial governments to preserve something of the Africa they loved. Their vision of unspoilt Africa did not include people: when an area was declared a national park, the people who lived there were moved to the fringes. They had both hunted and conserved the animals for centuries; now hunting was forbidden and they needed new sources of food.

Areas suitable for national parks are not normally densely populated; they tend to be relatively infertile. Even if someone succeeded in growing crops, their efforts could be wiped out by one hungry or angry elephant. This created a circle of poverty around many game reserves, a scenario which worked in the interests of ivory and rhino-horn traders. People living on the verges of reserves would happily kill elephant or rhino for what was a fraction of the market price, but a fortune in local terms.

As you are no doubt aware, rhinoceros are close to extinction in most Africa countries. In Tanzania, there are 20 left in the Ngorongoro Conservation Area and at best a couple of hundred in the Selous. Africa's elephant population is now thought to number about half a million. Tanzania is home to a significant number of these. There are an estimated 30,000 animals in the Selous alone, and at least as many scattered in other reserves.

In the late 1980s the elephant situation seemed hopeless. In some reserves, herds had been poached to within 20% of their size ten years previously. In the Selous, up to 20,000 were killed in a two year period. Most African governments lacked the finance to arrest this process; in some cases they also lacked the will, with strong rumours of corruption and the involvement of government officials. Anti-poaching units armed with old-fashioned rifles were fighting bands of poachers armed with AK47s, and losing. In 1988, I was driven through a part of Kenya's Tsavo East National Park, one of the worst hit reserves, with less than a quarter of its 1972 population of 17,000 animals left. We saw more elephant corpses than we did live animals; those elephant we did see ran off in terror at the approach of a vehicle.

A five-year moratorium on the world ivory trade was implemented in 1989. There is a wide consensus this ban has worked: elephant numbers are on the increase, and without a market poaching has virtually stopped. Southern African countries want this moratorium to be lifted. Herds in South Africa, Botswana and Zimbabwe are stable and growing, and as elephant are extremely destructive when overpopulated, excess animals are culled. This issue has been greatly misrepresented in Britain at least, where emotive and irresponsible newspaper columns and television programs have equated culling with murder. Obviously culling is not the ideal solution, but it is difficult to see a practical alternative. (The suggestion most often put forward is that the animals could be moved. To the Cotswolds? Or somewhere where African crops can be trampled?)

It has become evident to many conservationists that a complete change of approach is the only chance for the long term survival of Africa's large animals. Local people must be included in the process. If they benefit from the reserves, they will side with conservationists; if they do not they will side with the poachers. Attempts must be made to ensure that locals benefit from money raised by the reserves, that they are given meat from culled animals, and that wherever possible work is found for them within the reserve. In an increasingly densely-populated continent, reserves can only justify their existence if they create local wealth.

Zimbabwe is at the forefront of this more integrated approach to conservation. It is, by western standards, a poor country, and could use the revenue raised by selling elephant tusks which are at present gathering dust. Zimbabwean conservationists argue that they have the right to sell these on a legitimate market; that western countries would not be so keen to impose a moratorium if their commercial interests were at stake; that, ultimately, the west is yet again imposing its will on Africa.

Southern African countries suggest a cartel is created which sells only ivory from countries with stable elephant populations. Countries like Tanzania fear that such a cartel would be difficult to control, and may well lead to renewed poaching in their reserves. There is no simple solution to this conflict of interests. I believe it to be in the interests of most African countries that the moratorium stands for the meantime, but ultimately it should be lifted. Efforts should be made now to re-think conservation policies, so that when it is lifted the same old problems do not recur.

Africa does not belong to the west. I see no reason why Africans should conserve their wildlife for the sake of western aesthetics, unless they perceive it to be in their interest to do so. If some gun-happy soul with a Hemingway fixation is idiot enough to pay enough money to support a village for a year in order that he can hunt an elephant, good. If the meat from an elephant can feed a village for a week, and the money from the sale of the ivory be put back into conservation, good. If we westerners can drop the idealism and allow Africans to both conserve their wildlife *and* feed their bellies, only then is there a chance that our grandchildren will be able to see the Africa we want them to.

Just before going to the printers, I read a glowing review of a new book which addresses many of the issues raised above, called *At the Hand of Man: Peril and Hope for Africa's Wildlife* by Raymond Bonner (Alfred A Knopf 1993).

CONSERVATION AREAS

There are 12 national parks in Tanzania, and numerous other conservation areas. The most important of these fit broadly into three groups: the northern, southern and western reserves.

Northern reserves

The northern reserves are the focus of Tanzania's safari industry, which is based in the town of Arusha. The traditional northern safari includes visits to Serengeti National Park, the Ngorongoro Conservation Area and Lake Manyara National Park. With luck, a visit to all three will yield sightings of all the so-called big-five (lion, leopard, elephant, buffalo and rhino) and most other large African plains mammals.

The Serengeti is notable for its large migratory herds of wildebeest and zebra. It also harbours large numbers of predators; it is not unusual to see lion, leopard and cheetah in the same day. Although heavily touristed, the Serengeti is vast enough to handle it comfortably.

The centrepiece of the Ngorongoro Conservation Area is the magnificent 600m-deep crater after which it is named, the largest intact caldera in the world. Ngorongoro Crater supports large herds of ungulates and is said to have the world's densest lion population. It is the last place in East Africa where black rhinoceros are reasonably common. Ngorongoro is heavily-touristed, and because it is open and its area is limited, this does detract from many people's visit.

Lake Manyara National Park is the least compelling of this triad of reserves. Its once-famous elephant population has suffered badly at the hands of poachers, and its main claim to fame now are the tree-climbing lions which no-one ever seems to see. It is very scenic, however, and there is plenty of other game to be seen.

Many visitors incorporate visits to either Tarangire or Arusha National Park in a northern safari. Tarangire preserves a classic piece of African woodland, studded with plentiful baobabs. It is particularly rich in bird life. A number of localised species such as fringe-eared oryx and gerenuk are present, and elephant are abundant. Arusha National Park is the most low-key of the northern reserves, and considering its proximity to Arusha, it is surprisingly little-visited. Despite this, it has a number of attractive features, including Africa's fifth-highest mountain, Meru, and its own mini-Ngorongoro, Ngurdoto Crater.

Kilimanjaro National Park encompasses the peaks and higher slopes of Africa's highest mountain. Thousands of tourists climb it every year. Mount Meru in Arusha National Park is also popular with hikers.

Southern reserves

Tanzania's southern reserves are less spectacular than those in the north, but they have more of a wilderness atmosphere. The most important reserve in southern Tanzania is the Selous Game Reserve, the largest reserve in Africa. It is bordered by two national parks: Mikumi and the recently-proclaimed Udzungwa Mountains. A third national park, Ruaha, lies west of the Tanzam Highway.

With the exception of Udzungwa Mountains, the southern reserves are only really accessible if you go with an organised safari. These are generally more expensive than safaris to the northern reserves. You can, however, see something of Mikumi from the Tanzam Highway, and slow trains between Dar es Salaam and Mbeya pass through the Selous in daylight hours. The Udzungwa can be reached on public transport and once it is developed will be orientated towards hikers.

Western reserves

The western reserves are very different in character to those in the south and north of the country. They are low-key, have basic accommodation facilities only, and are time-consuming to visit. If you can afford the time, however, all are relatively easy to reach on public transport.

There are four national parks in western Tanzania: Gombe Stream, Mahale Mountains, Rubondo Island and Katavi. The first three are well-forested, noted for their chimpanzees, and can only be reached by boat. Katavi protects a similar habitat to the southern reserves, but is more remote.

HABITATS AND VEGETATION

The bulk of Tanzania is covered in open grassland, savannah (lightly-wooded grassland) and woodland. Most typical African species are at home in all these habitats, but there are exceptions.

The Serengeti Plains are an archetypal African savannah: grassland interspersed with trees of the acacia family. Most acacia are quite short, lightly-leaved and thorny. Many have a flat-topped appearance. An atypical acacia, the yellow-fever tree, is one of Africa's most striking trees. It is relatively large, has yellow bark, and is often associated with water. Combretum is another family of trees typical of savannah.

Much of central Tanzania is dry savannah; during the dry season this area is so barren it resembles semi-desert.

Woodland differs from forest in lacking an interlocking canopy. The most extensive woodland in Tanzania is in the miombo belt which stretches from southern and western Tanzania to Zimbabwe. Miombo woodland typically grows on infertile soil, and is dominated by broadleaved *brachystegia* trees. You may come across the term mixed woodland: this refers to woodland with a mix of *brachystegia*, acacia and other species. Many woodlands are characterised by an abundance of baobab trees.

True forests cover less than 1% of Tanzania's surface area, but are its most botanically-diverse habitat. The forests of the Usambara, for instance, contain more than 2,000 plant species. Most of the forest in Tanzania is montane. Montane forest is characteristic of a group of mountain ranges known as the Eastern Arc Mountains. These form a broken line from north to south, between 50km and 200km inland and include the Pare, Usambara, Uluguru, Udzungwa and Poroto ranges. The forests of the Eastern Arc mountains, characterised by a high level of endemism, form one of Tanzania's most ecologically-precious habitats. The most accessible montane forest is on the slopes of Kilimanjaro, Meru, the Udzungwa and the Usambara.

The lowland forests found in the extreme west of the country have strong affinities with the rain forests of Zaire. Three national parks contain extensive lowland forests: Gombe Stream, Rubondo Island and Mahale Mountains.

Other interesting but localised vegetation types are mangrove swamps (common along the coast, particularly around Kilwa) and the heath and moorland found on the higher slopes of Kilimanjaro and Meru.

ANIMALS

Mammals

Over 80 large mammal species live in Tanzania. On an organised safari your guide will normally be able to identify all the mammals you see. For serious identification purposes or a better understanding of an animal's lifestyle and habits, it is worth investing in a decent field guide or a book on animal behaviour. A number are available; see *Further Reading*. Field guides are best bought before you get to Tanzania.

In the listings below, an animal's KiSwahili name is given in parenthesis after its English name. The KiSwahili for animal is *mnyama* (plural *wanyama*); to find out what animal you are seeing, ask *mnyama gani?*

Predators

Lion (*simba*)   The largest African cat is the one animal everyone wants to see when they go on safari. Lions are the most sociable of the large cats, living in loosely-structured family groups (prides) which typically consist of between five and 15 animals. Lions normally hunt at night; their favoured prey are medium to large antelopes such as wildebeest, gazelle and impala. Females, working in teams of up to eight animals, are responsible for most hunts. Rivalry between male lions is intense: prides may have more than one dominant male working in collaboration to prevent a takeover and young males are forced out of their home pride at about three years of age. Pride takeovers are often fought to the death; after a successful takeover, it is not unusual for all the male cubs to be killed by the new dominant male. Lions are not active by day: they are most often seen lying in the shade looking the picture of regal indolence. Lions occur in most wooded habitats and are the most numerous large cat in savannah. They are common in all the southern reserves and at Katavi, but are more readily seen in the open savannah of the Serengeti and Ngorongoro Crater.

Leopard (*chui*)   This is the most common and widespread large cat in Africa, often living in close proximity to humans, but because of its secretive, solitary nature it is rarely seen. Leopards hunt using stealth and power, often getting to within 5m of their intended prey before pouncing, and they habitually store their prey in a tree to keep it from hyenas and lions. They can be distinguished from the superficially-similar cheetah by their rosette-shaped spots and powerful build. Leopards are found in all habitats. They are

frequently seen in the Seronera Valley of the Serengeti, where they
spend their days hiding up in trees.

Cheetah (*duma*)   Cheetahs hunt using speed instead of stealth;
they are the fastest land mammals, capable of running at up to
70km/hour. Their diurnal hunting habits make them vulnerable in
areas where there are high tourist concentrations; it's difficult for
them to get close to animals when they are surrounded by vehicles.
Males are strongly territorial, and in the Serengeti they most
commonly defend their territory in pairs or trios. Cheetahs are the
least powerful of the large predators: they are chased from a high
percentage of their kills and 50% of cubs are killed before they reach
three months. Like leopards, cheetahs are heavily-spotted and
solitary, but their greyhound-like build, distinctive black tear-marks
and preference for grassland and savannah precludes confusion.
Cheetahs are found in most large reserves and are regularly seen
in the Serengeti.

Caracal (*sibamangu*) and **serval** (*mondo*)   The caracal is a medium-
sized lynx-like cat with a uniform reddish-brown coat and tufted ears.
The slightly larger serval has a pale spotted coat. Both are
widespread, with the serval favouring moister and more densely-
wooded terrain than the caracal. As both are nocturnal they are
rarely seen.

Civet (*fungo*)   This bulky, long-haired, cat-like creature has been
kept in captivity for thousands of years (its anal secretions were
used in making perfumes until a synthetic replacement was found)
but little is known about its habits in the wild. Civets are primarily
carnivorous, feeding on small animals and carrion, but they will also
eat fruit. Their grey-white coat is marked with large black spots
which merge into stripes towards the head. Civets are widespread
and common in most habitats, but they are rarely seen.

Genet (*kanu*)   The genets are a closely-related group of small cat-
like creatures with extraordinarily long tails. They are secretive and
little-known scientifically, but as they are attracted to human waste
they are often seen slinking around campsites after dark. There are
ten recognised genet species, but they are difficult to tell apart in the
wild. The small-spotted genet is the common genet in Tanzania.

Ratel (*nyegere*)   Also known as the honey-badger for its habit of
raiding bee hives, the ratel has a puppy-like head, black sides and
underparts and a greyish-white back. Ratels are adaptable and
widespread, and will eat whatever comes their way. They have a

symbiotic relationship with a bird called the greater honeyguide: the honeyguide takes the ratel to a bee hive, which the ratel then tears open, allowing the honeyguide to feed on the scraps. According to some sources, the ratel fumigates the bee hive with its anal secretions. Ratels are widespread, but uncommon and rarely seen.

Spotted hyena (*fisi*)   This is the common hyena in Tanzania and the most abundant large carnivore in most parts of Africa. Although dog-like in appearance, hyenas are more closely related to mongooses and cats than they are to dogs, and despite their image as scavengers, the spotted hyena is an adept hunter capable of killing an animal as large as a wildebeest. In ancient times, the spotted hyena was thought to be hermaphroditic; the female's vagina is blocked by a false but remarkably realistic-looking scrotum; the entrance is via an equally realistic-looking 'penis'. Most hyena species live in loosely-structured clans of around ten animals. Clans are led by females, which are stronger and larger than males. The spotted hyena is bulky with a sloping back, a light brown coat marked with dark brown spots and a exceptionally powerful jaw (used to crack open bones). It is common throughout Tanzania and frequently seen in daylight. The more secretive and uncommon striped hyena is found in some Tanzanian national parks, but is rarely seen. The aardwolf, a hyena which has become so specialised it primarily feeds on one type of termite, is thinly-distributed in the drier parts of Tanzania.

African hunting dog (*mbwa mwitu*)   These endangered animals are always found in packs, normally about 10 animals strong, and have cryptically-marked black, brown and cream coats. They are ferocious hunters, literally tearing apart their prey as it runs. Although widely-distributed and highly successful predators, hunting dogs are threatened with extinction: they are susceptible to canine disease and their highly social behaviour has made them vulnerable to epidemics. They are present in most national parks, but are thinly-distributed.

Jackal (*mbweha*)   Jackals are small dogs, not much bigger than a fox. They are adaptable and versatile hunters and scavengers, and are found throughout Tanzania. The common species is the black-backed jackal, which can be distinguished by a black and gold saddle. The uncommon golden and side-striped jackals are found in small numbers in the Serengeti. The bat-eared fox, which can be distinguished from any other small canine by its large ears and black eye-mask, is common in the Serengeti.

Primates

Chimpanzee (*sokwe-mtu*)   This distinctive black-coated ape is closely related to man. Chimpanzees live in the lowland forests of western Tanzania. They are found naturally in two national parks — Gombe Stream and Mahale Mountains — and have been introduced to Rubondo Island. Chimpanzees live in large family groups and have complex social behaviour, which has been extensively studied by Jane Goodall at Gombe Stream and Japanese researchers at Mahale.

Baboon (*nyani*)   Baboons are heavily-built greyish primates, superficially similar to monkeys but larger than any monkey species found in East Africa. Baboons live in large troops, and spend most of their time on the ground. Troops have a complex and rigid social structure, held together by matriarchal lineages. Males frequently move between troops in their search for social dominance. Baboons are omnivorous and highly adaptable, and are the most common and widespread primate in Africa. Several subspecies are recognised: the olive baboon is found in northern Tanzania, while the smaller yellow baboon is found in the southern reserves.

Vervet monkey (*tumbili*)   This light grey monkey has a black face and the male has distinctive blue genitals. The vervet is associated with a wide variety of habitats and is the only monkey you are likely to see outside of forests. Vervet monkeys are common in most Tanzanian national parks.

Black-and-white colobus (*mbega mweupe*)   In Tanzania, this most distinctive of monkey species is restricted to montane forests such as those on Kilimanjaro, Meru, Mahale, and most of the Eastern Arc ranges. It is a beautifully-marked animal with a primarily black body and long white tail. Black-and-white colobus live in small groups and are exclusively arboreal. They are capable of jumping up to 30m, a spectacular sight with their white tail streaming behind. A good place to see black-and-white colobus is on the Ngurdoto Crater rim in Arusha National Park.

Blue monkey (*kima*)   The most widespread forest-dwelling monkey is the blue (or samango) monkey, which is a uniform dark blue-grey colour except for its white throat and chest patch; the black face mask of the vervet precludes confusion between the two. The blue monkey is found in virtually all Tanzanian forests, from the fig forest of Lake Manyara to the montane forest of Mount Meru, Kilimanjaro and Ngorongoro Crater rim.

Several more localised monkey species are found in Tanzania. These include red colobus (*chondi*), redtailed (*nkunge*) and patas (*ngedere*) monkeys. The best national parks for keen monkey-watchers are Mahale Mountains, Gombe Stream, Rubondo Island and Udzungwa.

Bushbaby (*komba*)   This small nocturnal primate is common throughout Tanzania. Its piercing cry is one of the distinctive sounds of the African night — I have even heard a bushbaby in Dar es Salaam. If you want to see one, trace the cry to a tree, then shine a torch into it — you should easily pick out its large round eyes.

Antelope
Large antelope
All the antelope described below have an average shoulder height of above 120cm (4 ft), roughly the same height as a zebra.

Common wildebeest or **gnu** (*nyumbu*)   This bizarre and ungainly antelope is the most common large mammal in Tanzania. Wildebeest are widespread and usually found in large herds. In the Serengeti, the annual migration of over a million animals forms one of Africa's great spectacles. Five subspecies are recognised, of which three can be seen in Tanzania: the western white-bearded race lives in the Serengeti, the eastern white-bearded race is found east of the Rift Valley and north of the Rufiji River, and the Nyasa race occurs south of the Rufiji.

Hartebeest   Hartebeest are also rather ungainly looking. They have large shoulders, a sloping back and relatively small horns. Most hartebeest species are brownish in colour and live in small family groups. Liechtenstein's hartebeest (*kongoni*) is a dull yellow-brown animal found in southern Tanzania. The similar-looking Kongoni (*kongoni*) is largely restricted to the Serengeti Plains, as is the dark red-brown Topi (*nyamera*).

Waterbuck (*kuro*)   This shaggy-looking animal has a grey-brown coat and distinctive white ring around its rump. Waterbuck are common in small numbers throughout Tanzania and are normally seen in small family groups grazing near water.

Eland (*pofu*)   Africa's largest antelope has a bovine appearance. It is fawn-brown in colour, has a large dewlap and short spiralled horns, and sometimes has light white stripes on its side. Eland are widespread, but are thinly-distributed and often skittish. They are most normally seen in open or lightly-wooded grassland.

Kudu (*tandala*)   This very large antelope favours woodland habitats. It is grey-brown with thin white stripes. The male has a small dewlap and large spiralling horns. Greater Kudu (*tandala mkubwa*) are found in most parts of southern Tanzania, but are nowhere common. They are replaced by the rare and smaller lesser kudu (*tandala ndogo*) in northern Tanzania. Both species are present in Ruaha National Park, where they can be told apart by their size and the number of stripes on their torso (greater kudu have between six and ten stripes; lesser kudu have eleven or more).

Roan antelope (*korongo*)   The roan is a handsome animal with a light reddish-brown coat, short backward-curving horns and a small mane on the back of the neck. It could be mistaken for a female sable, but is paler and lacks the sable's well-defined white rump and belly. Roan are associated with miombo woodland. They are present in small numbers in the Serengeti, but are more common in the southern reserves and Katavi National Park.

Sable antelope (*pala hala*)   This striking antelope has a black (male) or chestnut-brown (female) coat, white underbelly and rump, and long backward-curving horns. Sable are associated with miombo woodland and are present in most southern Tanzanian reserves, where they are widespread but thinly-distributed.

Fringe-eared oryx (*choroa*)   These regal-looking antelope are ash-grey in colour and have distinctive scimitar-shaped horns. Oryx are found in dry habitats and are present in much of northern Tanzania. They are common in Tarangire National Park.

Medium-sized antelope
All the antelope listed below have a shoulder height of between 75 and 90cm. The male sitatunga has a shoulder height of around 110cm.

Gazelle (*swala*)   Gazelle are lightly-built antelope found in open grassland. Three species are found in Tanzania: Grant's gazelle (*swala granti*) and Thomson's gazelle (*swala tomi*) are both common on the Serengeti plains. Grant's gazelle is larger than Thomson's, and lacks the Thomson's black side-stripe. The distinctive gerenuk (*swala twiga*) is a red-brown gazelle with an extraordinarily long neck (hence its Swahili name, which literally means gazelle-giraffe). Gerenuk are adapted to semi-desert conditions and are occasionally seen in Tarangire National Park, Mkomazi Game Reserve and along the Arusha-Nairobi road.

Impala (*swala pala*)   These slender, handsome antelope are superficially similar to gazelle, but in fact belong to a separate family. Impala can be distinguished from any gazelle by their chestnut colouring, sleek appearance, and the male's distinctive lyre-shaped horns. They can jump up to 3m high and have been known to broad-jump over 10m. Impala live in herds of between 20 and a few hundred animals. They favour well-wooded savannah and woodland fringes, and are often abundant in such habitats.

Bushbuck (*pongo*)   Bushbuck are normally found in forests and riverine woodland. The male has a dark chestnut coat marked with whites spots and stripes. The female is lighter in colour; it is similar in appearance to a duiker but larger. Bushbuck are secretive, but common in suitable habitats.

Sitatunga   This semi-aquatic buck is similar in appearance to the bushbuck, but the male is larger and has a shaggier coat. Both sexes are striped. Sitatunga live in papyrus swamps and are found on Rubondo Island, where they are thought to interbreed with bushbuck, and at Biharimulo Game Reserve.

Puku   This golden-brown antelope, closely related to the Uganda Kob, lacks distinctive markings. It lives in marshy areas and on flood plains. In Tanzania it is known from the Rukwa area.

Reedbuck (*tohe*)   Reedbuck are grey-brown antelope with small crescent-shaped horns. They are usually seen in pairs near water and are found in most Tanzanian national parks. In northern Tanzania they are replaced by the darker mountain reedbuck (*tohe mlima*).

Small antelope
The antelope listed below all have a shoulder height of between 30 and 50cm, except for oribi and klipspringer which are slightly larger (55-60cm).

Klipspringer (*mbuze mawe*)   Klipspringer have dark, bristly coats which give them a speckled appearance. As their KiSwahili name suggests, they have goat-like habits: they are invariably found in the vicinity of koppies or cliffs. Their name means rock-jumper in Afrikaans. They live in pairs in suitable habitats throughout Tanzania.

Kirk's dik-dik (*digidigi*)   This is the most commonly-seen small antelope in Tanzania. It is uniform greyish-brown with a distinctive white ring around its eye. Dik-dik are usually seen singly or in pairs in tall grass or thick undergrowth.

Steenbok (*tondoro*)   This nondescript rusty-brown antelope is common in some southern reserves. It favours open country.

Oribi (*taya*)   Oribi are similar to steenbok but larger. They are found mainly in tall grassland and are most likely to be seen in the northern Serengeti.

Duiker   Duiker are a group of tiny forest-dwelling buck. Several species are present in Tanzania's forests, but they are elusive and seldom seen clearly enough to identify. Abbot's duiker (*minde*) is chestnut brown and has a tuft of red hair on its forehead. It is endemic to Tanzania and can be found in the forests of Kilimanjaro. Common duiker (*nsya*) are grey-brown and have a vaguely speckled appearance. They are widespread and less habitat-specific than other duikers. Red duiker (*pofu*) are very small and are light chestnut-brown in colour. Blue duiker (*kima*), the smallest African antelope, are greyish-blue. Blue and red duiker are both reasonably widespread. Ader's duiker is found only in two forests: Jozani on Zanzibar and the Sokoke in Kenya.

Other herbivores

Elephant (*tembe*)   The world's largest land animal is also one of the most intelligent and entertaining to watch. A fully-grown elephant is about 3½m high and weighs around 6,000kg. Female elephants live in closely-knit clans in which the eldest female takes a matriarchal role over her sisters, daughters and grand daughters. Mother-daughter bonds are strong and, because elephants live to a similar age to humans, they may exist for up to 50 years. Males generally leave the family group at around 12 years, after which they either roam around on their own or form bachelor herds. Under normal circumstances, elephants range widely in search of food and water, but when concentrated populations are forced to live in conservation areas, their habit of uprooting trees can cause serious environmental damage. Despite heavy poaching, Tanzania still has an awesome elephant population. They are extremely adaptable animals, so are common in most large game reserves and national parks, particularly the Selous, Ruaha, Tarangire and Katavi. They are less common in the Serengeti.

Black rhinoceros (*faru*)   These imposing creatures have been poached close to extinction in Tanzania, but are still likely to be seen in Ngorongoro Crater. There is said to be a significant population in the Selous, but they are probably extinct in all the national parks. The closely-related white rhinoceros is not found in Tanzania.

Hippopotamus (*kiboko*)   These lumbering aquatic animals are found in most stretches of water within reserves. Hippos spend most of the day submerged in water, but they emerge from the water at night in order to graze. They are strongly territorial, with herds of 10 or more animals being presided over by a dominant male. Hippo are abundant on the Rufiji River in the Selous Game Reserve. The best places to see them in northern Tanzania are the hippo pool in Lake Manyara National Park and the picnic site in Ngorongoro Crater. Hippo are still quite common outside of reserves, where they are responsible for killing more people than any other African mammal.

Buffalo (*nyati*)   The African buffalo is an adaptable and widespread animal. It lives in large herds on the savannah and smaller herds in forested areas. Herds are mixed-sex and are normally comprised of several loosely-related family clans and bachelor groups. Buffalo are found in virtually all Tanzania's national parks and game reserves.

Giraffe (*twiga*)   The world's tallest animal (up to 5.5m) is distinctive. Giraffe live in loosely-structured mixed-sex herds numbering between five and 15 animals. As herd members may be dispersed over 1km or so, they are frequently seen singly or in smaller groups. Giraffes' long necks gives them a slightly ungainly appearance when they amble; they look decidedly absurd when they adopt a semi-crouching position in order to drink. Giraffe are common throughout Tanzania, though they are not found in the Ngorongoro crater or in the Selous south of the Rufiji River. Only one subspecies, the Maasai giraffe, is found in Tanzania.

Burchell's zebra (*punda milia*)   Zebra are striped members of the horse family, common and widespread throughout Tanzania. They are often seen in large herds, but their basic social unit is the small, relatively stable family group, which typically consists of a male, up to five females, and their collective offspring. Zebra are often seen in the company of wildebeest. Two other species of zebra are found in Africa, but neither are present in Tanzania.

Pigs   The only pig you are likely to see is the warthog (*ngiri*), which is widespread and common in savannah and woodland. Warthogs are a uniform grey colour, and both sexes have impressive tusks. They are normally seen in family groups, trotting away briskly in the opposite direction with their tails raised stiffly and a determinedly nonchalant air. The bulkier and hairier bushpig (*nguruwe mwitu*) is found mainly in thickets and dense woodland; although widespread and reasonably common, it is not often seen due to its nocturnal habits and favoured habitat. The giant forest hog (*nguruwe*), the largest African pig, is an animal of true forest. It lives in suitable habitat throughout Tanzania but is rarely seen.

Elephant shrews (*sange*)   These bizarre rodents look like miniature kangaroos with absurdly elongated noses. A number of species are present in Tanzania, but they are secretive and nocturnal, so rarely seen. The giant elephant shrew of the Usambara is about the size of a duiker.

Hyraxes (*pimbi*)   These guinea pig-like animals look like rodents but are more closely related to elephant (though you are unlikely to have any difficulty telling them apart). Three types of hyrax are generally recognised, all of them found in Tanzania. Rock hyrax and bush hyrax both dwell on cliffs and koppies, and are often live alongside each other. Both species are brown, but the rock hyrax is larger than the bush hyrax and has coarser fur with a yellowish tinge. Bush and Rock hyrax are tame and common at Lobo and Seronera Lodges in the Serengeti. The tree hyrax is a nocturnal creature generally found in montane forests; though seldom seen, its shrieking call is unforgettable if heard.

Birds

Tanzania is a bird-watchers dream, with over 1,000 species recorded. Casual visitors will be stunned at the abundance of bird life: the brilliantly coloured lilac-breasted rollers and superb starlings, the numerous birds of prey, the giant ostrich, the faintly comic hornbills, the magnificent crowned crane — the list could go on forever.

For serious birders, virtually anywhere in Tanzania offers good birding; in many areas a reasonably competent observer could hope to see between 50 and 100 species in a day. Any of the northern reserves are recommended: Arusha and Lake Manyara National Park are both good for forest and water birds; the Serengeti and Tarangire are good for raptors and acacia and grassland species.

Forest is an especially important birding habitat. The forests of the Eastern Arc Mountains hold numerous endemics. Amani and the Udzungwa National Park are the most accessible places for seeing some of these. Miombo-associated species can be seen in the southern reserves: the Selous, with the advantage of the many birds which live along the Rufiji River, is particularly recommended. Western reserves such as Gombe Stream and Rubondo Island offer a combination of water and forest habitats, with the possibility of glimpsing one or two West African specials. If you visit Mwanza, don't bypass Saa Nane Island — in an hour there I saw five species

I've not seen elsewhere in Tanzania.

Field guides are discussed under *Further Reading*.

Reptiles

The world's largest reptile, the Nile crocodile (*mamba*), is common in most large rivers and lakes, except where it has been hunted out. On the Rufiji River, in Selous Game Reserve, we saw some of the largest crocodiles we have seen anywhere in Africa. Crocodile feed on a variety of fish and mammals; the latter they drag into the water, submerge till drowned, then store underwater for a period of time until suitably decomposed.

Hundreds of different snakes and lizards are found in Tanzania. Perhaps fortunately, snakes are generally shy and are very seldom seen. You can expect to see lizards everywhere, even in hotel rooms. Saa Nane Island near Mwanza is a prime spot for reptile enthusiasts, with colourful rock agama in abundance, a healthy population of water monitor (Africa's largest lizard which grows up to about 2m long), and a chance of seeing crocodile. Several species of chameleon are found in Tanzania, but even though they are common, even in towns, they are difficult to find unless you know where to look. You're most likely to see a chameleon by luck; when you are on safari you could ask your guide to try and find one for you. Don't expect your chameleon to change its skin colour to match its background. This is a myth. Colour change is triggered by emotion.

Cichlids

Lakes Nyasa, Tanganyika and Victoria vie with each other for the distinction of harbouring the most fish species of any lake in the world (though, since the introduction of the Nile Perch, many of Lake Victoria's endemics have become extinct; see Chapter Nine). The majority of these fish are cichlids, a group of colourful fish well-known to anyone who keeps a tropical aquarium (particularly the *mbuna* cichlids of Lake Nyasa). Many cichlid species are mouth-brooders: the eggs are fertilised and left to hatch in the female's mouth, after which the young are released into secluded rocky crevices where they are safe from predators. If you have a mask and snorkel, the best place to look for cichlids is near rocky stretches of shore on Lakes Nyasa and Tanganyika (see *Matema Beach*, Chapter Ten). You should be aware of the fact that areas favoured by cichlids may also attract crocodiles.

HIKING

In the 1980s, the only recognised hiking areas in Tanzania were Mount Kilimanjaro and more recently Mount Meru. Travellers who attempted to hike off the beaten track frequently met with suspicion, and if they did not have the required permits they risked being arrested. This no longer appears to be the case: while few travellers explore the hiking possibilities in Tanzania, the reports I have heard suggest there are few obstacles preventing them from doing so.

New hiking areas

It is not only Kilimanjaro and Arusha National Parks (Mount Meru) that allow walking. In the west of the country, Rubondo Island and Mahale Mountains (both described in Chapter Nine) can only be explored by foot, while the new and more accessible Udzungwa Mountains National Park (Chapter Eleven) is likely to have a couple of hiking trails open within the next two years. It is possible to hike in the Ngorongoro Conservation Area (Chapter Eight) with the permission of the Conservation Authority in Arusha. Hiking in national parks is relatively expensive as an entrance fee of $15 per 24 hours is charged along with a camping fee of $10 per night. You may only hike if you are accompanied by an armed ranger, which costs $10 per day.

Outside of the national parks, the most accessible areas for hiking are the Usambara Mountains (Chapter Six), the Mbeya Range and the Poroto Mountains (both described in Chapter Ten). As yet, none of these areas is explored by travellers with any frequency, but they are beginning to open up and it is relatively easy to get up-to-date information about them.

Right now there is probably no country in east and southern Africa with Tanzania's potential for truly off-the-beaten-track hiking. Meru and Kilimanjaro excluded, even the places mentioned above are seldom visited by travellers, and they are only the tip of the iceberg. For keen hikers with a sense of adventure, some of the more intriguing possibilities follow (chapter number given where there is further information in the main part of the guide): the Pare Mountains near Same, the Livingstone Range east of Lake Nyasa (Chapter Ten), Mahenge Mountain south of Ifakara, the Kitulo Plateau east of the Poroto (Chapter Ten), Mount Hanang west of Babati, the Mbizi Mountains between Sumbawanga and Lake Rukwa (Chapter Nine), the Uluguru Mountains near Morogoro (Chapter Eleven) and Ukerewe, Maisome and Kome Islands in Lake Victoria (Chapter Nine).

With so little information available on most of these areas, I'd be delighted to hear from anyone who does visit some of them.

Maps and equipment

In the national parks you may only walk when accompanied by a guide, so maps are probably not necessary. In the Poroto, Usambara and Mbeya mountains there are day hiking possibilities which would not require you to have detailed maps or specialist equipment. If you plan to undertake other hikes in these areas or to explore elsewhere, you will need good maps and equipment, and should ideally have some previous experience of wilderness hiking.

Essential equipment includes a compass, a tent, a sleeping bag and mat, warm clothing for areas at altitudes above about 1,500m, a stove and food, water bottles, and if you are hiking in the wet season, waterproof clothing. Unless you have a fair grip on the language already, a KiSwahili dictionary or phrase book will be more than useful.

You should be able to buy 1:50,000 survey maps of the area you plan to visit from the Department of Lands and Surveys in Dar es Salaam. This is a straightforward procedure and maps cost no more than $2 apiece. You must decide where you want to hike before you leave Dar es Salaam. You will not be able to get hold of maps elsewhere in the country.

Permits

As I understand it, provided you stick to roads and footpaths no special permission is needed to hike anywhere in Tanzania. This is not as limiting as it may sound. The roads that pass through the type of place listed above are unlikely to see more than a vehicle or two daily — if that.

I have heard too few reports from hikers to say with total confidence that you will not hit bureaucratic problems hiking in remote areas, but it seems unlikely. The attitude to tourists has changed greatly in recent years, especially since the ANC was unbanned in South Africa. We went to several remote areas in the course of researching this book and experienced nothing that suggests there is any great suspicion of travellers in places where people are not used to them.

Having said that, at the time of writing many of the places mentioned above have not seen hikers for years. You will be charting unknown territory; before you do this it would be wise to make enquiries, if only to let someone in authority know your plans and to check there are no temporary restrictions on the area you plan to visit. The district or regional headquarters is the best place to enquire. If an area falls in a forest reserve the local Forestry Department office would be more appropriate. If the area is too remote for there to be either, ask at the police station. It would be worth trying to get something in writing with an official stamp on it, just in case you are queried at some point.

If you pass through villages when hiking, it is polite to exchange greetings with the village chairman. You are also less likely to arouse suspicion if you do this. Be discreet with your camera. Never photograph villagers without asking first and don't photograph anything in the vicinity of bridges, railway lines, radio masts or any other government property.

It is forbidden to hike in national parks without a ranger or without paying the entrance fee. If you do the latter you could be arrested.

Chapter Three

Practical Information

TOURIST INFORMATION AND SERVICES

The main office of the Tanzania Tourist Corporation (TTC) is in Dar es Salaam, on Maktaba Street opposite the New Africa Hotel. The staff do their best, but their information is often out of date. The TTC is only worth visiting for information about Zanzibar or Dar es Salaam. The address is PO Box 2485, Dar es Salaam. Tel: (051) 27671/2/3/4/5.

There are TTC offices in London, New York, Stockholm, Milan and Frankfurt, and these may supply you with an information pack on the country.

The UK and US addresses are:
Tanzania Tourist Office, 78-80 Borough High St, London SE1, tel: 071 407 0566.
Tanzania Tourist Office, 210 E 42 Street, New York, NY 10017, tel: 986 7124.

WHEN TO VISIT

Tanzania's rainy season is between November and April. These months are warmer than May to October, but in most parts of the country only by a couple of degrees. Along the coast and in parts of northern Tanzania there are two rainy seasons: the short rains in November and December and the long rains from March to May.

Tanzania can be visited at any time of year. If you want to see the Serengeti at its best, don't come during the dry season — most of the animals will have migrated to the Maasai Mara across the border in Kenya. If you plan to explore the south coast or other remote areas, bear in mind that many roads become impassable during the rainy season. The rainy months are best avoided if you plan to hike.

PUBLIC HOLIDAYS

1 January	New Years Day
12 January	Zanzibar Revolution Day
5 February	Founding of the CCM
26 April	Union Day
1 May	International Workers Day
7 July	Peasants Day
9 December	Independence Day
25 December	Christmas Day

Other public holidays are Good Friday, Easter Monday, Idd-ul-Fitr, Islamic New Year and the Prophet's Birthday. These fall on different dates every year.

RED TAPE

Visas

Visas are required by all except citizens of Commonwealth and Scandinavian countries and the Republic of Ireland. They must be obtained in advance from a Tanzanian Embassy. The High Commission in London is currently requiring British citizens to buy a visa for travel to Tanzania. This may be a temporary quirk, or just a London one. The only safe advice is to check with your embassy or High Commission before you go.

A visitors pass, required by all visitors, is normally issued for free and without any fuss when you enter the country. You can obtain a visitors pass in advance at any Tanzanian Embassy, but it will cost around $40. Your visitors pass will probably be valid for up to one month. It can be extended at any Immigration Office with a minimum of fuss. This is best done in a small town; in Dar es Salaam or Arusha you will face a long queue.

Embassies abroad

There are Tanzanian embassies or high commissions in Angola, Belgium, Britain, Burundi, Canada, China, CIS, Egypt, Ethiopia, France, Germany, Guinea, India, Japan, Kenya, Mozambique, Namibia, Netherlands, Nigeria, Rwanda, Sudan, Sweden, Uganda, USA, Zaire, Zambia and Zimbabwe. Below are addresses of those you are most likely to need.

High Commission of the United Republic of Tanzania, 43 Hertford St, London, England W1Y 8DB. Tel: 071-499 8951; Fax: 071-491 9321.

Botschaft der Vereinigte Republik von Tansania, Theatreplatz 26, 5300 Bonn, Germany. Tel: 0228 358051-4; Fax: 0228 358226.

Embassy of the United Republic of Tanzania, 2139 R Street NW, Washington DC 2000, USA. Tel: 202 9396129.

Immigration and customs

The official requirements for entering Tanzania are an onward ticket and sufficient funds. This is only likely to be enforced if you arrive by air. If you are not carrying much money (less than US$1,000) try to bring a credit card; this is normally considered sufficient funds.

An onward ticket is a ticket out of Tanzania. A ticket leaving from another African country is just as good. You obviously won't have an onward ticket if you fly into Tanzania to start extended African travels and only plan to buy a ticket home at a later stage. Again, a credit card will help get you through.

One possibility is an MCO (Miscellaneous Charge Order). This is a blank air ticket, charged to the value of your choice and exchangeable world-wide for a variety of travel services. MCOs are normally refundable, but the terms should be checked with the individual airline.

If you think you might have problems with immigration (you don't have an onward ticket or credit card, don't want to buy an MCO and are short of cash) it is worth having a visa or visitor's pass for a neighbouring country stamped in your passport before you fly into Tanzania. This will help back up your claim that you plan to become another country's problem within a reasonable time span.

Having said all this, I met plenty of travellers who flew into Tanzania without an onward ticket, and none had a problem.

You no longer need to complete a currency declaration form when you enter Tanzania. Restrictions on South Africans and people who have a South African stamp in their passport have been lifted.

Bribery

Bribery is not much of an issue. There is said to be plenty of corruption in Tanzanian business circles, but it is unlikely to affect tourists. I have never been in a situation where I felt a bribe was being hinted at, nor have I heard of one from another traveller.

Bureaucracy

In the 1980s you often heard stories about travellers clashing with Tanzanian officials. Most incidents were camera-related: it was illegal to take photographs outside tourist areas, largely because of the number of ANC training centres in Tanzania at that time. It may have been paranoid to suspect every backpacker with a camera of being a spy, but as South Africa had used European passport holders disguised as backpackers to bomb an alleged ANC office in Zimbabwe, it was understandable. Things have relaxed greatly since South Africa unbanned the ANC. In our time in Tanzania we experienced nothing more sinister than mild abruptness; in general, Tanzanian officials will go out of their way to accommodate foreigners.

Some travellers behave as if they expect to be allowed to do what they like in African countries, as if they are above the law because they have a white skin and a foreign passport. This attitude is on the decline, but it still persists amongst some budget travellers. So, for the sake of clarity: if, for instance, you climb Kilimanjaro via an illegal route to avoid paying park entrance fees and are arrested, the person who arrests you is not being officious or bureaucratic, he is merely doing his job.

In remote parts of the country you may from time to time be approached by an immigration or police officer who wants to look over your passport. This happened to us a few times and in every instance it was handled in a relaxed, friendly manner. If it happens to you, expect to be asked where you have come from, where you are going, what you are doing in Tanzania etc. Don't read too much into this; it is the typical stuff of KiSwahili small talk. The officer concerned is as likely to be savouring an opportunity to practice his English as he is to have any professional interest in the trivia of your holiday. If you are in a rush, it can be a bit irritating to be cornered like this. There is no point in letting your irritation show. Smile, keep your answers simple, and you will soon be on your way.

GETTING TO TANZANIA

Flying

The following airlines fly to Tanzania from Europe or the United Kingdom: Aeroflot, Air France, Air Tanzania, British Airways, Gulf Air, KLM, Lufthansa and Swissair. African airlines which fly to Tanzania from elsewhere in Africa include Air Botswana, Air Tanzania, Air Zimbabwe, EgyptAir, Ethiopian Airlines, Kenya Airways, Royal Swazi, South African Airways and Zambia Airways.

There are plenty of flights from Europe to Dar es Salaam. It is often cheaper to fly with an airline that uses a less direct route, such as Aeroflot or EgyptAir. Most African airlines fly to London and they are often cheaper than European airlines. London is the best place to pick up a cheap ticket; many continental travellers buy their tickets there.

Most people fly into Tanzania at Dar es Salaam, but there are also international flights to Kilimanjaro Airport (between Arusha and Moshi), and to Zanzibar. It is relatively straightforward to visit northern Tanzania from Nairobi (buses between Nairobi and Arusha take eight hours). It is generally cheaper to fly to Nairobi than Dar es Salaam; on the other hand a high percentage of travellers get ripped off in their first few days in Nairobi, so it is not the greatest introduction to the continent. Nairobi is the best place to pick up cheap tickets out of East Africa. For short stays in East Africa, some of the best deals are charter flights to Mombasa (Kenya), a day's bus ride from Tanga or an overnight train ride from Nairobi.

Two London travel agents specialise in Africa: African Travel Systems (6 North End Parade, North End Road, London W14 OSJ, tel: (071) 602 5091) and Africa Travel Shop (4 Medway Court, Leigh Street, London WC1H 9OX, tel: (071) 387 1211, fax: (071) 383 7512).

Trailfinders (42-48 Earls Court Road, London W8 6EJ, tel: (071) 938 3366) and STA (117 Euston Road, London WC1, tel: (071) 465 0486, fax: (071) 388 0944) are both respected agents who do cheap flights worldwide, and are particularly worth speaking to for round-the-world type tickets. There are STA branches worldwide.

When you fly out of Tanzania, a $20 airport tax must be payed in hard currency. Travellers cheques are *not* accepted.

Overland

Both overland routes between Europe and East Africa appear to be difficult at present. Southern Sudan is closed to tourists, so if you want to use the Nile route you must fly from Khartoum to Nairobi. From what I hear, several overland truck companies have stopped using the Sahara route due to banditry. Possibly people are still getting through, but in six months in East Africa, I didn't meet anyone who had come overland from the north.

Since South Africa has moved away from apartheid, the Cape to Nairobi route has become an overlander's standard. Some people start this trip in East Africa, others start in South Africa — there's not a lot in it. The advantage of starting in the south is that you can adapt to African conditions in the more organised environment of South Africa and Zimbabwe before you hit the relative chaos of East Africa; the disadvantage is that you will have to put up with the most trying travel conditions of the trip towards the end, after the novelty of being in Africa has worn off. These days Johannesburg is almost as good as Nairobi for cheap air tickets, so that is not a factor.

A proliferation of overland truck companies run regular trips between southern Africa (normally Johannesburg or Harare) and East Africa. The advantages of travelling on an overland truck are that it will visit remote areas which you would be unlikely to reach otherwise, and that you will see far more than you would by travelling independently for the same period of time; the disadvantages are that you will be in the company of the same 10 to 20 other people for the duration of the trip, and that the truck will cut you off from everyday African life.

   Most of the people I've spoken to say their main reason for travelling on a truck is safety. It's worth saying, therefore, that this is by-and-large a safe and well-travelled region and that you will meet plenty of other single travellers. If you feel you would prefer to travel independently, don't let fear swing you in the opposite direction.

Border crossings

Tanzania borders eight countries. A brief outline of frequently-used border crossings follows:

To/from Kenya

Most travellers use the Namanga border between Nairobi and Arusha. There is plenty of transport on this route: you will get through in a day comfortably. If anyone in Nairobi tries to talk you into buying Tanzanian money, ignore them. There is a bank on the Tanzanian side of the border.

   Buses link Mombasa to Tanga and Kisumu to Mwanza. A growing number of passenger boats link Mombasa to Dar es Salaam.

To/from Uganda

The simplest option is the weekly ferry between Port Bell and Mwanza (see Chapter Nine). The other route is via Masaka and Bukoba. Regular minibuses run from Masaka to Kyotera, where the odd pick-up truck leaves for the Mutukulu border. At Mutukulu you can pick up a Landrover to Bukoba. There are overnight ferries between Bukoba and Mwanza (see Chapter Nine).

To/from Rwanda

The only route between Kigale and Mwanza is by road. There is public transport from Kigale to Rusumu border (expect to walk the last 2km). A basic but friendly guest house on the Tanzanian side costs $1.50 per person. From Rusumu, it is easy to find a lift on a truck to Geita. It takes a day to get to Geita. If you spend a night in

Geita, the Nwanenge and Lunguyai Guest Houses are both recommended. There are plenty of buses between Geita and Mwanza.

To/from Burundi

The straightforward option is the Lake Tanganyika ferry (see Chapter Nine). The trip can also be done in steps. Minibuses go from Bujumbura to the immigration office at Nyanza Luc and on to the border. At Kagunga, a 20-minute walk past the border, lake taxis run to Gombe Stream and Kalalangabo, 3km from Kigoma.

To/from Zaire

Cargo boats between Kigoma and Kalemie might sometimes carry passengers, but don't rely on this. Most people go via Burundi.

To/from Zambia

Zambia, the main gateway between East and southern Africa, can be reached by boat or rail. Tazara trains run twice-weekly from Dar es Salaam to Kapiri Mposhi, and are met by a bus to Lusaka. From western Tanzania, the easiest way to get to Zambia is on the Lake Tanganyika ferry (see Chapter Nine).

To/from Malawi

The turn-off to the Malawi border is 5km from Kyela, on the Mbeya road. From there you can either take a bicycle taxi to the border or wait for a lift. In Malawi, a bus to Karonga arrives at the border at 7.00pm and leaves at 6.00am. It is forbidden to stay overnight at the border so the bus is of no use to travellers. Most travellers get to Karonga on a truck.

WHAT TO BRING

This depends largely on how you plan to travel. The following suggestions are mainly aimed at independent travellers.

Backpacking and camping gear

A backpack is the only practical way to carry your luggage on public transport. An internal frame is more flexible than an external one. Ensure your pack is durable, that the seams and zips are properly sewn, and that it has several pockets. It is useful to carry a day pack.

Normally I wouldn't dream of travelling in Africa without a tent, but there are very few campsites in Tanzania. Nevertheless, it is advisable to carry a tent if you plan to travel or hike in remote areas. If you are going to camp, bring a sleeping bag and mat. Many parts of Tanzania are cold at night.

Clothes

If you are travelling with everything on your back, keep your clothes to a minimum. A sweater is essential; more than one if you are heading into the mountains. Bring a pair of trousers for walking and to wear in the evening. Light cotton trousers are cooler and more practical than jeans. A track suit will double as thermal underwear if you intend to do high-altitude hiking. A hat and sunglasses are recommended.

Whatever else you bring should be light, flexible, comfortable, and made of cotton. A few T-shirts, a pair of shorts and/or a skirt, and a few pairs of underpants and socks is adequate.

What shoes you should bring depends on the sort of travelling you will be doing. The normal combination is a pair of trainers or hiking boots and either sandals, flip-flops or light slip-on shoes. I don't like flip-flops or sandals as they offer little protection against thorns, biting insects or potholed pavements, but I seem to be in a minority.

Tanzania's large Muslim population finds it offensive for a woman to expose her knees or shoulders. Women who do so can expect to meet with a certain amount of hostility. It is difficult to make hard and fast rules about what to wear, but some generalisations may help. Shorts are out, except at beach resorts, in game reserves, and possibly in Dar es Salaam or Arusha where people are used to tourists. For women, trousers are frowned upon in some quarters but they are just about acceptable. The ideal thing to wear is a skirt which covers your knees. A shoulderless t-shirt which exposes your bra — or worse — is unlikely to go down well (you laugh: I met someone dressed like this who couldn't figure out why she was hissed at wherever she went).

Men, too, should be conscious of what they wear. Shorts seem to be acceptable, but few Tanzanian men wear them and it is considered more respectable to wear trousers. Walking around in a public place without a shirt is totally unacceptable.

Many Tanzanians think it is insulting for westerners to wear scruffy or dirty clothes. Quite accurately, they feel you wouldn't dress like that at home. It is difficult to explain that at home you also wouldn't spend three successive days in crowded buses on dusty roads with a limited amount of clothing crumpled up in a backpack. If you are travelling rough, you are bound to look a mess at times, but it is worth trying to look as spruce as possible.

Other odds and ends

This is a random series of observations on what is and isn't available in Tanzania.

Don't come without a torch, a towel, a day pack, and if you are camping, pots and other cooking equipment. You cannot buy camping Gaz in Tanzania.

If you wear contact lenses, bring all the fluids you need. They are not available in Tanzania. It is not necessary to carry a spare pair of glasses unless you already have one; they are cheap (around $10) and can be made up quickly in most Tanzanian towns. Bring your prescription though.

Locally-manufactured insect repellant is a joke. The stuff we used left a trail of insects glued to our arms. Bring some with you, preferably roll-on.

Loo paper is widely available and cheap, but most toilets don't have any (this includes communal toilets in upper-range hotels). Always carry a spare roll with you.

Sanitary towels are manufactured locally. They are available in most large towns, but it is advisable to carry some spares. Tampons are imported and available in large towns only.

Many older hotels have baths but no bath plugs. You might want to consider carrying your own bath plug (though bear in mind that it's unusual for budget and moderate hotels to have hot water; a splash is often preferable to a wallow anyway).

Some cheap guest houses don't supply you with a padlock. Bring your own just in case.

A collapsible umbrella offers useful protection against both sun and rain.

A travel alarm clock will be useful for all those 5.00am bus departures.

Books of any description are difficult to get hold of in Tanzania. Bring whatever field guides etc you want with you.

Binoculars

It's worth bringing binoculars. They will add greatly to your enjoyment of a safari by allowing you to look at birds and distant animals. If you are buying binoculars especially for the trip, the newer compact variety generally have a crisper image than traditional binoculars, and they will certainly add less weight to your luggage; on the other hand, compact binoculars are considerably more expensive than the traditional variety, and they have a smaller field of vision. If you are spending an extended period of time in Tanzania, bear in mind that dust, rain and bad roads will all take their toll; you have less to lose if you buy a cheapish (or even second-hand) pair. For most uses, 8x32 compact or 7x35 traditional binoculars are good enough; if you are interested in birds and have reasonably steady hands, I recommend 10x40 or 10x50.

MONEY

The unit of currency is the Tanzania shilling. This is divided into 100 cents. At the time of writing the exchange rate is roughly US$1 = Tsh340/- (bank rate) and US$1 = Tsh420/- (Bureau de Change rate). Throughout this guide prices are given in US dollars, calculated at the Bureau de Change rate.

Notes are printed in 1,000, 500, 200, 100, 50, 20 and 10/- denominations. There are also Tsh 10, 20 and 50/- coins. There are rumoured to be cent coins, but you are unlikely ever to see them (or find a use for them if you do).

Foreign exchange

Foreign money can be changed into Tanzanian shillings at any bank or Bureau de Change (known locally as forex bureaux). Banking hours are from 8.30am to 12.30pm on weekdays, and 8.30am to 11.30pm on Saturdays. In larger towns, some banks stay open in the afternoon. Most forex bureaux stay open till 3.00pm or 4.00pm.

Tanzania's currency was freed in early 1992 and since then a number of forex bureaux have opened, offering far more favourable rates than the banks. There are government-run forex bureaux at the main branch of the National Bank of Commerce in Arusha, Dar es Salaam, Mwanza and Namanga, and privately-run forex bureaux in Arusha, Dar es Salaam, Mwanza, Mbeya and Dodoma. By the time you read this there should also be forex bureaux in Tanga and Kigoma. You can change money at any time of day at Dar es Salaam airport.

Privately-run bureaux give the best rates. In Dar es Salaam there can be a variation of up to 10% in the rate offered by various forex bureaux. It is worth shopping around. Before you change a large amount of money, check the forex bureau has Tsh 500 or 1,000 banknotes.

Forex bureaux have killed the black market which previously thrived in Tanzania. Private individuals may give you a slightly better rate, but the official rate is so favourable it seems unfair to exploit this. In Dar es Salaam or Arusha you will be offered exceptionally good rates on the street. If you are stupid or greedy enough to accept these, expect to be ripped off.

There are plenty of forged $100 bills floating around Tanzania. Assume that anyone who suggests a deal involving a $100 bill is trying to unload a forgery.

At most overland borders there is nowhere to change money legally. You will have to change money with individuals. This is illegal, but as there is no option it is usually fairly open. If you can, get hold of some Tanzanian money in advance (ask travellers coming from Tanzania if they have some to swap). On overland crossings I always carry a small surplus of the currency of the country I am leaving (about $10 worth), and try to change this into the currency I need. I feel safer swapping African currencies than changing US dollars.

Most hard currencies are accepted in Tanzania, but it is simplest to carry US dollars. There is a big difference in the exchange rates offered for cash and travellers cheques (cash gets you about 10% more). It is worth having some cash, but bring the bulk of your money in travellers cheques as they can be replaced if they are stolen.

Some travel guides which include coverage of Tanzania claim that you are unlikely to use much local currency. Except at the very top of the range, this is rubbish and always has been. Most safari companies insist on being paid in hard currency, but the only other things that must be paid for in dollars are aeroplane fares, national park fees, airport and port taxes, and rooms at tourist hotels. Road, rail and ferry transport, meals, drinks, goods in shops and markets, and almost all moderate and budget accommodation can be paid for in local currency.

It is essential that you bring about US$200 in $5 and $10 bills for small payments that must be made in cash.

Credit cards

There are several advantages in carrying a credit card: it will help you through immigration, will reduce the amount of cash you need to carry, and would be useful if all your money was pinched. Having said that, except in Dar es Salaam, there are few places in Tanzania where credit cards are accepted. On the balance I think it is worth carrying a credit card, but only to use in emergencies.

Budgeting

Tanzania is a cheap country to visit, but some activities are quite expensive, most notably going on safari and climbing Mount Kilimanjaro. If you need to keep track of your expenses, it is best to operate on a dual budget: one for everyday expenses and one for special activities.

As a rough guide to day-to-day spending, a soda costs $0.25 and a beer $1, a meal in a *hoteli* costs less than $1 and a meal in a proper restaurant around $3. You can buy enough fruit to keep you going for a week for $1. A basic room costs up to $2, and a self-contained room in a moderate hotel around $5. Transport costs vary, but you should average out at under $3/day.

On $10 per day for one person or $15 for two, you could get around reasonably easily staying in local guest houses, eating at *hotelis*, going second class on trains and ferries, and probably still enjoying the odd minor extravagance.

On $15 per day for one person or $25 for two, you can travel in relative comfort. On a budget of $20 per day (two people), we stayed in moderate hotels about half the time, ate and drank what we felt like, and travelled first class on trains and ferries.

If you go on safari or climb Kilimanjaro expect to spend up to $100 per day for the duration of that activity. It is difficult to keep to a strict budget in Dar es Salaam or Arusha, as hotels are more expensive and there is more to spend your money on.

Notes on prices

All prices are in US dollars, calculated at the rate of US$1 = Tsh 400. The Tanzanian shilling has declined in value in the last few years, and if it continues to do so a price quoted in dollars is more likely to mean something in two years time than one in Tanzanian shillings. Having said that, the currency has stabilised since it was floated. If it remains stable while internal inflation increases, prices may increase for tourists.

All these prices were collected between July and December 1992. Where HC appears after a price it must be paid in hard currency.

GETTING AROUND

Air

Air Tanzania flies between Dar es Salaam and a number of other Tanzanian towns. It has a bad reputation for cancellations and overbooking. It is more reliable on regular routes, for instance to Kilimanjaro Airport or Zanzibar, than on flights to southern destinations such as Mtwara, Lindi and Songea.

There are flights between Dar es Salaam and the following towns:

	Resident	Non-resident
Kigoma	$87.00	$200.00
Kilimanjaro	$52.50	$123.00
Lindi	$38.50	$100.00
Mtwara	$45.00	$97.00
Musoma	$74.00	$185.00
Mwanza	$79.50	$192.00
Pemba	$28.50	$47.00
Songea	$51.25	$159.00
Tabora	$57.50	$141.00
Tanga	$30.50	$79.00
Zanzibar	$21.25	$43.00

Prices quoted for residents are US dollar equivalents, and may be paid in shillings. Non-residents must pay in US dollars.

Rail

There are three main railway lines in Tanzania. The northern line connects Dar es Salaam, Tanga and Moshi. The central line connects Dar es Salaam, Kigoma, Mwanza and Mpanda. The Tazara line connects Dar es Salaam, Mbeya and Kapiri Mposhi (Zambia).

Trains are the most reliable and comfortable way of getting around. I used Tanzanian trains about ten times and only once did a train leave more than a few minutes late.

There are three classes. First class is consists of two-berth compartments and second class consists of six-berth compartments. Men and women may not share a first or second class compartment unless they book the whole thing. Compartments vary in condition from acceptable to very tired-looking. Third class consists of seated carriages, but there are always more passengers than seats; it's only worth thinking about if you value neither your comfort nor your possessions.

Theft from train windows at night is not unusual. I have heard of someone whose rucksack was taken this way. Close the windows securely when you turn the light off. A block of wood is provided for this purpose; if you cannot find one in your compartment speak to the steward. Don't leave loose objects lying around the compartment; keep your luggage under the bunks. If you leave the compartment take all valuables with you.

All trains except those leaving Tanga have dining cars. Meals are good and reasonably priced. Beers and sodas are normally available.

If you travel first class and do not want to leave your cabin empty, the steward can bring meals to you. In second class I would have no hesitation about going to the dining car provided other passengers remained in the compartment. At many stations vendors sell snacks and meals through the window.

It is advisable to book train tickets three days to a week in advance. It is easier to get last minute bookings on trains heading towards Dar es Salaam than on trains leaving it.

You may read elsewhere that ticket officers sometimes refuse to issue a ticket without a bribe. The story is that you go to the booking office on the morning of departure, and are told there are no tickets. You offer a bribe and are told to come back later, when a ticket magically appears. This has happened to me on a few occasions, but minus the bribe. It turns out a number of tickets are automatically held for institutions such as the army, police, and hospitals until a few hours before departure. If they are not taken, they become available to the public. I've not heard or seen anything that supports the bribe story.

The Central Line

The central line runs from Dar es Salaam to Mwanza and Kigoma, stopping at Morogoro, Dodoma and Tabora. The train splits at Tabora: one half goes to Mwanza, the other to Kigoma. A third branch from Tabora to Mpanda is run as a separate service.

Trains leave Dar es Salaam on Tuesday, Wednesday, Friday and Sunday at 6.00pm. Trains in the opposite direction leave on Tuesday, Thursday, Friday and Sunday. They leave Mwanza at 7.00pm and Kigoma at 4.00pm. The full journey takes about 40 hours. Tickets can only be booked in advance at Dar es Salaam, Kigoma, Tabora and Mwanza. Elsewhere you will have to get on the train and hope for the best.

There is no direct service between Kigoma and Mwanza. You will have to take a train to Tabora, where you can make an onward booking. Extra carriages are added at Tabora, so most people have no problem getting through.

Trains to Mpanda leave Tabora on Monday, Wednesday and Friday. Trains to Tabora leave Mpanda on Tuesdays, Thursdays and Fridays. In both directions, they leave at 10.45pm and take 12 hours.

The Tazara Line

Two trains run every week between Dar es Salaam and Kapiri Mposhi (Zambia). These leave Dar es Salaam on Tuesday and Friday at 4.55pm, and take 36 hours. Three additional slow trains run every week as far as Tunduma. These leave Dar es Salaam on Monday, Thursday and Saturday at 11.00am.

All trains stop at Ifakara, Mbeya and Tunduma. Slow trains pass through the Selous Game Reserve during daylight hours. There is usually plenty of game to be seen.

The Northern Line

This line connects Dar es Salaam, Moshi and Tanga. Trains to Dar es Salaam and Tanga leave Moshi on Monday, Wednesday and Friday at 4.00pm. Trains to Dar es Salaam leave Tanga on the same days at 7.30pm. Trains to Tanga and Moshi leave Dar es Salaam on Tuesday, Thursday and Saturday at 4.00pm. Trains for Moshi leave Tanga on the same days at 7.30pm. All services are overnight and arrive between 6.00am and 9.00am.

Fares

Fares can be paid in local currency. Sample fares from Dar es Salaam to various destinations (in US dollars) follow:

	1st	2nd	3rd
Ifakara	6.20	4.25	2.25
Mbeya	12.65	8.80	4.05
Kapiri Mposhi	21.25	14.50	6.70
Morogoro	6.05	4.00	0.80
Dodoma	10.90	7.50	1.50
Tabora	18.00	11.50	2.15
Kigoma	25.40	17.60	3.00
Mwanza	25.00	17.50	2.95
Tanga	9.50	5.75	1.10
Moshi	12.50	7.90	1.50

In Dar es Salaam a 50% discount on the Tazara line is given to anyone with a student card. This takes a couple of hours. You must collect an application form from the Tazara station. You must then go to the Department of Education on Kivukoni Front where the form will be stamped. Finally you must return to the station to buy a ticket.

Lake and ocean

There are several useful ferry services in Tanzania. A few boats go daily between Dar es Salaam and Zanzibar. A weekly service connects Dar es Salaam, Mtwara and Mafia, and another connecting Dar es Salaam, Zanzibar, Tanga, Pemba and Mombasa started operating in early 1993. In Dar es Salaam, details of all ferries can be obtained from the booking offices near the port on Kivukoni Front. See Chapters Twelve and Thirteen for further details.

There are ferry services on all three great lakes, run by the Tanzania Railway Corporation. For details see Chapter Nine (Victoria and Tanganyika) and Ten (Nyasa).

Road

Road transport in Tanzania is wildly variable and often nightmarish. Only 10% of Tanzania's roads are surfaced, and many of these are badly potholed. The following roads are surfaced and in reasonable repair: Arusha to Tarangire, Arusha to Moshi, Moshi to Dar es Salaam, Mombo to Lushoto, Dar es Salaam to Tundumu, Makumbako to Songea, Mbeya to Kyela, Mwanza to Musoma, and Mtwara to Masasi via Lindi.

If you have the choice, use any mode of transport in preference to buses on dirt roads. These normally cover about 20km in an hour, so a 250km trip takes about 12 hours. I don't know how many travellers I have met who decided to travel between the north and south of the country via Dodoma instead of Dar es Salaam because it looks quicker on the map. It is no quicker and considerably less pleasant; ask anyone who has done it. Likewise, unless you are a masochist, don't think about using buses in the northwest of the country, an area with good rail and lake transport. Unfortunately, if you travel in the southwest or along the south coast, the odd bus-ride-from-hell is unavoidable.

On some routes there is no formal public transport. You will generally find a couple of open-topped pick-up trucks cover these routes. These tend to be overcrowded and overpriced.

You should be aware bus departure times are often given in Swahili time; read the section covering this in the Swahili appendix.

Fares

It is impossible to document the price of every possible route in the
country. To give you an idea of what to expect, here are some fairly
typical rides, the distance covered and mode of transport, and
approximate times and prices in US dollars. All road transport can
be paid for in local currency.

		Distance (km)	Hours	Price
Arusha/Dar es Salaam	bus	647	12-15	10.00
Arusha/Dar es Salaam	express bus	647	10-12	12.50
Arusha/Moshi	bus	85	2	1.50
Tanga/Lushoto	bus	154	6+	2.00
Mwanza/Arusha	bus via Serengeti	692	12-18	55.00*
Mwanza/Arusha	bus via Singada	855	36+	12.50
Tanga/Dar es Salaam	express bus	354	8	5.00
Mtwara/Dar es Salaam	bus	555	15+	6.00
Dar es Salaam/Morogoro	bus	196	4	2.00
Dar es Salaam/Iringa	bus	501	12	5.00
Morogoro/Iringa	minibus	305	7	3.50
Dar es Salaam/Mbeya	bus	851	15+	8.50
Dodoma/Iringa	bus	251	10+	2.50
Dodoma/Arusha	bus	687	20+	7.50
Mbeya/Kyela	bus	141	4	2.50
Mbamba Bay/Mbinga	pick-up truck	61	3+	3.00
Mbinga/Songea	bus	103	3	1.50
Songea/Njombe	bus	237	5	2.50
Mbeya/Sumbawanga	bus	322	8+	3.50
Sumbawanga/Mpanda	lift with truck	235	8+	5.00
Mpanda/Ikola	lift with truck	126	4+	4.00
Rusumu/Mwanza	lift with truck	400	18-48	10.00

*includes $30.00 in national park fees

Bookings

On busy routes, buses leave when they are full. There is no need to
book. On long hauls and quiet routes, there is normally a fixed
departure time, so it is advisable to book the day before you leave.
We were often given wildly inaccurate information about bus
schedules. Ask a few people; don't take the word of the first person
you speak to. In the main part of the guide I have given the current
situation regarding frequency of buses and whether booking is
necessary. Things change, however; you should make your own
enquiries.

Theft on buses

Wherever I have travelled in East Africa, I have handed my luggage to the conductor and let him get on with it. My bags have never been tampered with. Three months into this trip, I met a girl whose rucksack was broken into on Tanzanian buses four times in two weeks. I could not believe this was just a matter of luck, so in order to establish a pattern, I quizzed everyone I met about their experiences.

• The roof is the worst place for your luggage. Some conductors insist on putting it there (there is often no real option) but if possible try to get it into the body of the bus. If it does not fit on the racks, put it up near the driver.

• Avoid overnight buses. Almost all the theft stories I have heard relate to them. The Arusha-Dodoma and Dar es Salaam-Mbeya routes are particularly bad.

• Be wary of strangers who offer you food. I have heard of travellers being given drugged food and having their possessions taken while they are asleep (one incident each on the two routes mentioned above).

• Be vigilant when the bus is stationary. The snatch-and-grab experts who hang round most bus stations are not above grabbing something through the window. If anyone is hanging around, catch their eye so they know you are aware of them.

• Don't leave valuables on your lap. It sounds obvious; I met someone whose money belt was snatched from his lap while he was fiddling in his day pack.

Hitching

There is little scope for hitching in Tanzania. On routes where there is no public transport you may have to hitch, but generally this will be on the back of a truck and you will have to pay. Hitching is an option on the Arusha-Dar es Salaam-Mbeya road.

Car hire

Self-drive car hire is not really an option in Tanzania. It is expensive and vehicles are poorly-maintained. It is more normal and sensible to hire a vehicle with a driver; this can be done through most safari companies in Arusha and Dar es Salaam.

ACCOMMODATION

Most Tanzanian towns have a variety of moderately-priced and budget hotels. Even the smallest villages usually have somewhere you can stay for a dollar or so. Except in major tourist centres, there is little in the way of luxury accommodation.

I have divided accommodation into four categories: camping, budget, moderate and upper range. These categories are based more on feel than on price, but except in Dar es Salaam and Arusha, prices are reasonably consistent: budget is under $3, moderate from $3 to $10, and upper range anything above that. In Dar es Salaam and Arusha, budget is under $10, moderate up to $30, and upper range anything above that.

Remember that in KiSwahili, *hoteli* means restaurant; if you ask people for a hotel, you will get a *hoteli* (see *Swahili* appendix).

Camping

There are few campsites in Tanzania, and those that exist tend to be in national parks, where camping costs $10 per person. There are private campsites in the Arusha-Kilimanjaro area. If you ask at moderate hotels in out of the way places, you may be allowed to camp in their grounds for a fee.

If you are hiking in off-the-beaten-track areas, a tent will be a distinct asset. You should, however, be discreet; either set up well away from villages or else ask permission from the village headperson before you pitch a tent. I've not met many people who have camped rough in Tanzania, but it's hard to imagine there would be a significant risk attached to camping in rural areas, provided you didn't flaunt your presence or leave your tent unguarded for a lengthy period.

Budget

Most budget accommodation in Tanzania consists of guest houses. These are almost exclusively used by locals, and are remarkably uniform in design and price. The typical guest house is made up of cell-like rooms forming three walls around a central courtyard, with a reception area or restaurant at the front. Toilets are more often than not long-drops. Washing facilities usually amount to a lockable room and a bucket of cold water, though some have showers. There are perhaps five guest houses in the whole of Tanzania which have running hot water. Quite a few will supply you with a basin of hot water on request.

Tanzanian guest houses may be basic, but the majority are

reasonably clean and pleasant, and are good value when compared to similar establishments in neighbouring countries. We rarely paid more than $2 for a room in a Tanzanian guest house. We found that guest houses run by women or with a strong female presence were generally cleaner and more hospitable than those run by men. There is a strong town-to-town variation in guest house quality: in some towns a clean, freshly-painted room with mosquito nets and a fan is standard; in others — Iringa and Bukoba leap to mind — three-quarters of the places we looked at were totally unappealing.

In most medium-sized towns there are a couple of dozen guest houses, usually clustered around the bus station and often with little to choose between them. In such cases I have avoided making individual recommendations.

There are a handful of church-run guest houses and hostels in Tanzania. These are normally included under budget accommodation.

Moderate

This category covers everything that isn't a guest house or a so-called tourist hotel, and defies generalisations. Typically, a moderate hotel has self-contained rooms with cold running water, and can be paid for in local currency. Most moderate hotels include a continental breakfast in the price of a room, but this rarely amounts to more than dry bread and coffee.

Upper range

These are official tourist hotels, and must be paid for in hard currency. Prices vary wildly, but typically you will be looking at around $60 to $90 for a double room. This invariably includes breakfast. Tourist hotels are concentrated in Dar es Salaam, Zanzibar, Tanga and the Kilimanjaro-Arusha-Serengeti area. There are only a handful in the south and west of the country. Most hotels in this range have a lower rate for Tanzanian residents. This difference can be as much as 60% less, especially in hotels run by the TTC. All TTC hotels offer a 50% discount between the day after Easter Monday and the 30 June.

Staying with Tanzanians

Unless you travel off the beaten track or have addresses of friends, you are unlikely to stay with Tanzanians much. If you stay with expats, be sensitive to their way of life. People living in the sticks are often delighted to have fresh company, but not always. If people evidently have a busy lifestyle, try not to get in the way: play with their children (if they have any) and help around the house.

In the past travellers have taken it to be their right to stay with aid workers or at missions. This goes back to the days when comparatively few backpackers travelled in Africa and those who did received a level of hospitality which reflected their novelty. Those days are long gone, but the on-the-cheap attitude still persists in some quarters. Many expats have suffered from travellers overstaying their welcome; don't necessarily expect people to welcome you with open arms.

EATING AND DRINKING

Eating

If you are not too fussy and don't mind a lack of variety, you can eat well and cheaply almost anywhere in Tanzania. In most towns numerous local restaurants, called *hotelis*, serve unimaginative but filling meals for under US$1. *Hotelis* vary greatly in quality: I have had some very tasty meals in them, but as often as not gristle and sludge would be an appropriate description of what you are served.

Most *hoteli* food is based around a stew eaten with one of four staples: rice, *chapati*, *ugali* or *batoke*. *Ugali* is a stiff maize porridge eaten throughout sub-Saharan Africa. *Batoke* or *matoke* is cooked plantain, served boiled or in a mushy heap. In the Lake Victoria region, *batoke* replaces *ugali* as the staple food. The most common stews are chicken, beef, goat and beans. In coastal towns and around the great lakes, whole fried fish is a welcome change.

Mandazi, the local equivalent of doughnuts, are tasty when freshly cooked. They are served at *hotelis* and sold at markets. You can eat cheaply at stalls around markets and bus station. Goat kebabs, fried chicken, grilled groundnuts and potato chips are often freshly-cooked and sold in these places.

Cheap it may be, but for most travellers *hoteli*-fare soon palls. In most larger towns, there are what could be termed proper restaurants. These are normally within the reach of any budget, and would typically serve a variety of meat, steak and chicken dishes with potato chips or rice, and cost around $3 for a main course. There is considerably more culinary variety in Dar es Salaam and Arusha, where for around $5 you can eat very well.

At one time, walking around a Tanzanian market you would see little but onions and bananas. This has improved, and in most towns a reasonable variety of fruits, vegetables, pulses and beans can be bought, depending on the season. The most common fruits are mangoes, oranges, bananas, pineapples, papaya and coconuts. Fresh fruit is dirt cheap in Tanzania.

NOTE: KiSwahili names for various foods are given in the KiSwahili appendix.

Drinks

The most widely-drunk beverage is *chai*, a sweet tea where all ingredients are boiled together in a pot. Along the coast *chai* is often flavoured with spices such as ginger. In some places *chai* is served *ya rangi* or black; in others *mazewa* or milky. Sodas such as Coke, Pepsi, Sprite and Fanta are widely available, and cost about $0.25. In large towns you can often get fresh fruit juice.

The two main alcoholic drinks are beer and *konyagi*. *Konyagi* is a spirit made from sugar cane. It tastes a bit strange on its own, but mixes well. A bottle costs about $2.50, and a tot about $0.25. The local beers, Safari, Pilsner, and Guinness, come in 500ml bottles and cost around $1. Pilsner is OK, Guinness is unlikely to tempt any Irishmen to emigrate, and Safari, the most widely-available beer, is never better than drinkable. Kenyan beers are better, and are widely available north of Dar es Salaam. Around Mbeya, try Carlsberg Green, an excellent Malawian beer. Around Lake Tanganyika, another excellent beer, Zairian *Primus*, comes in 750ml bottles and costs about $1. In Dar es Salaam, a variety of Kenyan, South African and European beers are available, but they are quite expensive.

A variety of imported spirits are available in larger towns, often at ridiculous prices. In Tanga, we were drinking good Scotch whisky for $0.25 a tot.

SHOPPING

Until a few years ago it was difficult to buy anything much in Tanzania. One of my most vivid memories of Dar es Salaam in 1986 was walking into a general store where a lone shelf of teaspoons was the only stock. Things have improved greatly since then. In Dar es Salaam and most other large towns a fair range of imported goods is available, though prices are often inflated. If you have any very specific needs — unusual medications or slide film for instance — bring them with you.

Toilet roll, soap, toothpaste, pens, batteries and locally-produced food are widely-available. *Dukas*, the stalls you see around markets or lining roads, are cheaper than proper shops and are open seven days a week. Even in Dar es Salaam, we were rarely overcharged because we were tourists.

Shopping hours are normally between 8.30am and 4.30pm, with a lunch break between 1.00pm and 2.00pm.

Curios

A variety of items specifically aimed at tourists are available: Makonde carvings, batiks, musical instruments, wooden spoons, and various soapstone and malachite knick-knacks. The curio shops near the clock tower in Arusha are the best place to shop for curios. Prices are competitive and the quality is good. Prices in shops are fixed, but you may be able to negotiate a discount. At curio stalls, haggling is necessary. Unless you are good at this, expect to pay more than you would in a shop.

If you have an interest in African music, a good range of tapes is available at stalls in Dar es Salaam city centre. Most are of Zairian groups which are popular in East Africa: Loketa, Kanda Bongoman, Bossi Bossiana and the like. Cassettes sell for about $1.25.

The colourful *Vitenge* (the singular of this is *Kitenge*) worn by most Tanzanian women can be picked up cheaply at any market in the country.

Bargaining

It is commonly asserted that nothing in Africa has a fixed price. To an extent this is true; nevertheless, you need a certain amount of sensitivity to know when haggling is appropriate. Many travellers arrive in Africa expecting everyone to overcharge them and so they enter into all transactions with paranoid aggression; this is understandable but unnecessary.

There are no hard and fast rules as to when you should and shouldn't bargain. You must be responsive to each situation and judge it on its own merits. My own feeling is that the issue of bargaining has been misrepresented by travel guides in the past; it's worth discussing in some detail.

Anyone who regularly deals with tourists will be open to negotiation. This includes taxi drivers, safari operators and stall owners in Dar es Salaam and Arusha, and curio stalls anywhere. Where haggling is the norm, it is best viewed as something that can add an enjoyable new dimension to your holiday. With experienced hagglers you must appear to be firm. This doesn't mean you need to be ungracious; except in extreme situations, yelling and throwing tantrums is simply loutish.

In non-tourist areas, you will seldom be overcharged. Some

travellers challenge every price as a matter of course, often accompanied with accusations of dishonesty. Try, instead, to establish the going rate in advance: find out what locals pay (it helps if you can count in Swahili) or visit a few stalls before you buy (an inflated price will drop the moment you walk away). If someone is unwilling to barter, the probability is that they asked a fair price in the first place.

You should be wary of rigid advice; for instance, that you will normally be asked double the price the person will eventually settle for. In Kenya, I was once asked Ksh 200/- for a batik; I didn't want it so said Ksh 20/- as a joke. I got it for Ksh 30/-. At the other end of the scale, on about half the occasions when we used taxis in Dar es Salaam (where I would expect to be overcharged) we were asked the going rate straight off.

Do not assume that things will cost the same from one town to the next. As an example, in three successive villages we passed through on a bus, oranges cost Tsh 5/-, 10/- and 20/- (the price they were asking locals, not us). You'll often find large price differences from town to town for such commodities as beer, sodas and fruit — and even accommodation.

Above all, don't lose your sense of proportion. No matter how poor you may feel, it is your choice to travel on a tight budget. Most Tanzanians are much poorer than you will ever be and they do not have the luxury of choice. If you find yourself quibbling with an old lady selling a few piles of fruit on the roadside, stand back and look at the bigger picture. There is nothing wrong, occasionally, with erring on the side of generosity.

PHOTOGRAPHY

Tanzania's abundant wildlife, varied scenery and colourfully dressed people are a photographer's dream. Low speed 64 ASA and 100 ASA films are ideal, but for close-up shots of animals faster speeds such as 400 ASA may be better. Except in Dar es Salaam and Arusha, film is difficult to get hold of. If you use slide film, bring what you need with you.

If you are buying a camera especially for the trip, bear in mind that the simpler the camera is, the less there is to go wrong. Complex electronic gadgetry is highly sensitive to rain and dust. The most solid and reliable camera for African conditions is the Pentax K1000; a good second-hand one shouldn't cost more than £100 in London. For animal photography, a zoom lens is essential (200 magnification is adequate). Don't forget to bring a couple of spare lens caps and, if your camera uses one, a spare battery.

Until recently, photographing something outside of a game reserve could land you in trouble. This has relaxed in the last few years, but it remains illegal to photograph military installations or government buildings (bridges, stations etc). If in doubt, ask.

Many Tanzanians consider, quite rightly, that it is rude to photograph someone without permission. Most people will let you take their photo, but always ask first. If someone refuses or demands a fee, that is their prerogative.

MEDIA AND COMMUNICATIONS

Newspapers

The English language *Daily News* is available in Dar es Salaam and other major towns. It doesn't have much international news, but the local news can make interesting reading. The Kenyan *Daily Nation*, available in Dar es Salaam, Arusha and Mwanza, is better.

Stalls in Uhuru Avenue, Dar es Salaam, sell *Time* and *Newsweek*, as well as a variety of European, British and American papers. You can sometimes buy foreign newspapers at the bookstall in the New Arusha Hotel in Arusha.

Post

Post from Tanzania is cheap and reliable. Incoming post arrives surprisingly quickly, and the Poste Restante service in Dar es Salaam is amongst the best in Africa. There is a nominal charge for collecting letters. Mail should be addressed as follows:

BRIGGS, Philip
Poste Restante
Main GPO
Dar es Salaam
Tanzania

Suggest when people write to you they underline your surname, so that the letter doesn't get misfiled. It is advisable to check under both names when you visit the post office.

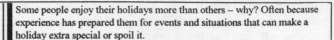

Chapter Four

Health and Safety

HEALTH

By Dr Jane Wilson, with additions by Philip Briggs
East Africa boasts a spectacular array of wildlife and it has an impressive array of diseases too. With some sensible precautions, however, your chances of catching anything serious are small. Most travellers who spend time in Africa become ill at some point, but this is most likely to be simple traveller's diarrhoea or a cold. Before you travel be sure to arrange the necessary immunisations and seek advice on which malaria tablets are sensible. In addition, consider how you will prevent mosquitoes from biting you.

Travel insurance

Don't think about arriving in East Africa without travel insurance. Make sure you take out a policy which will fly you back home or to Nairobi in an emergency. Medical facilities in Tanzania are not what you are used to at home, neither are they free. The ISIS policy, available in Britain through STA (Tel: 071 388 2266), is inexpensive and has a good reputation.

Immunisations

The wisest approach to preparing for a trip to Tanzania is to visit one of the many (38) British Airways Travel Clinics; phone 071 831 5333 for the nearest location. Each of these has a computer link with centres of tropical medicine, which is updated daily. It is thus easy to find out what you risk at the particular season and region you plan to visit. Meningococcal meningitis, for example, is a risk in Tanzania, but only during certain seasons in some parts of the country.

You will need an immunisation against Yellow Fever, and may be

required to show an international immunisation certificate as proof
of this. You should also have immunisations against Polio, Typhoid
and Tetanus, and take malaria prophylaxis. Hepatitis A immunisation
with the Havrix vaccine, launched in the UK in 1992 but not yet
available in some other countries such as the US, is also advisable.
The Havrix vaccine can be given by your G.P. or at any travel clinic
where it is more costly. Whatever you are charged it is a good
investment as you will have ten years protection against a disease
that could debilitate you for months. If you intend travelling far from
medical facilities, consider being immunised against rabies. The
cheapest way to arrange this is through a travel clinic as one vial
can be used for eight patients; your GP is unlikely to have as many
applicants unless you are travelling as a group.

Another useful source of information are the written health briefs
provided by the Medical Advisory Service for Travellers Abroad
(MASTA). Application forms for these can be obtained at any Boots
Pharmacy, or phone the Traveller's Health Line on 0891 224100 (you
must leave your address; they may not give information over the
phone). Recorded general advice is given on the Tropical Diseases
Health Line on 0839 337733.

Medical kit

Take a small medical kit with you. This should contain malaria
tablets, soluble aspirin or paracetamol (good for gargling when you
have a sore throat and for reducing fevers and for pain), plasters
(bandaids), potassium permanganate crystals or another favoured
antiseptic, iodine for water sterilisation and condoms or femidoms.
Any antibiotics that you think you may require will probably be
available where you need them and you are advised to seek medical
advice before taking them. If you are going to a remote part of the
country, you may like to carry three Fansidar tablets with you as a
cure in case you contract malaria.

Health problems

Travellers Diarrhoea

Diarrhoea afflicts at least half of those who travel in the tropics. The
best treatment is to stop eating solid foods, avoid alcohol, and take
only clear fluids. Only take blockers (such as Imodium or Lomotil or
Codeine Phosphate) if you do not have access to sanitation, for
example if you have to travel by bus.

The abdominal pains which are often associated with diarrhoea are
caused by the bowel trying to expel bad food. If the bacteria which

produce the poisons that cause these symptoms are deprived of food they will die out within 36 hours. Taking blockers will generally keep the poisons in your system and you will feel bad for longer.

Blockers are useful if bowel cramps continue for more than 48 hours, as they may do in the case of salmonella food poisoning, for example. It is dangerous to take blockers if you have dysentery (evidenced by blood, slime or fever with the diarrhoea).

It is important to drink a lot when you have diarrhoea. Paediatric rehydration fluids such as *Dioralyte* and *Rehidrat* are excellent, and you can make your own salt and sugar oral rehydration solution (see Box). If you are vomiting you can still absorb fluids and *Dioralyte* is absorbed better than other fluids. Drink slowly and in sips. Avoid drinks that are very hot or very cold; they will stimulate the bowel to open and may cause colic (belly ache). Drink a glass of rehydration solution, or any other liquid, each time your bowels open.

If you are vomiting, do not worry about the quantity you produce: the volume is never as much as it looks and provided you keep sipping slowly you will be replacing sufficient lost fluids (even if you have cholera!). Dehydration is the only serious complication of diarrhoea and vomiting and you will avoid this by drinking. In a temperate climate, if you are not eating, you need to drink about three litres per day to maintain the body's fluid balance. If it is hot, or you have a fever or diarrhoea, or you are at a high altitude you need to drink more than this.

Adults with stomach upsets associated with the production of a lot of sulphurous gas at both ends of the alimentary canal, and with abdominal distention, probably have Giardia. Take a course of Flagyl (metronidazole); 2g daily for three days. Abstain from alcohol while taking metronidazole or you will feel sick.

If you have diarrhoea with blood or you have a fever, it is sensible to organise a stool test and see a doctor. Provided that you are taking plenty of fluids, you need not be in a great rush to do this. In most cases no treatment will be required.

How to avoid diarrhoea

There are a great many myths about how diarrhoea is acquired, but most travellers become sick from contaminated food. Salads, especially lettuce, are always a likely source of diarrhoea. Foods which are freshly cooked or thoroughly reheated should be safe, and sizzling hot street foods are invariably safer than those served at buffets in expensive hotels. Ice cream is generally unsafe: it is an ideal medium for bacterial growth and is often not kept adequately frozen due to power cuts. Ice may have been made with unboiled water and could have been deposited at the roadside on its journey from the ice factory. Tap water is generally unsafe to drink, even

How to make oral rehydration fluid

People with diarrhoea or who are vomiting regularly need to take in more fluids or they will become dehydrated. When the intestine is upset absorbtion of fluids is less efficient. All solids, especially if they are greasy, are poorly tolerated and may cause colic. The ideal solution is a mixture of two heaped teaspoons of glucose and a three-finger pinch (less than a quarter of a teaspoon) of salt in a glass of cooled boiled water. Drink a glass of this at least every time your bowels open; more often if you want. If you feel nauseous or are actually vomiting, sip the drink very slowly. If glucose is unavailable, sugar, palm syrup or honey are good substitutes. If you can't get hold of any of these, or boiled water is unavailable, put a pinch of salt in any flattened sweet soda drink such as coke (which is available just about anywhere in Tanzania).

Any clear solution is OK to drink: sweet black tea and herbal infusions, drinks made from Marmite and Bovril and clear thin soups. The secret is to drink a combination of salt and sugar, so add a little salt to sweet drinks or sugar to salty drinks. The solution should taste no more salty than tears. Quantity is more important than constituents.

To get the proportions right you will find it useful to buy a plastic measuring spoon from Teaching Aids at Low Cost, PO Box 49, St Albans, Hants; tel 0727 53869.

when hotels claim it is drinkable. Bringing water to the boil kills 95% of bugs; boiling it for a further two minutes kills 99% of bugs. Boiling water renders it much safer than using iodine, which in turn renders it safer than using water purification tablets.

Sun and heat

The equatorial sun is vicious. It is difficult completely to avoid direct sunlight, but there is also no need to feel you must expose yourself: tanning ages your skin and can cause skin cancer. If you don't let your body get used to the sun gradually, you will end up with sunburn. If you carry things too far, sunstroke — a potentially fatal condition — is a possibility. Use sunscreen and build up your exposure slowly. Avoid exposing yourself for more than two hours in one day and stay out of the sun between noon and 3.00pm.

Be particularly careful of sunburn when swimming or snorkelling. An old T-shirt will protect your back and shoulders and shorts will take care of another vulnerable area, the back of your thighs.

Many people sweat a lot in Africa. You should drink more than usual to counter water loss and eat extra salt if your taste for it increases (salt tablets are useless). Prickly heat, a rash caused by sweat trapped under the skin, is a common symptom when you first arrive. It's harmless but it is nonetheless unpleasant. Wearing 100% cotton clothes will help, as will sploshing yourself regularly with cold water and avoiding excessive use of soap. People tend to sweat most at the coast; if you are suffering badly you could always head to a higher altitude or air-conditioning for a few days.

Always wear clothes made from natural fabrics such as cotton. These help prevent fungal infections and other rashes. Athletes foot is prevalent; wear thongs in communal showers.

Small cuts are inclined to go septic in the tropics, so if you cut yourself clean the wound by dabbing with a dilute solution of potassium permanganate 2-3 times daily. Antiseptic creams are generally not suitable for the tropics: wounds need to be kept dry and covered.

Malaria

Malaria kills about a million Africans every year, and of the travellers who return to Britain with malaria, 92% have caught it in Africa. You are 100 times more likely to catch malaria in Africa than you are in Asia. You should take all reasonable precautions against being bitten by mosquitoes and take malaria tablets meticulously. To do otherwise is foolhardy. The situation regarding which tablets to take is constantly changing and a G.P. may not have current information; you should seek advice from a travel clinic or phone 071 636 7921 for recorded information.

The *Anopheles* mosquitoes which transmit malaria emerge at dusk and tend to hunt at ground level. It is therefore advisable to wear long trousers and socks in the evening and to cover any exposed parts of your body with insect repellent, preferably a DEET-based preparation such as *Jungle Jell*. Mosquitoes can bite through thin socks, so it is worth putting some repellant on your ankles, even if they are covered. DEET-impregnated ankle bands (marketed by MASTA at the London School of Hygiene and Tropical Medicine; tel 071 631 4408) are quite effective, though they may get you some puzzled looks. If you are sitting in one place for some time, light a mosquito coil between your feet.

Like many insects, mosquitoes are drawn to direct light. If you are camping, never put a lamp near the opening of your tent; you will have a swarm of mosquitoes and other insects waiting outside when you retire. If you are staying in a hotel room, especially one that is poorly screened, be aware that the longer you leave your light on, the greater will be the number of mosquitoes that gather in the room.

At night, many hotels spray their rooms with insecticide, but this is not very effective. Mosquito nets afford good protection, but they are obviously less effective if, as is often the case in Tanzania, they are full of fist-sized holes (though even then they seem to keep most of the mosquitoes out). Mosquito coils reduce the biting rate and, even though strains of mosquito that are skilled at flying in turbulent air have evolved, it's worth switching on a fan if your room has one. Sleeping in a screened tent will protect, provided that no mosquitoes get in while the flaps are open. Some Tanzanian hotels have screened windows, but I've yet to stay in a room where the screening wasn't full of holes.

Even if you take your malaria tablets meticulously and take care to avoid being bitten, you might still contract a strain of malaria that is resistant to prophylaxis. If you experience headaches and fevers, or even a general sense of disorientation and flu-like aches and pains, you may have malaria. It is vital that you seek medical advice immediately. Local doctors see malaria victims the whole time; they will recognise it in all its various guises and know the best treatment for local patterns of resistance. Untreated, malaria is likely to be fatal; but even drug-resistant strains normally respond well to one or other treatment, provided you do not leave it too late. If it is not possible to get to a doctor, take three Fansidar tablets immediately, then travel to see a doctor (or follow the advice offered at the BA travel clinic since patterns of resistance are changing fast).

Malaria normally takes a few weeks to incubate, and for this reason you are advised to continue with prophylaxis for at least four weeks after you leave Tanzania. It is all too easy to forget to take your pills once you are back in the everyday routine of life at home, but you should make every effort to remember. If you display symptoms which could possibly be malarial, even up to a year after you leave Tanzania, get to a doctor and ensure they are aware you have been exposed to malaria; he/she may not think of it otherwise.

Sleeping sickness

This is carried by Tsetse flies. Symptoms include lethargy, local swellings and fevers. Chances of catching it are minimal, and it is easily treated.

Bilharzia or Schistosomiasis

This is caused by worms which spend part of their life inside freshwater snails and infect people when they swim or paddle in still or slowly-moving, well-oxygenated, well-vegetated fresh water. The first symptom of infection is an itchy patch where the worm entered, then perhaps a fortnight later, fever and malaise and, much later, blood in the urine or motions if you have a heavy infestation. Although there is a very good cure for bilharzia, drug resistance is emerging. It is wise to avoid infection.

Bilharzia is endemic in most of Africa. It is rife in Lake Victoria and present in parts of Lake Tanganyika. Matema Beach on Lake Nyasa is said locally to be free of Bilharzia, a claim that is supported by the roughness of the water and the absence of vegetation for a kilometre or so either side. I've been told that the rest of the Tanzania part of Lake Nyasa is free from Bilharzia; given how rough the lake is, this may well be the case, but it is difficult to verify and it would certainly be prudent to avoid swimming near reeds. For other fresh water, it's reasonable to assume that a fast-flowing mountain stream is very low risk, while a sluggish river or any lake is high risk.

If you dry off promptly after spending ten minutes or less in the water, the parasite does not have sufficient time to penetrate your skin and so does not infect you.

AIDS and venereal diseases

Both AIDS and venereal diseases are widespread in Tanzania. AIDS figures for Uganda make frightening reading, and there is every reason to believe that figures for Tanzania, if available, would be little better.

There is a great awareness of AIDS in the country. Most guest houses display posters warning of the disease, and sterilising needles is now normal medical procedure. It might be worth carrying your own needles if you are going to remote areas.

It barely needs saying that the risks involved in sleeping around, especially with prostitutes, are the same as anywhere in the world, only more intensified. If you cannot stick to a policy of celibacy, then carry condoms or femidoms. Using spermicide creams or pessaries will also help reduce the risk of infection.

Meningitis

This is a particularly nasty disease as it can kill within hours of the first symptoms appearing. The telltale symptom is a combination of a blinding headache and a stiff neck, and usually feverishness. A vaccination protects against the common and serious bacterial form in Africa, but not against all of the many kinds of meningitis. Local papers normally report any localised outbreaks. If you show symptoms, get to a doctor immediately.

Rabies

Rabies can be carried by any mammal. The domestic dog is the species which most often passes it on to man. The most common route of infection is a bite from an infected animal, but a scratch or even a lick on broken skin can do it.

The immunisation against rabies is highly effective, but once symptoms show, rabies is incurable, and the way that you die is so very horrible that most doctors advise a post-exposure booster dose. If you are not immunised and there is any possibility you have been exposed to a rabid animal, you should get to a doctor as soon as you can. This should be organised promptly, but since the incubation period can be over a year, don't think it's too late to get this done some weeks or even months after exposure.

The incubation period is determined by the distance the bite is from the brain; if you are bitten on the face (as is common with children) symptoms will appear in about ten days and you must seek medical help immediately. You can also acquire tetanus from animal bites and this will kill you more rapidly.

The message is to be fully immunised, especially if you intend visiting remote places or handling animals. Any wild animals that seem unusually tame should be assumed to be rabid and must not be handled.

Tetanus

Tetanus is caught through deep, dirty wounds and bites. Ensure that any wounds are thoroughly cleaned. Immunisation gives good protection for ten years, provided you do not have an overwhelming load of tetanus bacteria on board. Keep immunised and be sensible about first aid.

SAFETY

Theft

As in any country, there are parts of Tanzania where theft is a real risk. That said, it is considerably safer than many African countries, and I have heard of few instances of the kind of theft that would spoil a holiday. With a bit of care, I think you would be unlucky to experience any serious problems in this direction.

Mugging

Muggings are comparatively unusual in Tanzania. In all the time I spent in the country I heard of only one incident and even that was third-hand. Dar es Salaam and the roads connecting the beach resorts north of it are the main risk area, and Bagamoyo has a bad reputation. Never walk between the beach resorts except possibly in large groups. In Dar es Salaam, avoid back streets after dark. I always felt safe in the area immediately around Maktaba Street, but if crossing from, say, the New Africa Hotel to the Jumbo Inn after dark, I would play safe and get a taxi (this costs about $2; think of it as supplementary travel insurance). If you are mugged, the personal threat is minimal provided you hand over what is asked for.

Casual theft

The bulk of theft in Tanzania is casual snatching or pickpocketing. This is not particularly aimed at tourists (and as a consequence not limited to tourist areas) but you are fair game. The key to not being pickpocketed is not having anything of value in your pocket; the key to avoiding having things snatched is to avoid having valuables in a place where they are snatchable. Most of the following points will be obvious to experienced travellers, but they are worth making:

● Most casual thieves hang around bus stations and markets. Keep a close watch on your belongings in these places and avoid having loose valuables in your pocket or day pack.

● Keep all your valuables — passport, travellers cheques etc — in a money belt. One you can hide under your clothes has obvious advantages over one of the currently-fashionable codpieces which are worn externally.

● Don't carry your spending money in your money belt. A normal wallet is fine provided it only contains a moderate sum of money. Better still is a wallet you can hang around your neck. If I plan to visit a high risk area such as a busy market, I sometimes wear shorts under my trousers and keep my cash in the shorts pocket.

● Distribute your money throughout your luggage. I always keep the bulk of my foreign currency in my money belt, but I like to keep some cash and travellers cheques hidden in various parts of my pack and day-pack.

● Many people prefer to carry their valuables on their person. I think it is better to leave them in your hotel room. In all my African travels I have only once heard of a hotel room being broken into (that was in Nairobi, about the only place in East Africa where paranoia is apt), whereas I have met countless people who have been pickpocketed, mugged, or had possessions snatched from them.

• If you have jewellery that is of high personal or financial value, leave it at home.

• If you can afford it, when you first arrive in a large town catch a taxi to your hotel, especially if you arrive after dark.

• Avoid overnight buses. They have a bad reputation for theft. In Zanzibar and on overnight buses I have heard of people being given drugged food and robbed (more details about theft on buses are given under *Transport* in Chapter Three).

Con tricks

Dar es Salaam is not Nairobi as far as conmen are concerned. There are a few dodgy characters who hang around the New Africa Hotel trying to change money, but they are pretty transparent. You may encounter similar characters in Arusha, but you would have to be very gullible to get involved with them.

Documentation

The best insurance against complete disaster is to keep things well-documented. If you carry a photocopy of the main page of your passport, you will be issued a new one more promptly. In addition, keep details of your bank, credit card (if you have one), travel insurance policy and camera equipment (including serial numbers).

Keep copies of your travellers cheque numbers and *a record of which ones you have cashed*, as well as the international refund assistance telephone number and local agent. If all this information fits on one piece of paper, you can keep photocopies on you and with a friend at home.

You will have to report the theft of any item you wish to claim insurance against to the police.

One last thought

If you are robbed, the temptation is to chase the thief. If the items stolen are not of great value, you might want to think before you do this. Street justice is harsh: an identified thief is likely to be descended on by a mob, beaten, and quite possibly killed. I have met a few travellers who have found themselves in the bizarre position of having to save someone who has just ripped them off.

CREATURES GREAT AND SMALL

Some people arrive in Africa with images of man-eating lions, rampaging elephants and venomous snakes lurking around every corner. This idea can quickly be dispelled. Most animals avoid contact with people and the chance of being attacked is remote. Having said that, any animal large enough to kill a person might do so under the right circumstances. Wild animals should always be treated with caution and respect, and deliberately feeding or provoking them is highly irresponsible. Never assume that an animal isn't dangerous because it appears to be tame: the most dangerous animals are often those that have been hand-reared, or that have come to depend on the presence of humans for food or as security from predators.

Except for carnivores, which might attack for food, animals are only likely to attack humans if they feel threatened, and they are especially dangerous if they panic. The animals most likely to charge are hippo, rhino, elephant, buffalo and rhino, but even an antelope will attack in some circumstances, especially if it has young or is cornered. Many animals have what could be termed a fleeing and attacking circle: the closer you are when it first becomes aware of your presence, the more likely it is to choose confrontation over escape. If you see a large animal in the distance and want to approach it, use your common sense. If the animal is aware of your presence and you approach it reasonably openly and slowly, it is far less likely to panic than if it is initially unaware of your presence and you attempt to sneak up to it. If the animal becomes edgy or aggressive, remove the threat: back away slowly and calmly. Unless you are experienced or armed, it is foolhardy to approach an elephant or buffalo on foot; on the other hand, you would have to get very close to a giraffe or zebra before there was a remote chance of it attacking you. Never approach an animal in such a way that it might feel cornered (by a koppie or a lake, for instance); even a bushbuck will charge if it has no escape route. Be very cautious approaching a thicket or patch of woodland where, for instance, a buffalo or leopard might be hiding.

Most animals rely strongly on smell; whether you are trying to avoid an animal or approach it, the prevailing wind is an important consideration. If you want to get around an animal, it is far less likely to notice you if you stay upwind of it. If you want to approach the animal, you will get closer by staying upwind, but you are also more likely to startle it.

Before discussing specific animals, I should stress that the likelihood of an animal attacking you whilst you are in Tanzania is extremely small, certainly far less than the risk of being killed by malaria or in a road accident. The dangers associated with wild animals were greatly exaggerated by the so-called Great White Hunters, and many of the myths they created have stuck in the popular image. Nevertheless, in their haste to debunk the myths, many travel guides have gone to the other extreme and underplayed the potential risks. There are dangers associated with walking or camping where wild animals are present, and no matter how slight they may be, tourists should be aware of them.

Crocodiles
These are responsible for more deaths than any other African animal (apart from the mosquito!). They attack animals that are in or next to water and they are responsible for many deaths in river or lakeside villages where people have no option but to take their chances. If you keep a few metres between yourself and crocodile-infested water, the risk is small. Crocodiles are fast on land, so if they are out of the water don't sneak up too close. If you intend fishing or swimming, ask local advice; in many places all crocodiles large enough to attack an adult human have been hunted out.

Hippo
Hippo pose a very real threat to tourists. The danger is coming between a hippo and water. Their instinct when threatened is to head straight for water; they will mow down anything in their way. Always be alert when walking near a lake or river where hippo are present, especially at times when they are likely to be out of the water grazing (at night, in the early morning and late afternoon, and in overcast weather) and avoid walking in reed beds. If you are on foot and see hippo, it may be tempting to get as close as you can but it is more sensible to give them a wide berth. Hippo are not normally dangerous if they are in the water and you are on land, but be cautious.

Predators
Most large predators avoid contact with people and attacks are very unusual. You are safe in a vehicle, but be aware that most predators perceive a vehicle as a unit; if you are very close to a lion or leopard and do something that breaks the vehicle's outline, you may startle the animal and it could lunge at you. A tent offers good protection provided it is closed up properly and there is no meat in it. Never

sleep with your head poking out of a tent. If you have no tent, a head poking out from a sleeping bag may provoke curiosity in a lion or hyena. Sleep with your head against a tree or a wall, or towards a campfire. On foot, most predators will give you a wide berth. If one does take an interest in you, never run away — it is much faster than you are. Your best bet is to climb a tree. If there is no tree around, stand your ground and yell at it aggressively in the hope you will convince it that it has far more reason to be scared than you have.

Buffalo and rhino
In real terms, buffalo are the most dangerous land animal: they are common in many of the forests where people walk, and are less inclined to mock charge than, for instance, elephant. Solitary buffalo pose the greatest threat. If you encounter buffalo on foot, never try to approach them and don't run away unless you are actually charged. If they appear not to have seen you, walk away slowly and discreetly. If they have seen you, stand your ground or back off slowly and they will probably move on. If you are charged, try to get up a tree or an anthill; if none is available, run like hell. Rhino are as unpredictable as buffalo, if not more so, but their scarcity in East Africa makes it highly improbable you would ever encounter one on foot.

Elephant
Elephant can be very unpredictable and aggressive, especially lone bulls and mothers with young. There are few places in Tanzania where an unguided tourist on foot would be likely to encounter an elephant, but it could happen. In the vast majority of instances, the elephant will simply move on or ignore you, but never try to approach it.

It is impossible to give hard and fast advice about what to do if you are on foot and an elephant becomes aggressive: no two situations are the same and you will have to use your judgement as to what its intentions are. Elephant are highly intelligent when compared to buffalo or rhino, and they are more likely to react in an individual way. If an elephant charges you in earnest and without warning, there is probably little you can do but try to climb a tree or run away. Normally, however, an elephant will warn you off by trumpeting and/or mock charging.

When an elephant trumpets a warning, the odds are that it just wants you to clear off. Unless it is particularly bad-tempered, it is unlikely to charge unless you provoke it further. The most common advice is either to walk or back off calmly and quickly (but don't run), thereby removing the threat to the elephant, or else to stand your ground and try to frighten the elephant off by waving things at it and yelling aggressively. If one doesn't work, try the other, all the time looking for cover should it decide to charge.

If an elephant charges, climb a tall tree or, as elephants do not like steep inclines, make for a sharp rise or gulley. If there is no cover, you must gamble. If it is a mock charge, you are best standing your ground (but may still be all right if you run away); if it charges in earnest, the only chance you have is to run. On the balance, you are probably better running than standing your ground, but I've heard differing opinions.

Provided you are sensible, elephants pose little risk in campsites. They are unlikely to walk in if they are concerned about your presence and, unless there is fruit inside, they will almost always walk around a tent. It would be stupid to tease or feed an elephant, and if it hasn't seen you, don't attempt to sneak up on it. If elephants come into your campsite at night, don't take photos; a flashlight might startle them.

Elephant sometimes attack vehicles. Always approach them cautiously; if they show signs of aggression or edginess, back off gently and wait for them to pass. If they are at the side of the road and show no signs of aggression, make your way past them before you stop and watch. If you don't do this and another car comes up behind you, you will have no escape route should the worst happen. It's a question of judgement, but I would never switch off my engine in close proximity to an elephant.

Primates

Most primates are shy of people. At some campsites, however, baboons and vervet monkeys have become used to people. Vervet monkeys are unlikely to progress beyond being a nuisance, but baboons should be considered dangerous. I'm only aware of one place in Tanzania where baboons are a problem (Gombe Stream) but they are rampant in some Zimbabwean and Kenyan campsites. As tourism to Tanzania increases so will the number of places where baboons are a problem.

Baboons have sharp teeth and are very powerful and aggressive. They are capable of severely wounding an adult and have often been known to kill children. If baboon are present, don't leave food lying around or in your tent. Have a pile of stones next to you when you cook. If you have children, keep a close watch on them and never let them tease or play with baboons or monkeys.

When a baboon approaches you aggressively, it is largely bluff. Unlike the other animals discussed here, a baboon will not be after you but after your food. Once it has what it wants it will be off like a shot. Throw stones and yell aggessively to scare it off, but if this doesn't work don't try to call its bluff: should you provoke a confrontation you are bound to come off second best.

I've not encountered this in Tanzania, but in some parts of Africa troops of baboons or monkeys wait for tourists to feed them by the roadside. If a baboon or monkey is very tame or leaps onto your car, close the windows. If it gets into the vehicle it will panic and could seriously injure someone. When baboons and monkeys become too bold they often have to be shot; deliberately feeding one not only creates problems for other tourists, it may well sign the animal's death warrant.

Chimpanzees are capable of killing a person and could easily do so if they felt sufficiently threatened. Unhabituated chimps are too shy and localised to be a cause for concern, but it would be an error to assume that habituated chimps are tame. Chimp viewing at Gombe Stream and Mahale Mountains is well organised. There is no danger provided you obey your guide.

Snakes

Snakes pose less of a threat than many people imagine (in South Africa, for instance, they are responsible for a mere five deaths a year). They are shy, secretive creatures, and most species are completely harmless to people.

For off-road walking, solid shoes reduce the risk of being bitten (50% of snake bites occur below the ankle). Long, loose trousers will help prevent a snake from sinking its fangs in to you. Treading heavily (as opposed to loudly) warns snakes of your approach; they will generally scoot off. An exception is the puff adder — this slothful creature is responsible for a large proportion of snakebite deaths.

Snakes often shelter under rocks or in thickets. If you want to move a rock, kick it over before you pick it up. Likewise, when you collect firewood, be cautious.

If you see a snake, wait and let it pass. If it actually rises to strike at you, the most common advice is to stand dead still: a snake is more likely to strike if you make a sudden movement. This is all well and good, but I have once had a snake rear its head at me, and twice been with someone else who has. Each time instinct won over logic and the person concerned beetled off as quickly as possible in the opposite direction. This tactic worked perfectly well.

Most snakes are non-venomous and venom is dispensed in only about 50% of bites by venomous snakes. The chances are that if you are bitten you will not come to any harm. The victim should be kept still and calm and the bitten area should be washed with clean soap and wiped gently with a clean cloth to remove any venom from the skin surface. Swelling is a feature of envenomation and it is wise to remove any rings, bangles or watches etc. The victim must then be prevented from moving the bitten limb, preferably by splinting, to slow the absorbtion of the venom and also reduce pain. The victim should then be taken promptly to a doctor, with the offending snake if possible, though only if it can be captured without risk. If you kill the snake, be aware that a decapitated head can envenomate. The victim will then be kept under observation and if signs of envenomation begin, an antivenin can be administered. Antivenin must only be given if and when signs of envenomation occur.

Meanwhile:

DO NOT give alcohol or aspirin, but paracetamol is safe.
DO NOT cut, incise, or suck the wound.
DO NOT apply potassium permanganate.
DO NOT panic; it is likely that no venom has been dispensed.

Insects

Except for mosquitoes, which carry malaria and various other nasty diseases, most insects are relatively harmless. If you stay in cheap hotels, you will sooner or later sleep on a mattress infested with either fleas or bedbugs. These may not be the most pleasant bed companions, but there is little point in worrying about them unduly: they are mainly harmless (fleas do carry plague) and in my experience their bites only itch for a short time. I found that if either bedbugs or fleas became a problem, my sleeping mat made a good barrier.

If your sleeping bag becomes infested with biters, turn it inside out and leave it in the sun or sprinkle it with an insecticide.

Sleeping in an enclosed mosquito net, such as the ones put out by Long Road in the USA (Tel: 510 450 4763) will eliminate all nocturnal insect problems. (See advert on page 66.)

Part two

Chapter Five

Dar es Salaam

INTRODUCTION

Dar es Salaam is Tanzania's largest city and most important port, and although it may not be the capital of Tanzania for much longer (Dodoma is scheduled to become the capital before the end of the century), it seems likely to remain the commercial and social heart of the country for the foreseeable future. The city draws extreme reactions from travellers, most of whom either love it or hate it. It is my favourite East African city, with all the hustle and bustle of Nairobi, yet none of that city's underlying aggression.

Dar es Salaam's distinctive character comes from the cultural mix of its people and buildings, and the sloth-inducing coastal humidity which permeates every aspect of day-to-day life. German, British, Asian and Arab influences are all evident, but it is fundamentally a Swahili city. Dar es Salaam is a friendly place. People are willing to pass away the time with idle chat and will readily help out strangers, yet you are rarely hassled, except around the New Africa Hotel where money-changers froth into action every time a tourist walks past.

I first visited Dar es Salaam in 1986. Then it looked decidedly down at heel. The streets were acneous with potholes and the pavements were lifeless, shops had given up the pretence of having anything to sell, water ran for about an hour every day, and except for the odd overland traveller crossing between Kenya and southern Africa, tourists were something of a novelty. In 1988, when I next passed through, things were still pretty torpid, but there were definite signs of recovery.

It was extremely heartening to return in 1992 and find a lively, bustling city, comparable in many ways to Nairobi. Most of Dar es Salaam's buildings could still do with a scrub and whitewash, but the streets have been resurfaced, the pavements are alive with peddlers and colourful impromptu markets, the shops are well-stocked, water runs more often than not — and tourists are flocking back.

History

By coastal standards, Dar es Salaam is a modern town. Until 1862, when Sultan Majid of Zanzibar first visited the area, it was the site of an insignificant fishing village called Mzizima. Majid was so impressed by the natural harbour and surrounding scenery he decided to establish a trading centre. A coral palace called Dar es Salaam (haven of peace) was built in 1866 and a small Arab settlement was established. In 1870, after Majid died, his successor Barghash abandoned all plans for further development.

In 1877 Dar es Salaam was proposed as the starting point for the construction of a road by the anti-slaver Sir William Mackinnon. He hoped the road would encourage legitimate trade between the coast and Lake Nyasa. Known as Mackinnon's Road, the project never took off and was abandoned after 112km had been completed.

Dar es Salaam acquired real significance under German rule. In 1887 a camp was established; four years later the fledgling city was the capital of German East Africa. Between 1893 and 1899 several departments of the colonial government were established there and in 1898 a Roman Catholic Cathedral was built. The construction of the central railway consolidated Dar es Salaam's position; by 1914, when the line was completed, Dar es Salaam was the country's most significant harbour and trading centre.

Dar es Salaam was attacked and captured by a British boat soon after the outbreak of World War One. When German East Africa became Tanganyika, Dar es Salaam remained the capital, and its importance has never been challenged. Dar es Salaam is now the country's economic hub, with a population of almost two million.

GETTING THERE AND AWAY

Dar es Salaam has good local and international links. Details of transport to other parts of the country are given throughout this guide, under the relevant town or area. A brief overview follows:

Air

There are air links between Dar es Salaam and many African and European cities, and domestic flights to most large Tanzanian towns. Further details are under *Air* in Chapter Three.

The airport is 13km from the city centre. A shuttle bus to the airport, run by Air Tanzania, leaves from in front of the New Africa Hotel every other hour between 8.00am and 4.00pm, and returns every other hour between 9.00am and 5.00pm. An up-to-date

timetable is posted at the New Africa. You can also get to the airport
on a 67 bus. There is a taxi rank at the airport.

Airlines

	Address	Tel
Aeroflot	Eminaz Mansion, Samora Ave	46005
Air France	Peugeot House, cnr Upanga/UWT	46653/4
Air India	cnr Upanga/UWT	46803
Air Tanzania	ATC Building, Ohio Street	46643
Air Zaire	IPS Building, cnr Samora/Maktaba	20836
British Airways	Coronation House, cnr Samora/Maktaba	46025
EgyptAir	Matsalamat Building, Samora Ave	46806
Ethiopian Airlines	TDFL Building, Ohio Street	20868
Kenya Airways	Tanganyika Motors Building,Upanga Rd	46875-7
KLMT	DFL Building, Ohio Street	46497
Lufthansa	Peugeot House, cnr Upanga/UWT	46813-5
Pakistan Airlines	IPS Building, cnr Samora/Maktaba	46820/1
Sabena	Mbwana Salum, Ugweno Street	50476
Swissair	Luther House, Sokoine Drive	46816
Uganda Airlines	IPS Building, cnr Samora/Maktaba	46818/9
Zambia Airways	IPS Building, cnr Samora/Maktaba	46662

Mozambique, Royal Swazi, Somali and Saudi Arabian Airlines are
represented by Holiday Africa in the TDFL Building on Ohio Road
(Tel: 30395). A number of other airlines which only do occasional
flights are represented by Air Tanzania.

Boat

There are several boats between Dar es Salaam and Zanzibar every
day, and reasonably regular services to Pemba, Mtwara, Tanga and
Mombasa (Kenya). Boats to Mafia, Lindi and Kilwa are rare. All the
commercial boat operators have kiosks near the harbour on Sokoine
Drive. If you are heading for a place where there is no regular
service and have no joy at the harbour, try the Tanzanian Coastal
Shipping Line (Tel: 26192).

Rail

Trains to northern and western destinations such as Moshi, Tanga,
Mwanza and Kigoma leave from the central station on Sokoine Drive.
Bookings to these destinations should also be made at this station.
Trains to southern destinations such as Ifakara and Mbeya leave
from the Tazara Station 5km from the city centre. The booking office

for southbound trains is at Tazara Station. Buses there leave from the Post Office (Posta).

Details of all train services are under *Rail* in Chapter Three.

Bus

There are buses between Dar es Salaam and virtually every town in Tanzania. There is no central bus station in Dar es Salaam; buses leave from all over the city centre. There is a semblance of a pattern, but it should not be viewed too rigidly.

Buses to Arusha and Moshi leave from the large bus station on the corner of Morogoro Road and Libya Street, as do most buses to coastal destinations south of Kilwa. Most buses to Tanga, Iringa, Mbeya and Songea leave from Mnazi Mmoja on UWT Street. Buses to Bagamoyo, Morogoro and Kilwa generally leave from the backstreets around Kariakoo Market. Most buses to western destinations such as Dodoma, Tabora and Mwanza leave from Msimbazi Street, a few blocks from the market.

If in doubt, the best place to make enquiries is the Morogoro Road/Libya Street bus station. It is the biggest and the most central bus station, and people seem to have a helpful attitude to travellers.

There is a simple way to navigate through the chaos. Taxi drivers are familiar with the bus system, often speak good English, and, in my experience, are very helpful. Enlisting some knowledgeable support is well worth the price of a taxi-fare (about $1.50 within the city centre). If you want to leave immediately, a taxi driver is far better equipped than you to cut through the bullshit, find the next bus to leave, and make sure you get a seat.

WHERE TO STAY

Although there are plenty of hotels in the city centre, budget hotels tend to fill up early in the day. If you arrive late in the afternoon it may be easier to settle for something more expensive and look for a cheap room the next morning.

Although things have improved recently, there are still regular water and electricity cuts in Dar es Salaam. Electricity cuts are generally localised and only last a couple of hours, but water only runs for about half the day in most parts of town. If there is running water when you get a room, shower while the going is good.

UPPER RANGE

There are four hotels in this range in the city centre. All offer self-contained rooms with hot showers and air-conditioning. There is little to choose between them; I have heard both good and bad about them all. If you are not committed to staying in the city centre, the Oyster Bay Hotel and beach hotels further out of town are better value for money.

The TTC-run New Africa and Kilimanjaro offer a 50% discount between Easter and 30 June and cheap rates for residents all-year.

Kilimanjaro Hotel   (PO Box 9574, Tel: 46528). Overlooking the harbour, this is the best hotel in the city centre. It has its own generator, a swimming pool, and an excellent restaurant. $77/87/92 HC single/double/triple or $13/16/19 for residents.

New Africa Hotel   (PO Box 9314, Tel: 46546). This was built on the site of Dar es Salaam's oldest hotel, the Kaiserhof, in the 1960s. The verandah is a popular meeting point, but the hotel itself lacks atmosphere. $68/78 HC single/double, or $9/10 for residents.

Motel Agip   (PO Box 529, Tel: 46551/5). The Agip, situated behind the New Africa, has a modern transatlantic atmosphere. The service is good and the restaurant is excellent. $79/80 HC single/double.

Embassy Hotel   (PO Box 3152, Tel: 30006). After the Kilimanjaro, many people regard this as the best hotel in the city centre. It has all the usual facilities, a good restaurant, and a swimming pool. $70/80 single/double.

Oyster Bay Hotel   (PO Box 2261, Tel: 68631). This is on a beach 6km from the city centre. It has a good restaurant and a popular bar and disco. All the rooms face the sea and are air-conditioned. $95/110 HC s/c single/double.

MODERATE

There are a number of hotels in this range, all very similar in quality and price. Rooms are self-contained with fans and mosquito nets, and in some cases air-conditioning. Most enforce payment in a hard currency.

Hotel Continental   (PO Box 2040, Tel: 22481). The best value in its range. Air-conditioned rooms cost $13.75 double, payable in shillings.

DAR ES SALAAM - Key to Maps

West Central

3. HOTEL MAWENZI
4. ZANZIBAR
    GUEST HOUSE
6. SAFARI INN
7. JAMBO INN
9. CITY GUEST HOUSE

11. TRAFFIC LIGHT
     MOTEL
12. HOLIDAY HOTEL
14. DELUXE INN
16. HOTEL TAMARINE
17. HOTEL
     INTERNATIONALE
18. HOTEL
     CONTINENTAL
19. KIBODYA HOTEL

2. NIGHTS of ISTANBUL
5. PIZZERIA
8. IMRAM REST.

21. SUPREME REST.

1. KARIAKOO MARKET

13. MNAZI MMOJA
     BUS STATION
15. CLOCK TOWER

East Central

24. YMCA
25. YWCA
28. HOTEL EMBASSY

31. MOTEL AFRIQUE
38. TWIGA HOTEL

47. NEW AFRICA HOTEL

51. AGIP MOTEL
52. LUTHER HOUSE
53. SKYWAY HOTEL
57. KILIMANJARO HOTEL

23. BUSHTREKKER
29. The CAFETARIA

32. PANDYA REST.
33. COSY CAFE
35. COFFEE SHOP
36. THE ALCOVE
37. SALAMANDER
39. SNO-CREAM

41. SHALAMAR REST.
43. HAPPY SNACKS
56. CHINESE REST.

22. NYUMBA YA SANAA GALLERY
26. SECOND-HAND BOOKSHOP
27. POST OFFICE
34. EXTELCOM HOUSE

42. FERRY OFFICES
44. IPS BUILDING
45. ASKARI MONUMENT
46. SUPERMARKET
48. TANZANIA TOURIST BOARD
49. AIR TANZANIA

54. BRITISH COUNCIL
55. NIC BUILDING
58. NATIONAL MUSEUM
59. MAP OFFICE

ACCOMMODATION

RESTAURANTS

OTHERS

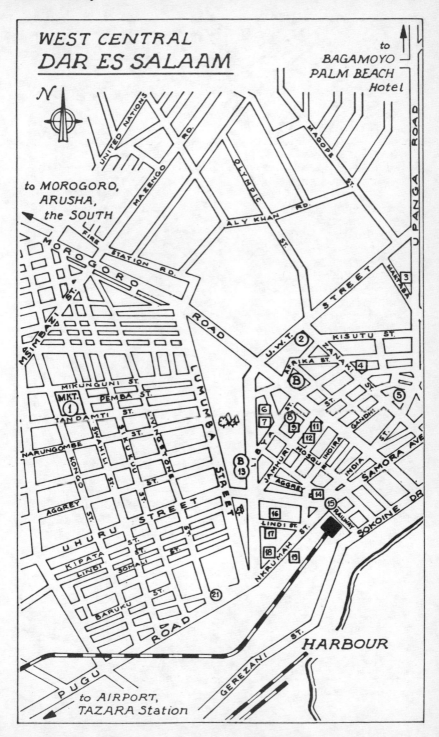

WEST CENTRAL
DAR ES SALAAM

N

to
BAGAMOYO
PALM BEACH
Hotel

to MOROGORO,
ARUSHA,
the SOUTH

HARBOUR

to AIRPORT,
TAZARA Station

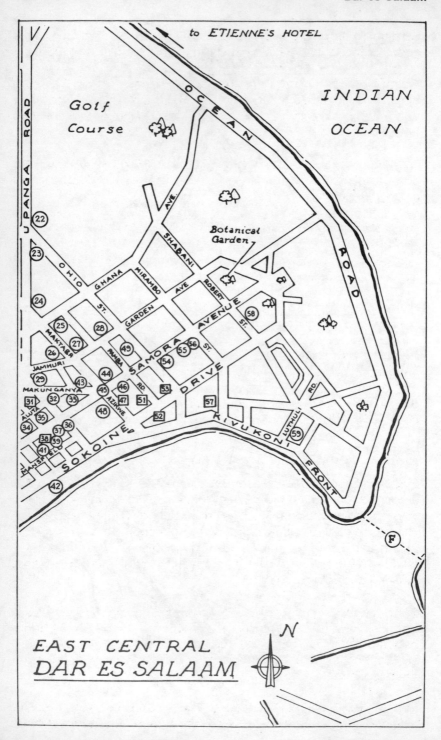

to *ETIENNE'S HOTEL*

INDIAN OCEAN

Golf Course

Botanical Garden

EAST CENTRAL DAR ES SALAAM

Starlight Hotel   (PO Box 3199, Tel: 23845). Air-conditioned rooms here cost $22.50 double, payable in shillings. It is popular with expats.

Twiga Hotel   (PO Box 1194, Tel: 46578). One of Dar es Salaam's older hotels, this has a convenient position, a pleasant atmosphere and a horribly creaky lift. $20/25 HC single/double or $15.00/17.50 for residents.

Hotel Skyway   (PO Box 21248, Tel: 46566/27601). This is also conveniently central and is friendly and clean. $22/25 HC single/double.

Hotel Mawenzi   (PO Box 322, Tel: 29922/46561). Since its recent refurbishment, the Mawenzi has become one of the more popular hotels in its range. Rooms are large and air-conditioned. $25/30 HC single/double or $8.75/10.50 for residents.

Motel Afrique   (PO Box 9482, Tel: 46557/8). This has a convenient position and comfortable rooms. $30 double or $12 for residents.

Palm Beach Hotel   (PO Box 1520, Tel: 22931/28891). This atmospheric hotel is about 20 minutes walk from the city centre. It has a large balcony where barbecues are held in the evening. Rooms are shabby but air-conditioned. $11/25 single/double, payable in shillings. Single rooms are not self-contained.

BUDGET

Finding a cheap vacant room in Dar es Salaam involves a fair amount of footwork. A few places stand out as good value but these are generally popular so you may have to book a day ahead. There is a bunch of scruffy hotels around the Morogoro Road bus station and the clock tower, but even these are often full. If you find a room, take it. You can always look for something better later and make a booking for the next day.

YMCA   (PO Box 767, Tel: 26726). The rooms here are clean enough but basic and have no fans or mosquito nets. In the past it had a bad reputation for theft, but the room I saw looked reasonably secure. Poor value at $10 HC single or double, but worth a try if you are desperate.

YWCA   (PO Box 2086, Tel: 22439). The YWCA is pleasant, popular, safe and convenient, and its canteen is a good place to meet other travellers. Only women and couples are accepted. Rooms are clean and have mosquito nets and fans. The rooms for couples are partitioned in such a way that the fan, lights, and any nocturnal noises are shared with another couple. $4/5/7 single/double(couple)/double(women sharing).

Luther House (PO Box 389, Tel: 32154). This is convenient and popular. It is booked solid days in advance, but is worth enquiring about if you are spending a while in Dar es Salaam. Rooms are clean and have hot water. $3.25/4.50 s/c single/double.

Jambo Inn (PO Box 5588, Tel: 35359/35531). This clean, friendly hotel has become very popular in recent years. A good restaurant is attached. $5/8 s/c single/double, or $10 for an air-conditioned double.

Safari Inn This is around the corner from the Jambo Inn and similar in standard. $6.25/7.50 s/c single/double.

Kobodya Hotel (PO Box 1019 Tel: 32937/31470). This is similar in standard to the Jambo Inn, but less popular with travellers. It is often booked solid days in advance. $6.25 s/c double.

Etienne's Hotel (PO Box 2981, Tel: 20293). This laidback old hotel is 20-minutes walk from the city centre. Rooms are large, have fans and hot water, and the staff are friendly. The overgrown grounds add to an air of faded colonial seediness. It has a restaurant, but the barbecue at the nearby Palm Beach Hotel is a more attractive proposition. $7/9 single/double or $12 s/c double.

Salvation Army (PO Box 1273, Tel: 51467). This is on Kilwa Road, about 3km from the town centre. If you don't mind staying out of town, it is as good value as anything in Dar es Salaam. Rooms are spotless and there is a swimming pool. $4 double.

Other hotels in this range include the grotty **City Guest House** ($1.00/1.25 single/double), the similar **Zanzibar Guest House** ($1.50/2.00 single/double), the marginally more savoury **Holiday Hotel** ($2/3 single/double), and the relatively pleasant **Traffic Light Motel** ($5/6 single/double), all near the Morogoro Road bus station. There are a few acceptable places near the clock tower: the **Deluxe Inn** ($5/6 single/double), the **International** ($4 double) and the **Tamarine** ($3/4 s/c single/double).

WHERE TO EAT

Dar es Salaam has restaurants to suit all tastes and budgets, and more had opened every time we visited the city. Typical opening hours are lunch between 12.00 noon and 3.00pm and dinner between 7.00pm and 10.00pm. Generally food is of a high standard and good value for money. It would be impossible to list every restaurant and *hoteli* in Dar es Salaam; you might well want to adventure beyond the following recommendations.

UPPER RANGE

We found the best value to be at upper range hotels rather than specialist restaurants. The open-air restaurant on the top floor of the **Kilimanjaro Hotel** has a great view over the harbour, and the food and service are excellent. Main courses cost around $5, three-course set menus cost $6.25.

The restaurant in the **Motel Agip** lacks the view of the Kilimanjaro, but is similar in price and standard, and has a more varied menu. You could also try the grill on the second floor of the **Embassy Hotel**; it serves the best steaks in town for around $4. A lot of tourists eat at the **New Africa Hotel**, but its difficult to see why. Main courses start at around $3 and a three-course set menu costs $5; it's fair value, but you can get better food for a similar price elsewhere.

The Alcove is a well-established Indian restaurant. It was popular with budget travellers in the mid-1980s and although there is more competition these days, it is still the place to head for if you feel like a good Indian or Chinese meal. A main course with rice costs around $6. The **Nights of Istanbul** specialises in Indian and Turkish dishes. It is highly-rated but the prices are steep for Tanzania: around $10 for a main course.

The Bushtrekker is similar in standard and price to the restaurants in the Kilimanjaro and Agip. Getting there at night involves walking down a long stretch of unlit road. Take a taxi.

MODERATE TO CHEAP

The **Chinese Restaurant** in the basement of the NIC Building on Samora Avenue serves a wide range of Chinese, Indian and Western dishes for around $3. The food is tasty and portions are enormous. The **Motel Agip Snack Bar** is popular with both locals and tourists. Jacket potatoes ($1.25) are a definite attraction and the cappuccino is good, but otherwise it's pretty ordinary. The **Pizzeria** is the place to go if you want a pizza. Expect to pay up to $5.

For Indian food try **The Shalamar**. The food is tasty but portions are mean (my curry was a lonely chicken wing floating in a pool of sauce). A curry with rice costs $3.25. The *hoteli*-like **Imram Restaurant** is much better value. There are two good Indian vegetarian restaurants. The buffet dinner at **The Pandya** is good value at $3.25. The food at **The Supreme** is as good if not better, and a meal shouldn't set you back more than $2.

The restaurant at the **Hotel Skyway** serves three-course lunches and dinners for $2.50. The menu is predictable, but the food is more than adequate. Good value. The restaurant on the top floor of the **Twiga Hotel** offers good views over the city. The food is fair, and reasonable value at $3 a main course.

Cosy Cafe has a pleasant atmosphere, and specialises in steaks and other grills. Main courses cost up to $4. **The Salamander** has a deserved reputation for serving the best lunches in town. Meals such as fish and chips and spaghetti bolognese cost $1.50. Snacks are also served. It is closed in the evenings. **Happy Snacks** is a fast food joint. The food is erratic but you can fill up for around $1. **The Cafeteria** is similar in price and style, but the food is less greasy.

In the mid-1980s, when the city's other ice-cream parlours served nothing but orange juice spiced with flies, the **Sno-Cream Parlour**'s extravagant interior and marvellous sundaes were decidedly surreal. It looks less out of place these days, but still serves the best sundaes in the country for around $1.

The **TCB Coffee Shop** on the ground floor of Extelcomms House is a good place for a coffee and snack during shopping hours.

USEFUL INFORMATION

The Tanzania Tourist Corporation (TTC) office opposite the New Africa Hotel is open on weekdays and Saturday mornings. We found the staff helpful, but not that knowledgeable when it came to off-the-beaten-track destinations.

The **telephone area code** for Dar es Salaam is 051.

Getting around

There are taxis all over the place. A good place to find one is in front of the New Africa Hotel, though you are more likely to be overcharged there than elsewhere. The standard price for a ride within the city centre is about $2. There is a good bus service in Dar es Salaam. Most buses leave from the post office.

Maps

The Department of Lands and Surveys building is on Kivukoni Front, about 100m past the Kilimanjaro Hotel. Their map office is not in this building but in a small office tucked away behind a building on the block before it. I had been told buying maps could be a drawn-out process, but I found the staff helpful and the office surprisingly well-stocked. If you plan to hike off the beaten track, 1:50,000 maps of areas such as the Pare, Poroto, Usambara and Udzungwa mountains are available.

The kiosk in the foyer of the New Africa Hotel usually stocks maps of Dar es Salaam and Tanzania; if they don't have what you want, try the TTC office or the bookshop in the Kilimanjaro Hotel.

Books

Most bookshops in Dar es Salaam (and in Tanzania for that matter) only stock textbooks. For fiction, try the second-hand bookshop on Maktaba Street opposite the post office, or any of several stalls around the Agip and New Africa Hotel. The kiosk in the New Africa is your best bet for glossier books, but it has a limited range. There is also a bookshop on the ground floor of the Kilimanjaro Hotel.

The British Council library and reading room has plenty of up-to-date British newspapers and magazines. Membership costs $2.50 per month. You can sometimes buy recent European and American newspapers at the stalls on Samora Avenue near the Salamander Restaurant.

Hairdressers

There are unisex salons on the ground floor of the Kilimanjaro Hotel and in the YMCA building.

Shopping

Although it has improved greatly in recent years, Dar es Salaam is some way short of being a shopper's paradise. Locally-produced goods are cheapest at stalls like those lining Maktaba Street. The supermarket on Samora Avenue (see map) is one of many so-called luxury shops, selling a variety of imported foodstuffs and toiletries at inflated prices. There are several clothes shops and fruit stalls along Zanaki Street. The most colourful place to buy these sort of things is Kariakoo Market (described under WHAT TO DO). Curio stalls in Dar es Salaam are very expensive when compared to those in Arusha.

Money

Most people change money at one of the numerous forex bureaux which sprang up after the exchange rate was floated. Forex bureaux give better rates than banks and are open for longer hours. Rates vary considerably, so shop around before you change large sums. I cannot recommend individual bureaux: the one giving the best rate in town when we first visited Dar es Salaam had dropped almost as low as the bank rate three months later. There are plenty of forex bureaux on Samora Avenue and Zanaki Street.

If you need to change money after the bureaux have closed, you can do so at the airport. It's also possible to do this at any hotel which takes payment in dollars, providing you stay at that hotel. Do not change money with street dealers. There is no black market worth talking about in Dar es Salaam, but there are plenty of conmen.

Rickshaw Travel on UWT Street (PO Box 1889, Tel: 29125/35079, Fax: 29125/35456) is the Tanzanian representative of American Express. It can provide financial services such as emergency cashing of cheques and foreign exchange, and is open from 8.00am to 5.00pm Monday to Saturday.

Embassies and diplomatic missions

Embassies and high commissions in Dar es Salaam are listed below. Most are open mornings only and not at all at weekends. Typical hours are 9.00am to 12.30pm, but this varies considerably.

Country	Address	Tel
Algeria	34 Upanga Road	46250
Angola	IPS Building, cnr Maktaba & Samora	46168
Argentina	953 Msasani Peninsula	41628
Austria	20 Samora Ave	46251
Belgium	NIC Building, Samora Ave	46194
Brazil	IPS Building, cnr Maktaba & Samora	46191
Britain	Hifadhi House, Samora Ave	46300
Bulgaria	232 Malik Road	23787
Burundi	1007 Lugalo Road	46307
Canada	Pan Africa Insurance Building, Samora Ave	46000
China	2 Kajifcheni Close	67586
CIS (ex USSR)	73 Kenyatta Drive	46368
Cuba	313 Lugalo Road	46315
Cyprus	City Drive	23513
Czechoslovak	69 Upanga Road	46251
Denmark	Bank House, Samora Ave	46318
Egypt	24 Garden Ave	32158

Finland	NIC Building, Samora Ave	46324
France	cnr Bagamoyo & Kilimani	46329
Germany	NIC Building, Samora Ave	46334
Greece	Parthenon Hall, Upanga Road	46252
India	NIC Building, Samora Ave	46341
Indonesia	299 Upanga Road	46347
Iran	Mazengo Road	32788
Iraq	NIC Building, Samora Ave	25728
Ireland	TDFL Building, cnr Upanga & Ohio	46852
Italy	316 Lugalo Road	46352
Japan	1008 Upanga Road	46356
Kenya	NIC Building, Samora Ave	46362
Korea	46B United Nations Road	46831
Libya	386 Mititu Street	46254
Madagascar	143 Malik Road	46255
Malawi	IPS Building, cnr Maktaba & Samora	46673
Mexico	2052 Kimara Street	23935
Mozambique	25 Garden Ave	46487
Netherlands	ATC Building, Ohio Road	46391
Nigeria	3 Bagamoyo Road	66682
Norway	Extelcomms House, Samora Ave	46443
Pakistan	149 Malik Road	27971
Poland	4 Upanga Road	46294
Rwanda	32 Upanga Road	46502
Somalia	539 Kalenga Road	50717
Spain	99B Kinondoni Road	46506
Sudan	64 Upanga Road	46509
Sweden	Extelcomms House, Samora Ave	46443
Switzerland	17 Kenyatta Drive	66006
Uganda	Extelcomms House, Samora Ave	46256
USA	36 Laibon Road	66010
Yemen	353 United Nations Road	46834
Zaire	438 Malik Road	46350
Zambia	Cnr Ohio Road & City Drive	46383
Zimbabwe	439 Malik Road	46259

Tour operators

Most tour operators in Dar es Salaam specialise in visits to the southern reserves described in Chapter Eleven. It is more normal to organise northern safaris in Arusha. It is also cheaper, as most tour operators in Dar es Salaam are in the middle to upper range. Some tour companies can do day trips to Bagamoyo. Safaris can usually be arranged through the owners of various camps in the Selous; see Chapter Eleven for details of these.

Bushtrekker Safaris, PO Box 5350, tel: 31957.
Holiday Africa, Africa Street, PO Box 2132, tel: 30700.
Kearsley Travel, Indira Gandhi St, PO Box 801, tel: 20607/8/9, fax: 35012.
Savannah Tours, in the Kilimanjaro Hotel, PO Box 6247, tel: 25273, fax: 41652.
State Travel Service, Samora Ave, PO Box 5033, tel: 29291, fax: 29295.
Takims Safaris, Jamhuri Street, PO Box 20350, tel: 25691/2/3, fax: 46130.
Valji & Alhibai, Bridge Street, PO Box 786, tel: 20522, fax: 46401.

WHAT TO DO

Dar es Salaam is an interesting city, but not one that offers much in the way of conventional sightseeing. It is worth taking a stroll around the harbour area, and through the backstreets between Maktaba Road and the station. There are several old German buildings in the older part of town around the national museum and botanical gardens.

If you have a couple of days to kill in Dar es Salaam, you might want to spend them at Kunduchi Beach (covered later in this chapter) or Bagamoyo (see Chapter Six).

Kariakoo Market

A huge variety of clothes, foodstuffs, spices and traditional medicines can be bought at this lively and colourful covered market which extends onto the surrounding streets in the form of a chaotic miscellany of stalls. The name *Kariakoo* derives from the British Carrier Corps, which was stationed in the area during World War Two.

National Museum

This is one of the better museums I have visited in Africa. The natural history section is a predictable collection of stuffed birds and animals, but the section on early hominid development has some of the world's most important fossils. The history displays upstairs have a good selection of exhibits dating back to the era of European exploration and German occupation. If you plan to visit Kilwa Kisiwani, don't miss the display of coins, pottery and other artefacts found during excavations there. Entrance costs $1.

The area around the museum is notable for its pre-1914 German buildings, recognisable by their red-tiled roofs. The botanical gardens, started in 1906, and State House, built by the British in 1922, are both worth a look. From State House, if you walk back to town along Kivukoni Front, you will be rewarded by good views of the city and harbour. You will also pass the 19th-Century Lutheran Church which is the oldest building in the city.

Nyumba ya Sanaa

This well-known gallery was founded by a nun, and is now housed in an unusually-designed building, erected in 1983 with the help of Norwegian funding. It exhibits arts and crafts made by handicapped people. A variety of carvings, batiks and pottery items can be bought. The standard of craftsmanship is generally regarded to be high. There is a cafe in the complex.

Oyster Bay

This is the closest swimming beach to the city centre. It is a reasonably attractive spot and very popular at weekends. The Oyster Bay Hotel, which overlooks the beach, is a pleasant place to have a drink. Oyster Bay is difficult to get to using public transport. A taxi from the city centre will cost around $2.50.

Village Museum and Mwenge Market

The Village Museum consists of life-size replicas of huts built in architectural styles from all over Tanzania. It is open daily from 9.30am to 6.00pm. There is an entrance fee of $0.50 as well as a photographic fee of $1.25 (or $5.00 for video cameras).

The nearby Mwenge market is a traditional Makonde carving community. It is one of the best places to buy these unique sculptures (covered in more detail under *The Makonde Plateau* in Chapter Twelve). Prices are negotiable.

Both are along the Bagamoyo road, about 10km and 13km from the city centre respectively. To get there, you could board a bus heading towards Bagamoyo and ask to be dropped off. City buses and matatus leave from the post office.

Nightlife

Bars The most popular place for an evening drink is the verandah of the New Africa Hotel. The outdoor bar at the Motel Agip has less character, but it's quieter and the service is better. Further afield, the Oyster Bay and Palm Beach Hotels both get lively at night, but you will need a taxi to get to either of them.

Discos and live music   There is a disco in the New Africa Hotel on Wednesday, Friday and Saturday nights. The entrance fee is quite steep but there is often a live group. A more earthy place is the disco at the Imperial Hotel on Samora Avenue near the clock tower. There is always the possibility that one of the better-known Zairian groups will be in town for a one-off gig. Ask around. The most popular disco in Dar es Salaam is at the Oyster Bay Hotel; you will need to take a taxi there.

Cinema and theatre   There are six cinemas in Dar es Salaam. If you are a fan of Indian, kung-fu or gungho American war films you will be in your element. Stallone is a massive figure in Tanzania; his face is printed on shopping bags and painted on shops and restaurants. If enthusiastic kids yell "Rambo" at you don't let it go to your head — they would yell it at Bambi if he happened to be passing.

The only theatre in Dar es Salaam is the *Little Theatre* near Oyster Bay.

KUNDUCHI BEACH

This is Dar es Salaam's major resort. Most people visit it to relax on the sandy beaches, which are marred only by concrete piles at regular intervals, apparently to control erosion. It is possible to hire a boat to one of the many small islands dotted along the coast.

Getting there

A shuttle bus to the hotels on Kunduchi Beach leaves from in front of the New Africa Hotel at 9.00am, 12.00 noon, 2.00pm and 5.00pm on weekdays, and every other hour between 9.00am and 5.00pm on weekends. It stops first at the Kunduchi Beach Hotel, followed by Silversands, Rungwe Oceanic Hotel and the Bahari Beach Hotel. It then returns directly to the city centre.

The trip out takes about an hour. Timings for the return trip are vague. If, for instance, you want to return to Dar es Salaam on the bus which leaves the New Africa at 9.00am, it could pass your hotel any time between 9.45am and 10.15am.

There are ordinary buses to Kunduchi village, from where you could walk to one of the hotels. This is not recommended; thefts and muggings are a common occurence on roads between the hotels. Stick to the shuttle service.

Where to stay

There are four hotels, all on the beachfront.

UPPER RANGE

Bahari Beach Hotel (PO Box 9312, Tel: 47101). This coral and thatch hotel, constructed in traditional Swahili style, is the top of the range. It has attractive grounds. Facilities include a restaurant, swimming pool, and live music on Sundays. Air-conditioned chalets cost $90/110 HC s/c single/double, or $30/35 for residents. Day visitors are charged $1.25.

Kunduchi Beach Hotel (PO Box 9313, Tel: 47621/23491). This is also a pleasant hotel. All rooms are air-conditioned and sea-facing. There is a restaurant and swimming pool; boat hire can be organised. $43/53 HC s/c single/double or $9/10 for residents.

MODERATE

Rungwe Oceanic Hotel (Tel:47815). Accommodation is in comfortable huts, with a fan, mosquito nets and hot water. Rungwe is a lively place; it has a bar, a restaurant and a disco. $11.25 s/c double. The campsite is popular with overland trucks and costs $1.25 per person.

Silversands Hotel This hotel, run by the University of Dar es Salaam, is a bit run-down but nevertheless pleasant. Facilities include a restaurant and bar. Air-conditioned rooms cost $8 s/c double. There is a rather shabby and not very secure looking campsite attached.

Kunduchi Ruins

These ruins are a short walk from the Kunduchi Beach Hotel. Little is known about their history. One of the ruined buildings is a 16th-Century mosque. The main point of interest is an 18th-Century graveyard set amongst a grove of baobab trees. The graves at Kunduchi are notable for being marked by inscribed stone obelisks — a feature not found at any other Swahili graveyard of this period. Pottery collected at the site suggests the town was wealthy and had trade links with China and Britain.

104

Chapter Six

The north coast and Usambara

INTRODUCTION

This chapter covers the coast between Dar es Salaam and the Kenyan border, and the Usambara Mountains between Tanga and Moshi. It is an area with no major tourist attractions, but it offers several minor delights normally bypassed by visitors in their haste to reach Kilimanjaro or the northern safari circuit. Unlike similar destinations in western and southern Tanzania, these are all within easy reach of short-stay visitors.

The largest town on the north coast, Tanga, has been the country's second-largest port since German times. The Omani-founded settlements of Bagamoyo and Pangani lie between Tanga and Dar es Salaam, as does the little-visited Sadani Game Reserve.

The Usambara Mountains lie north of Tanga, between the coast and the main Dar es Salaam-Moshi road. The only large town in the mountains is Lushoto, but smaller settlements such as Amani, Soni and Mlalo are all of interest. The most important centres on the Tanga-Moshi road are Muheza, Korogwe, Mombo and Same.

Climate

The north coast has a typical coastal climate: hot and humid, with short rains in November and December and long rains between March and May. The Usambara is higher and cooler than the coast, but has a similar rainfall pattern.

Getting around

Regular buses run along the main roads between Dar es Salaam, Tanga and Moshi. Transport off this road is less regular, but there are daily buses to Amani, Lushoto and Pangani, and from Dar es Salaam to Bagamoyo.

The Dar es Salaam-Moshi road was in a sorry state for years, but it has recently been re-surfaced; at the end of 1992, only the 50km stretch north of Mombo still needed work. Buses from Dar es Salaam to Moshi take eight to 10 hours. The road between Tanga and Segera is poor, but there are plans to re-surface it. The only other tar road in the region connects Mombo to Lushoto.

Trains between Dar es Salaam and Moshi stop at Korogwe, Mombo and Same, though not at a particularly convenient hour. Tanga is connected to Dar es Salaam and Moshi by rail. See *Rail* in Chapter Three for details.

In an ideal world you could travel from Dar es Salaam to Tanga along the coast, taking in Bagamoyo, Sadani and Pangani along the way. Unfortunately, transport between Bagamoyo and Pangani verges on the non-existent. Unless you have a 4x4 vehicle, the coastal route is only worth attempting in the dry season, and even then only if you are an optimist with plenty of time on your hands.

BAGAMOYO

Bagamoyo, 70km north of Dar es Salaam, was the centre of the 19th-Century slave trade. It was an important base in the first years of German rule, but little development has taken place since the then. Bagamoyo is dominated by Arab and German buildings in various states of disintegration. This stagnation has given it a fascinating museum-like quality.

History

The 12th-Century town of Kaole, 5km from Bagamoyo, had strong trade links with Kilwa during the Shirazi era, and was evidently wealthy. It must also have enjoyed some prosperity during the Portuguese and Omani periods; most of its decorative graves were erected years after the Portuguese invasion.

Bagamoyo itself was a minor fishing village until the late 18th Century when it became the terminus for the northern slave caravan route. By the mid-19th Century approximately 50,000 slaves were shipped from Bagamoyo to Zanzibar annually. Various meanings have been attributed to the name Bagamoyo; *to lose hope* or *where the heart lays down its burden* are two of them. These relate to Bagamoyo being the last place of rest on African soil for captured slaves awaiting shipment.

Many European explorers passed through Bagamoyo, including Burton, Speke, Grant, Stanley and Livingstone. Their publicising of the horrors of the slave trade led to the Holy Ghost Fathers establishing a mission there in 1868. The church they built in 1873 is the oldest in East Africa. It seems fitting that after his death at Lake Benguela in 1873, the preserved body of Livingstone — who called the slave trade the 'open sore of the world' — was carried 1,600km by his porters to the Holy Ghost Mission before being shipped to Zanzibar and England.

The Germans built their headquarters at Bagamoyo in 1888. Stanley arrived there in 1889 after a three year trip to what was then the Equatoria Province of Egypt (the area north of Lake Albert) and was struck by how it had grown since German occupation. He brought with him the Emin Pasha, the German-born British officer who had defended Equatoria since the fall of Khartoum in 1885. Having survived this, the Emin Pasha — drunk at the time, and notoriously short-sighted — celebrated his safe arrival with a near-fatal fall from the balcony of the officer's mess to the street below. He spent the next six weeks in the mission hospital recovering from head injuries.

The Germans deemed Bagamoyo's harbour too shallow for long-term use and moved north to Tanga. The town remained an important regional centre for some years — its most impressive building, the State House, was built in 1897 — but since the turn of the century, its importance has declined steadily.

Getting there and away

Regular buses to Bagamoyo leave Dar es Salaam from outside Kariakoo Market. The road up is outrageously bad; expect the trip to take four hours. People do visit Bagamoyo as a day trip from Dar es Salaam, but with two long bus trips either side it is not an attractive prospect. In any case, Bagamoyo deserves an overnight stay.

Where to stay

The only tourist hotel is the **Gogo Beach Hotel**, on the beach about 1km out of town. It is very new and rather lacks character, but this should improve with time. It has a restaurant and bar, and the chalets look comfortable. $30/40 HC s/c single/double.

The moderately-priced **Badeco Beach Hotel** is on the beachfront, a short walk from the town centre. It has a relaxed, friendly atmosphere. Meals are cooked on request and there is a bar. Rooms are basic but clean and have mosquito nets. $4/5 single/double.

The **Alpha Motel** near the bus station has clean rooms and a restaurant. $1.25/1.90 single/double. There are other guest houses, but they are only worth looking at if you are desperate.

What to see

In the town centre there are a few buildings with carved wooden Zanzibar doors. The most impressive building is the State House, which now serves as a customs office. The unusual two-storey building near the Badeco Hotel, currently being restored, is the one from which the Emin Pasha fell in 1889. Also near the Badeco is the tree from which the Germans hanged Africans they considered rebellious, and a graveyard for German soldiers. The building which is now the police station used to be where slaves were held prior to being shipped to Zanzibar.

The Holy Ghost Mission   This 19th-Century mission should be your first port of call. The church, built in 1873, is still standing and a small museum has fascinating displays on every aspect of Bagamoyo's past. Entrance is free, but a donation is expected. The mission is 3km out of town. The avenue that leads to the mission has a reputation for muggings; leave your valuables behind and either go in a group or with a guide.

The beach   It is difficult to imagine a beach which conforms more closely to the archetype of a tropical paradise than the one stretching for miles either side of Bagamoyo. We stayed at the Badeco where, unless they have a new cassette by now — or maybe it's deliberate — Bob Marley's *Redemption Song* comes over the speaker perhaps a dozen times a day: a chilling reminder that tens of thousands of slaves were shipped from this beach. If you cannot quite abandon yourself to hedonism in these circumstances, it is still worth wandering along the beach between the Badeco and Gogo Hotels. The old beachfront slave market now sells fish; the white sands in front of it are lined with picturesque fishing dhows. I was enchanted by the legions of ghostly white crabs which scuttle along the beach after dusk.

Kaole Ruins   In Shirazi times, Kaole was the largest trading centre between Kilwa and Mombasa. The main ruins date mainly from the 13th Century and include what is thought to be the oldest mosque on the East African mainland. There is also an Omani-era graveyard. Kaole is an hour's walk south of Bagamoyo; the most straightforward route is along the beach, but there is a risk of being mugged on the way. Find a guide or leave your valuables behind, preferably both. Kaole can be reached by road. The caretaker is enthusiastic and knowledgable.

Bagamoyo Art College   This art college, 100m south of the Badeco

Hotel, is housed in a stunning building constructed from traditional materials. Most weekends the students put on a free show of traditional music, dancing and mime. When we visited it, this was attended by what looked like the entire population of Bagamoyo and there was plenty of audience participation.

SADANI GAME RESERVE

This is the nearest game reserve to Dar es Salaam, yet one of the least visited in Tanzania. I have met only one person who has been to Sadani, a safari operator in Dar es Salaam. It is not easy to reach unless you have your own vehicle; we tried from Pangani and Bagamoyo without any luck. If you have the time and initiative, however, I have read and heard enough to suggest it is worth pursuing.

Sadani is the only East African coastal reserve to harbour large mammals and it is said to be the one place where elephant can still be seen bathing in the Indian Ocean. It protects a wide variety of habitats, including mangrove swamps, coastal thickets and acacia woodland. Animal numbers have been depleted by poaching, but this is said to be under control and there is still enough game left in the surrounding area for populations to replenish themselves naturally. Resident mammals include lion, leopard, elephant, zebra, roan antelope, giraffe, oryx and buffalo.

The small but ancient village of Sadani lies within the reserve on the Pangani-Bagamoyo road.

Getting there and away

Long-term plans to develop Sadani include clearing an air strip, but until this materialises the only easy way to get there is in a 4x4 vehicle. The route via the Dar es Salaam-Moshi highway and Miono is more reliable than the coastal road through Bagamoyo.

Getting to Sadani on public transport appears to be difficult. If you decide to give it a go, be prepared to get stuck along the way. According to the TTC office in Dar es Salaam, the odd vehicle runs from Bagamoyo to Sadani. This was news to everyone we spoke to in Bagamoyo; there we were told to catch a bus from Dar es Salaam to Miono (10km east of the Moshi road) where we could catch a pick-up truck to Sadani. The Miono road is favoured by private vehicles so is probably the better one to try. I doubt there is anywhere to stay in Miono and there is a good chance of getting stuck overnight. Take a tent.

Where to stay

Boldly marked on virtually every map of Tanzania published in the last thirty years, the ex-government rest house in Sadani village has spent the last two-thirds of this period quietly attempting to biodegrade. It is functional, but camping in the grounds may be preferable to taking a room ($1.50 double). Bring food with you.

PANGANI   *BUSES GO 3 TIMES DAILY TO TANGA.*

The mouth of the Pangani River has been a trading centre for centuries. It was known as Muhembo in Shirazi and Portuguese times. Some sources claim it was the site of Rhapta, a town described in the 1st Century document *Periplus of the Erythraen Sea*, but the Rufiji Delta is a more likely location. The modern town, on the north bank of the river, was settled by the Omani in about 1820. Pangani was the terminus for slave caravans to modern-day western Kenya. For much of the 19th Century it rivalled Bagamoyo and Kilwa Kivinje in importance.

Pangani has an attractive situation. The banks of the Pangani River are heavily forested and a gorgeous beach stretches north of the estuary as far as the eye can see. The town itself is Arabic in feel, and several buildings are said to date back to the slave trade. The harbour is quite busy, with the main economic impetus apparently coming from traditional fishing. Otherwise Pangani is relaxed and sleepy, and like so many coastal towns, it does not quite seem to belong in the 20th Century.

Getting there and away

There are a couple of buses daily each way between Tanga and Pangani. You could also try to hitch; a good place to wait is the turn-off to Baobab Beach (see *Tanga*) as you can stay at the hotel if you have no luck.

The roads heading south from Pangani to Bagamoyo and the Dar es Salaam highway are little-used. There is no public transport along them. If you want to hitch southwards from Pangani, take the ferry across to the south bank of the river and wait there. Don't expect anything to happen in a rush.

Where to stay/eat

None of the lodgings in Pangani has any significant virtue other than cheapness. The **Pangadeco Beach Hotel** is in a good position and if renovated would be the place to stay, but at present it is dirty, run down, and the rooms don't lock. The cleaner **Riverside Inn** and **Paradise Guest House** are both on the river front near the bus terminus and cost 0.90/1.40 single/double. A few *hotelis* along the river serve basic meals such as chicken and chips. There is a bar at the Pangadeco.

Excursions

Most travellers who visit Pangani do so to take a boat up the Pangani River. There is some wildlife in the area, and crocodile are regularly seen. The river is lined with forest so bird watching is good. Pangani District Council charters a boat that carries up to 10 people for $4 per hour. Details are pinned up at the Pangadeco's bar. It you want to cut costs by getting a group together, ask around at the Bandorini Hotel in Tanga.

TANGA

Tanga is Tanzania's third-largest town and second-busiest port. It is one of my favourite East African towns. There is little to do there, but it has a relaxed, friendly atmosphere and is a pleasant place to hang out. If, like many travellers, you never stray beyond the town centre of quiet, potholed streets lined with German and Asian buildings, Tanga is deceptively sleepy. The hub of Tanga's commercial activity lies away from the centre, in the grid of colourful, crowded streets around the bus station. There is also a well-preserved residential area which sprawls attractively along a wooded peninsula east of the town centre.

History

There is little record of Tanga before Omani times and it was dwarfed by Pangani for most of the 19th Century. Tanga was settled by the Germans when Bagamoyo's harbour proved too shallow. The first school in German East Africa was built at Tanga in 1893, and a railway line to Moshi was started in the same year.

When Dar es Salaam replaced Tanga as the capital, the Germans saw no reason to abandon Tanga the way they had Bagamoyo. Its excellent harbour and the coming rail link to the fertile foothills of Kilimanjaro (the Moshi line was only completed in 1911) guaranteed its survival. Tanga remains the second largest port in Tanzania; most of its business comes from sisal exports.

Tanga was the scene of a tragically farcical British raid in the

PANORI HOTEL

(NEAR PORT SIDE & LHOTY)

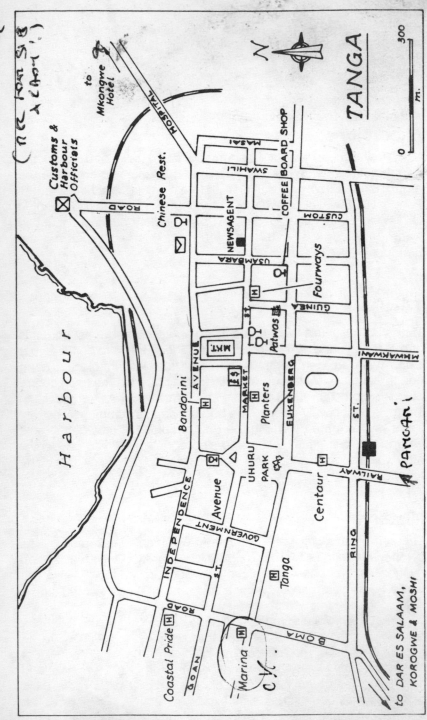

opening stages of World War One. Still seasick after a long voyage from India, 8,000 Asian recruits leapt ashore, got bogged down in the mangroves, stumbled into a swarm of ferocious bees and finally triggered off trip-wires rigged up by the Germans. By the time the raid was aborted 800 British troops were dead and 500 wounded. In the confusion 455 rifles, 16 machine guns and 600,000 rounds of ammunition were left on the shore — a major boon to the Germans. This battle forms a pivotal scene in William Boyd's excellent novel *An Ice-cream War*.

Getting there and away

Trains connect Tanga to Dar es Salaam and Moshi (see *Rail* in Chapter Three), as do regular buses. The bus station is 1km from the town centre. Make enquiries and a booking the day before you want to leave. There are daily buses to Pangani and Lushoto.

There are dhows between Tanga and Pemba every week or so, but they are unreliable and dangerous. The Sea Express and Flying Horse boats which at present connect Dar es Salaam to Zanzibar should have expanded their service to include Pemba, Mombasa and Tanga by the time you read this.

Where to stay

[handwritten: KINGFISHER LODGE, 32 k on Pangani Road. $135 per night — Ipob Res !!]

UPPER RANGE

Mkonge Hotel (PO Box 1544, Tel: (053) 44541). Tanga's top of the range hotel is 1km from the town centre on Hospital Road. Its pleasant grounds face the sea, it has a good restaurant and bar, and hosts a popular disco at weekends. Air-conditioned rooms cost $30/40 HC s/c single/double.

[handwritten: recommended]

Inn by the Sea (PO Box 2188, Tel: (053) 44613). Rooms at this *[handwritten: 18,000 : £]* attractively situated hotel, next to the Mkonge, cost $20 HC s/c double or $10 for residents.

[handwritten: 7000 TSh — for double ! 12000 TSh — air conditioning !]

MODERATE

Marina Hotel (PO Box 835, Tel: (053) 44362). This is the best hotel in its range. Facilities include hot running water in the rooms, a restaurant and bar, and evening video shows. The staff aren't particularly friendly but you can't have everything. Double rooms with fans cost $6.25 s/c; those with air-conditioning cost $10 s/c. This includes a good breakfast.

Tanga Hotel   (PO Box 602, Tel: (053) 45857). This colonial-style hotel is a bit run-down, but agreeable in a dopey kind of way. The restaurant is pretty good. $6.25 s/c double with fan.

BUDGET

The places listed here are dearer than budget hotels in other parts of Tanzania. There are several cheaper guest houses around the bus station, but I have not met a traveller who has used one, and would instinctively be wary of that area after dark.

Bandorini Hotel   This hotel is geared towards travellers and is often full. The helpful manager is a good source of up-to-date local travel information. Rooms have fans and mosquito nets, and some have balconies. $2.75/3.75 s/c single/double.

Planters Hotel   Planters has been a travellers hang-out for years. It is run-down but pleasant, and has huge rooms and a large communal balcony from where you can watch Tanga go by. $2.75/4.50 single/double and $5.75 s/c double.

Fourways Hotel   This newish hotel is geared more to local businessmen than travellers. The staff are friendly and the rooms clean. $3.25/3.75 s/c single/double.

Centaur Hotel   This was finished but not yet open when we were in town. I expect it will be similar to the Fourways.

Coast Pride Hotel   The rooms here are basic, but they are clean and have fans. $2.50 double.

Where to eat

Most of the hotels mentioned above have a restaurant attached, but none is anything special. The **Chinese Restaurant** has a varied menu (not just Chinese food) and is very reasonably priced at around $1.50 for a main course. You can eat indoors or in the garden.

The **Patwas Restaurant** serves a good range of snacks such as samosas and kebabs. The passion fruit juice is excellent. The nameless restaurant around the corner has a similar menu and is cheaper but the food is not as good. The **Coffee Marketing Board Shop** serves cheap coffee and a limited range of snacks.

Excursions

Amboni Caves

These limestone caves 8km north of Tanga are the most extensive in East Africa. Local people knew about the caves years before Europeans discovered them in 1940; they believe the main cave is inhabited by a fertility god and still leave offerings to this deity. The guide has gathered an admirable collection of anecdotes and tall stories. Amboni lies just off the Tanga-Mombasa road; any vehicle heading towards Mombasa can drop you off near the entrance.

Baobab Beach Hotel

Baobab Beach Hotel lies on a beach surrounded by mangroves and lined with palms and — surprise — baobabs. It is a relaxing spot, with an outdoor bar and a reasonably-priced restaurant. The hotel hires out rowing boats ($1.25/hour), windsurfers ($2.50/hour), paddle-skis ($0.75/hour) and a minibus ($0.25/km). Rooms are clean and the staff efficient. $3.75/4.50 s/c single/double banda, or $5.00/6.25 s/c single/double cottage.

Baobab Beach is 8km from Tanga. Any bus to Pangani can drop you at the turn-off, from where you can either walk the 3km to the hotel or wait for a lift. There is a slight risk of theft walking in this area, but according to hotel staff, you are fine if you stick to the road.

You can save a lot of mucking about by getting a taxi straight through from Tanga. This will cost around $5. Another option is to visit Karamjee Travel next to the Chinese restaurant (PO Box 1563, Tel: (053) 40459), which does bookings for the hotel and may have a vehicle heading out that way.

Tongoni Ruins

These are the ruins of a Shirazi town which peaked in the 14th and 15th centuries. Even in its heyday Tongoni was probably a minor town, but it was certainly prosperous — its graveyard houses the largest concentration of historical tombs on the East African coast, many of which are threatened by the sea. There is also a ruined mosque at the site.

Tongoni is about 20km south of Tanga. To get there catch any bus heading to Pangani and ask to be dropped off at the village of Tongoni. The ruins are 10 minutes walk from the main road. There is a caretaker. Try to get to Tongoni early in the day; there will not be much transport back to Tanga later, and there is nowhere to stay.

THE USAMBARA MOUNTAINS

This is the most accessible of the Eastern Arc Mountain Ranges, and the best-known scientifically. Research at the botanical garden at Amani started in 1902. Despite severe encroachment in some areas, significant stands of montane forest remain. These forests, like all those in eastern Tanzania, are characterised by a high level of endemism. The general ecology of the eastern Tanzanian mountains is more fully discussed under *Udzungwa National Park* in Chapter Eleven.

The western and eastern Usambara are very different in character. The western Usambara is cultivated and relatively densely populated; the eastern Usambara is forested except where the indigenous vegetation has been replaced by tea plantations. Access to the Lushoto in western Usambara is via a tarred road from Mombo. The most accessible place in the eastern Usambara is Amani, about 30km from Muheza on the Tanga-Moshi road.

History

The Usambara has been occupied by Bantu-speakers for a few thousand years. The people of the mountains, the Shambaa, have a tradition of welcoming refugees from other areas, and until recent times had a loose political system similar to the *ntemi* of western Tanzania. The probable impetus for forging greater unity was the threat posed by the 18th Century Maasai occupation of the plains west of the range.

The first Shambaa leader was Mbegha, the self-styled *Lion King*, who probably originated from the *ntemi* area of western Tanzania. Mbegha united the area peacefully by taking a wife from each major clan, then placing her son in charge of that clan. His army, formed from refugees, seems likely only to have been used in defence. Under the rule of Mbegha's grandson, Kinyashi, the Shambaa became more militarised. Their greatest leader was Kinyashi's son, Kimweri; under his rule the Shambaa controlled much of the area between the Usambara and the coast.

Kimweri's capital at Vuga, near the modern settlement of Soni, was too deep in the mountains to have had much contact with Kilimanjaro-bound caravans. One of Kimweri's sons, Semboja, the chief of Mazinde, on what is now the main Moshi-Dar es Salaam road, came to exert considerable influence over passing traders. By 1867 he had built up a stockpile of arms large enough to enable him to overthrow Kimweri's successor at Vuga. This event split the Shambaa into several splinter groups, and although the leadership was retained by Semboja, he controlled a far smaller area than did his predecessor. The Shambaa figured heavily in the Abushiri uprising of 1888/9, but after Semboja's son, Mputa, was hanged in 1898, they offered little further resistance to German occupation.

The Usambara was popular with European farmers. Lushoto, originally called Wilhelmstal, was considered a possible capital in the early days of the colony. Evidence of German architectural styles can be seen throughout the region.

Amani

In 1902 the Germans established an agricultural research station at Amani and set aside the surrounding area as a botanical garden. Amani is now an important medical research centre, housed in buildings dating to the German and British colonial era. The botanical garden, said to be the second largest in the world, still exists. Amani has the genteel appearance of an English country village transplanted to the African jungle: it is surrounded by montane forest and teems with animal life. The area is scheduled to become a nature reserve.

Amani is exceptionally attractive to anyone with an interest in hiking or natural history. Wandering around the forest-fringed village is an ideal way to see species such as black-and-white colobus and blue monkey. The area supports numerous endemic plant species, including nine varieties of African violet, and is renowned for its colourful and abundant butterflies, many of which are also endemic.

The bird life around Amani is fantastic. The conspicuous and beautiful green-headed oriole is restricted to a handful of montane forests between Tanzania and Mozambique. Other Amani specials include the Uluguru violet-backed, banded green and Amani sunbirds, and a variety of robins, bulbuls and starlings. The Nduk eagle owl is only found in the Usambara. Many endemics are forest fringe species, so are likely to be seen in the village. Abercrombie and Kent (see safari company listings in Chapter Eight) do occasional bird watching tours to Amani.

Getting there and away

Amani is reached from Muheza on the Tanga-Moshi road. There are guest houses in Muheza should you need to spend a night. The bus to Amani leaves Muheza at 2.00pm, but it may not run after heavy rains. If you want to try hitching, wait in front of the courthouse 1km from the town centre, opposite a sign that reads *Amani Medical Research Centre 32km*.

The drive to Amani is spectacular. From Kisiwani, 7km before Amani, the dirt road climbs through the forest in a succession of tight hairpin bends. In a bus this is nerve-wracking; I was convinced we were the unwitting victims of a pilot scheme, doomed to failure after a maiden attempt. We got there in the end, however — the bus has been doing this route safely for years.

When we left Amani, we could not find a bus back to Muheza, so walked the 7km to Kisiwani. The road passes through forest all the way; we saw plenty of monkeys, butterflies and birds. It is marginally easier to get a lift at Kisiwani than it is at Amani, as roads to the various tea estates in the area branch off between the two. There is regular transport to Muheza from Bambani, a village about two hours walk from Kisiwani.

Where to stay/eat

The rest house in Amani, run by the medical centre, is a well-maintained post-war colonial building. The cosy lounge is heated by a log fire in the evenings and houses a library of yellowing and improbably-titled books. Space in the rest house is limited. If you have a tent you can camp in the garden, but otherwise it is advisable to phone in advance. Ask for Amani exchange; they will connect you to the rest house.

Rooms cost $3.75, inclusive of a good breakfast and dinner. Lunch is an extra $1.25. There is nowhere else to eat. The bar at the Welfare Club, which serves as a school during the day, has a pleasant atmosphere.

There are plans to establish a campsite at Kisiwani and to convert the disused station building there into an information centre.

Walks and hikes

You are free to explore the extensive network of roads and paths surrounding Amani. There is also plenty to be seen from the grounds of the research centre. Details of walks and hikes can be obtained from the IUCN office 500m from the rest house.

A good short walk through the forest starts from behind the IUCN office. You initially follow disused and overgrown German roads, then a footpath, and come out at a viewpoint over the surrounding hills. We saw some interesting birds, a snake and a giant elephant shrew on this walk. The view when you reach the top gives an idea of the extent of deforestation in the area.

Provided you stick to roads and footpaths, no special permission is needed for longer hikes. It is advisable, however, to notify the IUCN of your plans. If you want to hike wild you need written permission from the Forestry Office in Tanga or Kwamboro.

The following hike is relatively straightforward, covers about 20km, and can be done in two days. From Amani, follow the dirt roads past Derema and Bulwa tea estates. From there you follow disused roads through the villages of Mgambo and Zeria to Kilonga Ngua. From Kilonga Ngua a reasonable dirt road leads to the main Marombo-Korogwe road. You should be able to pick up a lift to Korogwe at the junction. You will need a tent.

A map is recommended for the above hike and essential for any other route. Maps are available from the Department of Lands and Surveys in Dar es Salaam. I'm told a couple of villages are marked inaccurately on the Amani map; someone at the IUCN should be able to point out any errors.

Korogwe

The largest town on the Moshi-Tanga road is unremarkable except for its Usambara backdrop. It is, however, a useful overnight stop when crossing between the eastern and western Usambara.

The only vaguely upmarket hotel is the **Korogwe Traveller's Inn** on the main Tanga-Moshi road. It is perfectly adequate, and has a well-stocked bar and restaurant. $5.00/7.50 s/c single/double.

There are several cheaper lodgings to choose from. The **New Savari Guest House**, 100m from the bus station, is very reasonable. Clean double rooms with mosquito nets cost $2. The **Miami Guest House** next door is similar.

Mombo

This scruffy little town on the Moshi-Dar es Salaam road is the jumping-off point for trips into the western Usambara. Most buses between Dar es Salaam and Moshi stop here for lunch. None of the more basic guest houses in Mombo give the impression that accommodation is their primary function. Try instead the **Usambara Inn**. Its exterior gives new meaning to the expression run-down (it looks derelict), but the rooms are clean, spacious and have a fan and sink. $1.75/2.50 single/double. A restaurant and beer garden are attached.

Lushoto

The largest town in the Usambara is a strange and slightly anachronistic place. Many buildings on the main street date to the early part of the century, when Lushoto provided weekend relief for settlers farming the dry, dusty Maasai Steppe below. The still-significant settler community adds to the time-warped feel; we drove in on a Sunday and saw a couple of young girls walking to church in clothes that would not have looked out of place in an Edwardian period drama.

If the main street calls to mind an Alpine village, the sideroads, lined with mud-and-thatch homesteads, are pure Africa. So, too, is the vibrant market where colourfully-dressed Shambaa women sell their goods. The vegetation around Lushoto reflects these contradictions; papaya trees subvert neat rows of exotic pines and eucalyptus, which in turn are interspersed by patches of lush indigenous forest alive with the raucous squawking of silvery-cheeked hornbill.

You can take in most of what Lushoto has to offer in a couple of hours, but plenty of short walks and day trips can be done using the town as a base.

Getting there and away

The tar road between Mombo and Lushoto offers splendid views in all directions. Direct buses between Tanga and Lushoto are slow. Instead catch an express bus or train as far as Mombo, from where the odd minibus runs to Lushoto — or you could try to hitch.

Where to stay/eat

The colonial-style **Lawns Hotel** is the only upmarket hotel in Lushoto. The rooms are comfortable but seem overpriced at $6/12 s/c single/double. The similarly-priced **Oaklands Hotel**, 10km out of town on the Mlalo road, is considered better by locals. It is not a practical option without your own transport. Far better is the hotel at Soni Falls (see *Excursions*).

A lot of travellers stay at the **Kilimani Guest House**, which is good value at $0.75 per person, and has a reasonable restaurant and bar. Our strong impression was that the staff were sick of travellers, but this might have been a temporary thing. There are other similarly-priced places: the **Milimani Guest House** (a conspicuous brown building on the hill above the bus station with a red and white brick front) or the **nameless guest house** next to it. The **Green Valley Hoteli** near the market serves good, cheap snacks and meals.

Excursions

The area around Lushoto, riddled with footpaths and winding roads, is open to gentle exploration or — if you have the appropriate maps — longer hikes. The area is scenically varied, with steep-sided valleys covered in euphorbia, pine plantations, small patches of indigenous forest, and cultivated Shambaa homesteads.

Irente viewpoint

An attractive short walk from Lushoto takes you to a stunning viewpoint at the edge of the Usambara overlooking the Maasai Steppe. It is possible to organise a guide to take you there, but once you are out of Lushoto it is easy enough to find your own way. Ask people to direct you to Irente farm. From there it is ten minutes walk through Irente village to the viewpoint. The round trip takes two to three hours. Look out for the Egyptian vultures which apparently nest on the cliffs below the viewpoint. It is also worth scanning patches of indigenous forest on route for forest birds.

Soni Falls

The waterfall at Soni is pretty but nothing special, but the hotel overlooking it is a pleasant base for exploring the Usambara. **Soni Falls Hotel** is clean, friendly, and good value at $5 s/c double. Meals are excellent and good value at $2, but must be ordered in advance. The relaxed bar is lit by a log fire in the evenings.

Of the guest houses in Soni village, **Msufino Lodgings** looks the best. Rooms are clean, there is a bar and restaurant, and hot water is provided. $0.75/1.00 single/double.

Soni village is 30 minutes drive from Lushoto along the Mombo road. There is a fair amount of traffic; you shouldn't wait long for a lift in either direction. Soni Falls Hotel is signposted from the Lushoto road less than 1km from the village.

Mlalo

Beyond Lushoto a dirt road skirts the highest peak in the Usambara, Magambo (2,230m), passes through an extensive patch of indigenous forest, then, almost 30km from Lushoto, dramatically descends the side of a valley into a rural sprawl called Mlalo.

Mlalo is bizarre. It has an insular, almost other-worldly feel that made us feel like a pair of Indiana Joneses entering a misplaced Mediterranean mountain kingdom. Initially, I was struck by the unusual style of many of the buildings: two-storey mud houses with intricately-carved wooden balconies which seem to show both German and Arab influences. The town apparently sprawls for miles, yet even in its nominal centre rural homesteads cling precipitously to steep-sided hillocks. There is no electricity; at night the surrounding hills are lit up by lamps bobbing up and down and flickering like fireflies.

The residents of Mlalo seem a bit unsure about tourists; we felt a sense of unease all the time we were there. Wherever we walked people stopped what they were doing to stare at us. In one guest house I enjoyed the unique experience of a Tanzanian saying

'KiSwahili Kidogo' to me, rather than the other way round. I don't regret visiting Mlalo, but I was profoundly relieved when I left.

Getting there and away

There are two buses a day between Lushoto and Mlalo, leaving Lushoto in the early afternoon and Mlalo at around 7.00am. The bus ride takes two hours or so. This means that you will probably have to overnight in Mlalo if you visit it.

Where to stay/eat

The guest houses are near the bus stop. Outside **Lonido Guest House**, a sign proclaims that 'Lonidi is the only alternative for accommodation in Mlalo. Other alternatives are a mere miscalculation'. We gladly risked miscalculation and stayed instead at the **Afilex Hotel**, which was very clean, as friendly as you could hope for in Mlalo, and had the distinct advantage of a manageress who spoke a bit of English. A double room costs $1.25 and lamps are provided.

The restaurant at the Afilex is recommended, despite the fact that the entire staff sat in dead silence and stared at us while we ate. There is a bar and *hoteli* opposite the Afilex.

MKOMAZI GAME RESERVE

Mkomazi Game Reserve is the southern extension of Kenya's vast Tsavo National Park, and it may well be proclaimed a national park itself in the future. In the mid-1980s Mkomazi was badly overgrazed, but recent attempts at restoration have met with success. A significant number of animals have returned from Tsavo; most large African mammals are present. Mkomazi is still rarely visited by tourists, but there is a rundown campsite as well as a small private camp.

The town of Same on the Moshi-Tanga road is the obvious base for a visit to Mkomazi. You can stay at the **Elephant Motel** ($10 s/c double), which is also the best place to get details about Mkomazi, or to find out about hiring a vehicle to take you into the reserve. Mkomazi is two or three hours drive from Arusha, close enough to be added to a safari from that town.

124

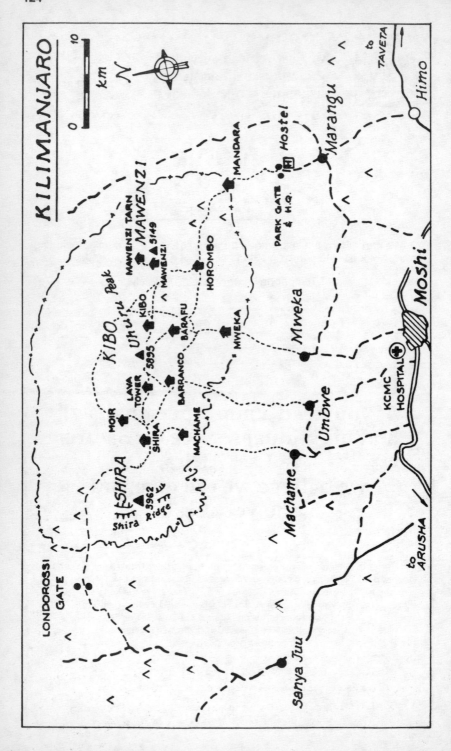

Chapter Seven

Kilimanjaro

INTRODUCTION

This chapter covers Africa's best-known and highest mountain, Kilimanjaro, and the nearby town of Moshi. Kilimanjaro is the highest mountain in the world which can be climbed by ordinary tourists. Thousands attempt to reach its peak every year. The fertile lower slopes support one of the most densely-populated rural areas in Tanzania.

History

Kilimanjaro's fertile soils have attracted people from all over East Africa for centuries. Ancient stone tools of indeterminate age have been found on the lower slopes, as have the remains of pottery artefacts thought to be at least 2,000 years old. Between 1,000 and 1,500 years ago, Kilimanjaro was the centre of an Iron Age culture spreading out to the coastal belt between Pangani and Mombasa.

Kilimanjaro is now home to the Chagga, a Bantu-speaking group whose ancestors first arrived in the area 500 years ago. The Chagga have no tradition of central leadership. As many as 100 small chiefdoms existed in the mid-19th Century. They are efficient agriculturalists, and the lower slopes of Kilimanjaro are covered in their disused dams and irrigation furrows. Because they have always produced a food surplus, the Chagga have a long history of trade with the Maasai and other local groups, and later with Arab caravans.

The first written reference to Kilimanjaro is found in Ptolemy's 4th-Century *Geography*. It is also alluded to in an account written by a 12th-Century Chinese trader, and by the 16th-Century Spanish geographer, Fernandes de Encisco. These allusions fired the curiosity of 19th-Century geographers, who outdid each other in publishing wild speculations about the African interior.

In 1848, Johan Rebmann, a German missionary working in the Taita Hills, was told about a very large mountain reputed to be covered in silver and to host evil spirits which would freeze anyone who tried to climb it. It was called Kilimanjaro. When Rebmann visited it, he immediately recognised the silver to be snow. His observations, published in 1849, were derided by European experts who thought it ludicrous to claim there was snow so near the equator. Only in 1861, when an experienced geologist, Von der Decken, saw and surveyed Kilimanjaro, was its existence and that of its snow-capped peaks accepted. Chagga legend suggests that no local person ever successfully climbed Kilimanjaro before Hans Meyer and Ludwig Purstscheller reached its summit in 1889.

Climate

The higher slopes of Kilimanjaro are cold at all times. Moshi is relatively low-lying (813m) and has a typical equatorial African climate: hot during the day and cool at night. Kilimanjaro can be climbed at any time of year, but the rainier months are best avoided. The heaviest rains fall between March and May.

MOSHI

In addition to being the gateway to Kilimanjaro, Moshi is the centre of an important coffee-growing area. The town itself is unremarkable, but it is blessed with one of the most imposing settings imaginable, the snow-capped peaks of Kilimanjaro rising more than 5km above it.

Prior to the arrival of the Germans, Moshi was the capital of Rindi, who came into power in about 1860 and, largely through his diplomatic skills, became one of the most important chiefs in the area. By allying with the Maasai, Rindi extracted large taxes from passing caravans. He made a favourable impression on John Kirk, the British Consul in Zanzibar, and signed a treaty with Carl Peters in 1885. When the first German colonial forces arrived at Kilimanjaro in 1891, Rindi assured them he ruled the whole area. At his insistence, they quelled his major rival, Sina of Kibosha.

Getting there and away

Moshi can be reached by rail, air or road. Air Tanzania flies regularly between Dar es Salaam and Kilimanjaro Airport (off the main Arusha road). A shuttle-bus between Moshi and the airport leaves from the Air Tanzania office next to the Moshi Hotel.

There are three trains every week between Moshi and Dar es Salaam and Tanga; see *Rail* in Chapter Three for details.

Buses between Dar es Salaam and Moshi take about eight hours.

Several buses leave in each direction every morning. There are regular buses between Moshi and Tanga.

There is a steady flow of traffic between Arusha and Moshi. The trip takes under two hours by bus. Buses to Arusha, Marangu and other local destinations leave when they fill up, but buses further afield have fixed departure times and should be booked in advance.

Where to stay

UPPER RANGE

Keys Hotel   (PO Box 993, Tel: (055) 2250). About 1km from the town centre, this is the most attractive hotel in its range. It has a bar and restaurant, and is a good place to arrange Kilimanjaro climbs. $50 HC s/c double, or $12.50 for residents. A discount is given if you arrange your climb with the hotel.

Moshi Hotel   (PO Box 1819, Tel: (055) 3071). Conveniently situated in the town centre, this TTC hotel has a bar and a restaurant. $47 HC s/c double, or $11 for residents. Rooms using communal showers cost $22/31 HC single/double, or $4.60/6.30 for residents.

MODERATE

YMCA   (PO Box 85, Tel: (055) 52362). This long-time travellers favourite has recently priced itself out of the budget range. It is clean and well-run, and some rooms face the mountain. There is a canteen and a swimming pool (usually empty). Trans-Kibo in the foyer arrange reliable Kilimanjaro climbs. The YMCA is a good place to meet travellers. $10/13 HC single/double.

Coffee Tree Hotel   This is convenient and good value. There is a reasonable restaurant on the top floor. Rooms are large and clean. $4.50/8.75 s/c single/double. Rooms using communal showers cost $3.25.

Green Cottage Inn   This family-run place, 1km from the town centre, is cosy or claustrophobic depending on your tastes. $3.75/5.00 single/double, or $7.50 s/c double.

New Kindoroka Hotel   This is the most pleasant and reasonably-priced of several modern hotels on the grid of streets around the market. $7.00/7.50 s/c single/double, or $4.50/6.25 for rooms using communal showers.

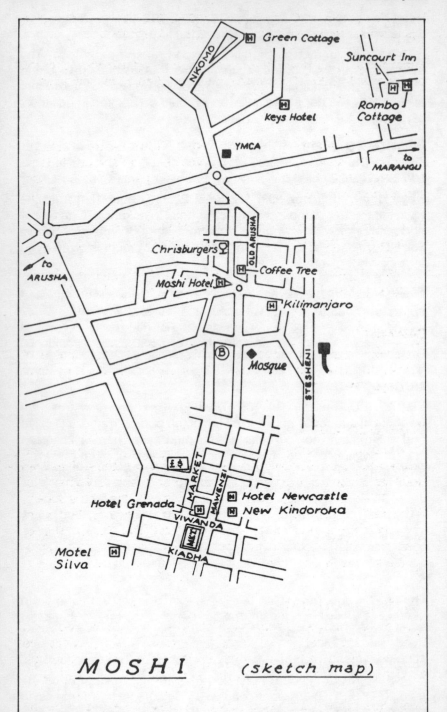

MOSHI   (sketch map)

Hotel Newcastle (PO Box 2000, Tel: (055) 53203) Near the market, this is similar to the New Kindoroka. $15 HC s/c double.

Motel Silva This new hotel has clean, comfortable rooms, but is overpriced. $12/20 HC s/c single/double or $10/13 for residents.

BUDGET

Rombo Cottage Inn This is 1km from the town centre and worth the walk. The staff are friendly, the rooms are clean and comfortable and have fans. Facilities include a good restaurant, a bar, a lounge, and a shady verandah. $2 s/c double.

Sun Court Inn Next door to Rombo Cottage, this is a good option if that is full. It has a bar. $2/3 s/c single/double.

Kilimanjaro Hotel Rooms at this conveniently-situated hotel are a bit dank, but seem reasonably clean. $2/4 s/c single/double.

CAMPING

The campsite at the **Golden Shower Restaurant**, about 2km out of town on the Marangu road, costs $2 per person. You can camp at the **Keys Hotel** for $5 HC per person.

Where to eat

For a snack, try **Chrisburgers**, which serves eggburgers, samosas and excellent fruit juice. The restaurant on the top floor of the **Coffee Tree Hotel** has a commanding view of Kilimanjaro, and serves solid meals for under $2. **Rombo Cottage Inn** is similar in price and the food is superb.
   The best restaurants in Moshi are the **Golden Shower**, 2km out of town on the Marangu road, and **Keys Hotel**. The Golden Shower has a particularly good menu. Main courses cost around $4. Three-course set meals are served at the Moshi Hotel.

Useful Information

Foreign exchange There was no forex bureau in Moshi in December 1992, but this is likely to change. For now, the best place to change money is the bank opposite the clock tower. You will get a much better rate in Arusha or Dar es Salaam.

Shopping There is a good market in Moshi, but shops do not compare to those in Arusha and Dar es Salaam.

MARANGU

Marangu is 8km south of the main gate to Kilimanjaro National Park. It has an alpine feel, with a babbling mountain stream running alongside the main road. Marangu used to be a popular base for organising Kilimanjaro climbs, but unless you are looking at top-of-the-range prices Moshi is a better bet these days. If you organise a climb in Moshi there is no reason to visit Marangu; most companies will organise transport to the entrance gate. If you are not climbing the mountain, Marangu would be a pleasant place to spend a few days as a base for day walks were it not for the high price of accommodation.

Getting there

Buses between Moshi and Marangu leave when they are full, which is every hour or so.

Where to stay/eat

The cheapest rooms in Marangu costs $30. If you have a tent, camping is an option, and cheap rooms are available in Kibo on the Moshi-Dar es Salaam highway.

UPPER RANGE

Kibo Hotel (PO Box 137 Moshi, Tel: (055) 52503 or dial 900 and ask for Marangu 4). This well-established hotel 1km from the village has pretty flowering gardens, a relaxed atmosphere, and a good restaurant. Kilimanjaro climbs organised here are not cheap, but have an impeccable reputation. $84/105 HC s/c single/double, or $56/70 for residents.

Marangu Hotel (PO Box 40 Moshi, Tel: dial 900 and ask for Marangu 11). Like the Kibo, this is a comfortable old hotel with a solid reputation. It is 5km from Marangu on the Moshi road. $70/100 HC s/c single/double, including dinner and breakfast.

MODERATE

Babylon Bar & Hotel This is 500m and signposted from Marangu Post Office. In itself, it's a reasonable place, but at $30/45 HC s/c double/triple it must rank as the worst value for money in Tanzania. A similar room in Moshi costs well under $5.

Pentecostal Church Hostel This hostel next to the Marangu Hotel is more pleasant than the Babylon. Prices are negotiable.

CAMPING

The best place to pitch a tent is at the Kibo Hotel. This costs $6 HC per person and entitles you to use the hotel's facilities. You can camp at the Babylon Bar for $10 HC per person.

MOUNT KILIMANJARO NATIONAL PARK

At 5,895m, Mount Kilimanjaro is the highest mountain in Africa. It is also the highest free-standing mountain in the world, rising 5,000m above the surrounding plains, and the only mountain of its size that can be climbed with comparative ease by non-mountaineers. On the rare occasions when it is not blanketed in clouds, Kilimanjaro's distinctive silhouette and snow-capped peaks are one of the most breathtaking sights in Africa.

Kilimanjaro has three peaks: Kibo (5,895m), Mawenzi (5,149m) and the smaller Shira (3,962m). The area of 756km² lying above the 2,700m contour has been a national park since 1977. Parts of the lower slopes are protected in forest reserves.

No-one knows for sure where the name Kilimanjaro comes from, or even whether it is Swahili, Maasai or Chagga in origin. *Kilima* is Swahili for *little mountain* (a joke?); njaro is similar to the Chagga word for caravan (the mountain was an important landmark on the northern caravan route), the Maasai word for water (it is the source of most of the region's rivers) and the name of a Swahili demon of cold.

In geological terms, Kilimanjaro is a new mountain. The vents which formed its peaks first erupted about one million years ago. Shira collapsed 500,000 years ago, but Kibo and Mawenzi continued to grow until more recently. Shira plateau formed 360,000 years ago, when the caldera was filled by lava from Kibo after a particularly violent eruption. Kibo is now dormant, and no-one knows when it last displayed any serious activity. Chagga myths which suggest there have been eruptions in the last 500 years do not tally with the geological evidence. The myths may have been handed down by previous occupants of the area.

Vegetation and biology

There are five vegetation zones on Kilimanjaro: the cultivated lower slopes, the forest, heath and moorland, alpine, and the barren summit zone. Vegetation is sparse higher up due to lower temperatures and rainfall.

Lower slopes The lower slopes of the mountain were probably once forested, but they are now mainly cultivated. The volcanic soils make them highly fertile and they support a dense human population. The most biologically-interesting aspect of the lower slopes is the abundance of wild flowers, seen between Marangu and the park entrance gate.

Forest The southern slopes above 1,800m and below 3,000m receive up to 2,000mm of rainfall annually. As a result they are densely forested. This is the most biologically-interesting zone. In addition to numerous plant species, the forest supports a fair amount of wildlife. The most commonly-seen animals are black-and-white colobus and blue monkey. Antelope species include three types of duiker, and the beautifully-marked bushbuck. Leopard, bushpig and porcupine are common but rarely seen. Other large mammals present in small numbers include eland, buffalo and elephant. The forest is home to many varieties of butterfly, and, as with all East African forests, it is rich in bird life. Most forest birds are difficult to spot. An exception is the large, raucous silvery-cheeked hornbill.

Moorland This semi-alpine zone lies between 3,000m and 4,000m. It is characterised by heath-like vegetation and abundant wild flowers. As you climb into the moorland, two distinctive plants become common. These are *Lobelia deckenii*, which grows to 3m high, and the groundsel *Senecio kilimanjarin*, which grows up to 5m high and can be distinguished by a spike of yellow flowers. This zone supports low animal densities, but a number of large mammals have been recorded. Klipspringer are quite common on rocky outcrops. Hill chat and scarlet-tufted malachite sunbird are two birds whose range is restricted to the moorlands of large East African mountains. Other localised birds are lammergeyer and Alpine swift. Because it is so open, the views from the moorland are stunning.

Alpine This semi-desert zone lies between 4,000 and 5,000m, and receives an annual rainfall of under 250mm. The ground often freezes at night, but ground temperatures may soar to above 30°C by day. Few plants survive in these conditions; only 55 species are present, many of them lichens and grasses. Large mammals have been recorded, most commonly eland, but none are resident.

Summit This is the arctic zone above 5,000m. It receives virtually no rainfall, and there is little permanent life other than the odd lichen. Two remarkable records concern a frozen leopard discovered here in 1926, and a family of hunting dogs seen in 1962. The most notable natural features at the summit are the inner and outer craters of Kibo, a 120m-deep ash pit, and the Great Northern Glacier, which has retreated markedly since it was first seen by Hans Meyer in 1889.

Climbing Kilimanjaro
Kilimanjaro can be climbed with relative ease by any reasonably fit adult. This does not mean climbing it is a picnic; adequate preparations are necessary and there are serious health risks attached to being at such a high altitude. Neither is the climb cheap. You are looking at a bottom-line price of around $250 per person, and between $400 to $500 if you use a reliable operator.

But as the highest point in Africa, Kilimanjaro's peak offers an irresistible challenge to many people. Dozens of tourists, ranging from teenagers to people in their sixties, set off up its slopes every day. For those who reach it, being at the summit of Kilimanjaro is often the highlight of their trip.

Routes

The vast majority of people who climb Kilimanjaro use the Marangu Route. There are several other routes, but they are far more expensive to climb, not least because the hut fees along them are almost triple those on the Marangu Route ($40 as opposed to $15). The huts on these routes are in poor condition. Nevertheless, if you have no budget restrictions, it is worth thinking about using another route. Marangu has become busy in recent years and many people complain it is overcrowded.

Marangu route
Day one: Marangu to Mandara Hut On an organised climb you will be dropped at the park entrance gate 8km past Marangu. The path to Mandara passes through forest. There is a high chance of rain in the afternoon, so set off early. Foot traffic is heavy along this stretch, and shy forest animals are rarely seen. If your guide will go that way, use the parallel trail which meets the main trail halfway between the gate and the hut. The walk takes up to four hours. Mandara hut (2,750m) is an attractive collection of buildings with room for 200 people.

Day two: Mandara Hut to Horombo Hut You continue through forest for a short time before reaching the heather and moorland zone. There are good views of the peaks and of Moshi from here. The walk takes up to six hours. Horombo hut (3,720m) sleeps up to 120 people. It is in a valley and surrounded by giant lobelia and groundsel. If you do a six-day hike, you will spend a day at Horombo to acclimatise.

Day three: Horombo Hut to Kibo Hut The vegetation thins out as you enter the desert-like alpine zone, and when you cross the saddle Kibo peak comes into view. This six to seven-hour walk should be done slowly: many people start to feel the effects of altitude. Kibo Hut (4,703m) is a stone construction which sleeps up to 120 people. Water must be carried there from a stream above Horombo. You may find it difficult to sleep at this altitude, and as you will have to rise at around 1.00am the next morning, many people feel it is better not to bother trying.

Day four and five: Kibo Hut to the summit to Marangu The penultimate day starts at around 1.00am. It is marginally easier to climb the scree slope to Gillman's Point on the crater rim when it is frozen. This is a six-hour walk; an early start improves your chances of reaching the summit early enough to catch the sunrise. From Gillman's Point it is a further two-hour round trip along the crater's edge to Uhuru Peak, the highest point in Africa. From the summit it is downhill all the way to Horombo Hut where you will spend your last night on the mountain, before descending to Marangu the next day. Expect to arrive in Marangu in the mid-afternoon.

Mweka route
This is the steepest and fastest route to the summit. There are two huts along it: Mweka (3,000m) and Barafu (4,600m). Both are unfurnished uniports which sleep up to 16 people. There is water at Mweka but not at Barafu. This route starts at the Mweka Wildlife College, 12km from Moshi. From there it takes about eight hours to get to Mweka Hut, then a further eight hours to Barafu. You will reach the rim at Stella Point, a six-hour walk from Barafu and one hour from Uhuru Peak.

Machame route
This is considered to be the most scenic route and is relatively gradual. It starts at the village of Machame, where there is a guest house. From Machame it is a two-hour walk to the park gate, a further two hours to the trail head, then four or five hours through the forest to Machame Hut (3,000m). There is war near this hut, which sleeps up to 12 people. It is a five-hour walk to Shira Hut (3,800m) which is near a stream and can sleep up to eight people.

From Shira, a number of options exist: you could spend your third night at Lava Tower Hut (4,600m), four hours from Shira, but the ascent to the summit from there is tricky and only advisable if you are experienced and have good equipment. Another option would be to spend your third night at Barranco Hut (3,900m), then go on to Barafu Hut (4,600m) and ascend to the crater from there (see Mweka Route).

Shira route
This route crosses the Shira Plateau west of Kibo. You need a 4x4 to do it, as it is 19km from the gate to the trail head. You can either camp at the trail head or walk the 4km to Shira Hut. The views from the Shira Plateau are excellent, and there is some game to be seen. If you use this route, spend two nights at Shira in order to acclimatise before you continue. For routes from Shira Hut, see the Machame Route.

Umbwe route

This short, steep route is one of the most scenic. It is often used as a descent route. Umbwe route descends from Barranco Hut, and comes out at the village of Umbwe. It is possible to sleep in two caves on the lower slopes along this route.

Park fees

The reason why Kilimanjaro is so expensive to climb boils down to park fees. There is an entrance fee of $15 per day and a rescue fee of $20 per person per trip. Huts on the Marangu Route cost $15 per person per night; huts on other routes cost $40. Each guide and porter costs around $5 per day (this includes their entrance and hut fees). Park fees for one person doing a five-day ascent with two porters and a guide amount to around $210. All these fees are considerably lower for residents.

You are expected to tip the guides and porters. The company you go with can give you an idea of the going rate is, but around $5 per day per guide/porter per climbing party is fair.

Maps and further reading

A map is not generally considered to be necessary if you use the Marangu Route, but it is for any other. *The Walker's Guide and Map to Kilimanjaro* by Mark Savage (African Mountain Guides, 32 Sea Mill Crescent, Worthing, UK, tel: (0903) 37565) is popular and reliable, and has useful information printed on the back. You may be lucky and pick up a second-hand copy in Arusha, but it is better to buy one before you visit Tanzania.

A 60-page national parks handbook *Kilimanjaro National Park* has accurate small-scale maps. It is worth buying for its detailed route descriptions and background information, and is available from the National Park office in Arusha for $2.50.

Before you leave home — or as a memento when you get back — try to get hold of *Kilimanjaro* by John Reader (Elm Tree Books, London, 1982). Although it is superficially a coffee-table book, it offers a well-written and absorbing overview of the mountain's history and various ecosystems. The photographs are good too.

Preparations

Two climatic factors must be considered when preparing to climb Kilimanjaro. The obvious one is the cold. Bring plenty of warm clothes, a windproof jacket, a pair of gloves, a balaclava, a warm sleeping bag and an insulation mat. During the rainy season, a rain jacket and rain trousers will come in useful. A less obvious factor is the sun, which is fierce at high altitudes. Bring sunglasses and sunscreen.

Other essentials are water bottles, a first-aid kit, and solid shoes or preferably boots. Most of these items can be hired in Moshi or at the park gate, or from the company you arrange to climb with. I've heard varying reports about the condition of locally-hired items.

Health

Do not attempt to climb Kilimanjaro unless you are reasonably fit, nor if you have heart or lung problems. Bear in mind, however, that very fit people are more prone to altitude sickness because they ascend too fast. If you have any cold-like symptoms, wait until you are better before you climb.

Above 4,000m you may not feel hungry, but you should try to eat. Carbohydrates and fruit are recommended, rich or fatty foods are not. You should drink plenty of liquids, and will need enough water bottles to carry several litres of water to Kibo Hut. If you dress in layers, you can take off clothes before you sweat too much, thereby reducing water loss.

Few people climb Kilimanjaro without feeling some of the symptoms of altitude sickness: headaches, nausea, fatigue, sleeplessness and swelling of the hands and feet. You can do a lot to limit these. Give yourself time to acclimatise by taking an extra day over the ascent, eat and drink properly, and try not to push yourself. If symptoms become severe, descend immediately. Even going down 1000ft is enough to start recovery.

Pulmonary and cerebral oedema are altitude-related problems which can be rapidly fatal if you do not descend. Symptoms of the former include shortness of breath when at rest, coughing up blood, and gurgling sounds in the chest. Symptoms of the latter are headaches, a general lack of co-ordination, disorientation, poor judgement and even hallucinations. The danger is that the sufferer often doesn't realise how sick he/she is and may argue against descending. You are less likely to get these problems if you ascend slowly.

Hypothermia is a lowering of body temperature usually caused by a combination of cold and wet. Mild cases usually manifest themselves as uncontrollable shivering. Put on dry warm clothes and get into a sleeping bag; this will normally raise your body temperature sufficiently. Severe hypothermia is potentially fatal: symptoms include disorientation, lethargy, mental confusion (including an inappropriate feeling of well-being and warmth!) and coma. In severe cases the rescue team should be summoned.

A $20 rescue fee is paid by all climbers upon entering the national park. The rescue team ordinarily covers the Marangu route only; if you use another route their services must be organised in advance.

Arranging a climb

A number of operators in Moshi and Marangu offer Kilimanjaro climbs. It is also possible to make your own arrangements with a registered guide. Most companies offer a comprehensive package, but I suggest you clarify what you are paying for prior to parting with any money. A package should include a registered guide, two porters per person, park fees, food, and transport to and from the gate. If you are in a group, ensure that one porter is also registered as a guide. Then if someone in your party has to turn back the rest can still continue.

The normal length for a climb is five days. Think about adding a sixth day to acclimatise at Horombo Hut. This will reduce the risk of altitude sickness and increase the likelihood of making the peak. It is daft to team up with strangers just to cut 5% off the price. If you hike on your own or with people you know, you can dictate your own pace and there is less danger of personality clashes developing mid-climb.

I can recommend four companies. The best value at present is Keys Hotel (Moshi), which does a five-day climb for $340 per person and a six-day climb for $420 per person. Keys is a relative newcomer to the business, but it has a good reputation, both in Moshi and with tour operators in Arusha.

Trans-Kibo, based in the Moshi YMCA, has been organising reliable climbs for years. The charge is $440 for a five-day climb for one climber, $420 per person for two, and $400 per person for three or more. An additional $80 per person is charged per extra day.

The Kibo and Marangu Hotels (both in Marangu) are the most experienced of all, but they charge around $460 per person for a five-day climb. They do, however, supply reliable equipment. Marangu Hotel offers a do-it-yourself deal whereby you organise food and equipment and they organise porters and guides. This works out at between $350 and $400 per person depending on group size. Some people claim the poor food supplied by tour companies is a factor in the illness people experience on the mountain, so organising your own food may not be a bad idea.

All these companies should be able to organise climbs along less-used routes. If none can meet your needs, try Tropical Tours in Arusha (see Chapter Eight).

Plenty of outfits in Moshi organise climbs for around $250 per person. You can get a similar price dealing directly with a guide at the park gate or in Marangu. Be wary of either option — as with organising a safari in Arusha, if you go for the cheapest price you take your chances. On safari, the worst that can go wrong is you lose time through breakdown; on Kilimanjaro, you could literally die. I have also heard reports of people arranging a climb through bogus guides and porters, and being left stranded halfway up the mountain minus their possessions. If you make private arrangements, check your guide *is* registered; he will have a small wallet-like document to prove this.

If you are organising your own climb, there is dormitory accommodation at the park entrance gate.

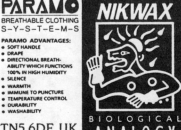

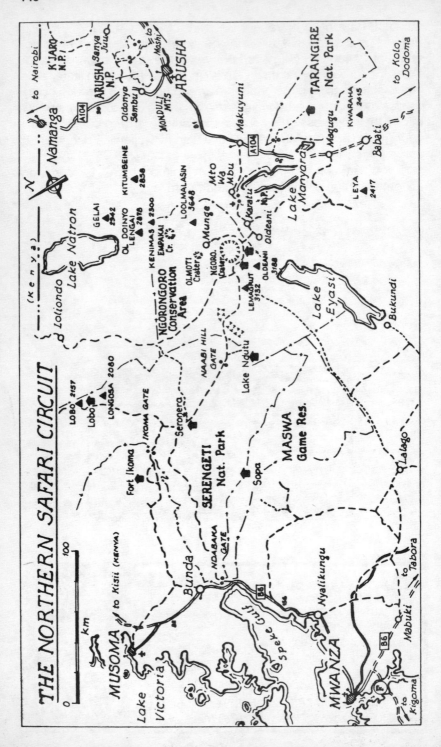

THE NORTHERN SAFARI CIRCUIT

Chapter Eight

The northern Tanzania safari circuit

INTRODUCTION

The reserves between Arusha and Lake Victoria need little introduction. They are the best-known and arguably the finest anywhere in Africa.

The world-famous Serengeti Plain, a vast sea of grass dotted with granite koppies, plays host to Africa's greatest wildlife spectacle: the annual migration of more than a million wildebeest and zebra. Nearby, the Ngorongoro Crater is a spectacular 600m-deep volcanic caldera; its floor supports large herds of virtually every large African mammal.

East of this, Lake Manyara National Park protects a large shallow lake on the Rift Valley floor. The less-celebrated Tarangire National Park preserves an area of acacia woodland notable for its dense elephant population.

The base for exploring this area is the town of Arusha. Northeast of the town, Arusha National Park, though less well-known than the block of reserves described above, protects a wide variety of animals and Africa's fourth-highest peak, Mount Meru.

Climate

The highlands around Ngorongoro Crater and Mount Meru receive a high rainfall and are cold at night. The rest of the area is warm and relatively dry. Rainy seasons are in November and December, and from March to May. Game viewing in the Ngorongoro Crater and Lake Manyara is good at any time of year. Tarangire is best between July and December, and the Serengeti between November and March.

Getting around

Access to the Serengeti, Ngorongoro and Manyara is via the B142, a dirt road which leaves the Dodoma-Arusha road at a village called Makuyuni. The B142 by-passes Lake Manyara at the village of Mto wa Mbu, then snakes up the side of the Rift Valley wall, passes through Karatu, and climbs to Ngorongoro Crater rim. From the crater it descends onto the Serengeti plains, passing through the park headquarters in the Seronera valley before reaching Bunda on the main Musoma-Mwanza road.

It is 80km from Arusha to Makuyuni, 37km from Makuyuni to Mto wa Mbu, 25km from Mto wa Mbu to Karatu, and 18km from Karatu to the village on the crater rim. Seronera lies about halfway along the 300km stretch of road between the crater and Bunda.

Tarangire National Park is just off the main Arusha-Dodoma road about 30km south of Makuyuni. Arusha National Park lies off the main Arusha-Moshi road near Usa River.

A couple of buses run every week between Arusha and Mwanza via the B142. These can drop you off along the way, or pick you up if arrangements are made in advance. Buses run daily between Arusha and Karatu, and the Ngorongoro Conservation Authority plans to introduce a service between Arusha and the crater rim, which will run in each direction on alternate days.

THE MAASAI

The area covered in this chapter is the home of the Maasai, a Nilotic-speaking people who arrived in Tanzania from what is now the Sudan about 300 years ago. The Maasai have aroused western awe and curiosity since the 19th Century, when they acquired a reputation amongst slave traders and explorers as fearsome warriors. Caravan routes studiously avoided them, and areas like the Serengeti were amongst the last parts of East Africa ventured into by Europeans.

Maasai remain the most instantly recognisable East African people, though their modern reputation rests as much on their continued proud adherence to a traditional lifestyle as to any of their past exploits. Maasai men drape themselves in red blankets, carry long wooden poles, and have red-ochred hair. The women's actual dress is not dissimilar to the *Vitenge* favoured by most Tanzanian women, but they cover themselves in all manner of beaded jewellery.

Maasai are traditionally pastoralists. They believe their God, who resides in Lengai Volcano, made them the rightful owners of all the cattle in the world; a view which, in the past, has made life difficult for neighbouring herders. This arrogance does not merely extend to cattle. They scorned agriculturalist and fish-eating peoples, and were equally disrespectful of Europeans, calling them *lloredaa enjekat* — Those who confine their farts with clothing. The Maasai now co-exist peacefully with their non-Maasai compatriots, but they show little interest in changing their lifestyle.

The Maasai's main diet is a blend of cow's milk and blood, the latter drained — it is said painlessly — from a strategic nick in the animal's jugular vein. They are reluctant to kill their cattle for meat; the animals are more valuable to them alive. Despite the apparent hardship of their chosen lifestyle, many Maasai are wealthy by any standards. Our safari driver pointed out a not unusually large herd of cattle that would fetch the market equivalent of three new Landrovers.

Despite appearances, the Maasai, like us, are living in the 1990s. Large parts of their traditional grazing grounds have been given over to conservation; in the Serengeti and Tarangire they are no longer allowed to graze their cattle.

In some ways, the Maasai are just another cog in the tourist industry, albeit an unwilling one. Herds of snap-happy tourists leap out of minibuses and landrovers to capture their image on film, on the one hand swooning at their noble savagery — *Real Africa!* — on the other shoving a camera at them as though they were just another one of the big five.

There are Maasai who deliberately hang around at places like Ngorongoro waiting for tourists. If you want to photograph a Maasai, you must ask permission and should also be prepared to pay for the privilege. Because of this, many tourists complain that the Maasai are 'overcommercialised'. I don't know whether such people believe the Maasai's first priority should be to pander to the aesthetic requirements of tourists, or whether they are just outraged at not getting something for nothing. Either way, we create the demand and the Maasai satisfy it. If they expect us to pay, that's just good capitalism, something the West has been keen to encourage in Africa. If you don't like it, save your film for another subject.

ARUSHA

Arusha is the gateway to Ngorongoro and the Serengeti, and like Moshi its skyline is dominated by a mountain: the 4,556m-high Mount Meru. In itself, Arusha is a very ordinary medium-sized African town. It was founded as a German garrison in 1900, and grew rapidly as it became the centre of an important farming area and, more recently, the country's safari industry.

Everything in Arusha seems to revolve around safaris. The competition is fierce; there are touts on every street corner offering the best price in town. This can become wearing, but on the whole business is conducted in a leisurely manner. I found Arusha very relaxed and pleasant once I settled in.

Electricity and water are both problems in Arusha. I have never spent a day in the town when there wasn't an electricity and/or water cut at some point.

Getting there and away

The most popular way to get between Arusha and Dar es Salaam is via the railway which terminates at Moshi. You can book for trains to Dar es Salaam at Arusha's otherwise unused station.

Arusha is connected to Dar es Salaam, Moshi and Nairobi by good tar roads. These carry regular transport. Express buses between Arusha and Dar es Salaam are worth the extra expense.

Air Tanzania fly regularly between Dar es Salaam and Kilimanjaro Airport (halfway between Arusha and Moshi).

There are daily buses between Dodoma and Arusha. The road is in a poor state and the ride can take up to 20 hours.

Getting between Arusha and Mwanza is covered in detail under Mwanza in Chapter Nine.

Where to stay

UPPER RANGE

The upper range hotels in Arusha town centre are convenient, but no more than ordinary. If you are spending an extended time in the area, there are more attractive hotels along the Moshi road.

New Arusha Hotel   (PO Box 88, Tel: (057) 3241). This is the best hotel in its range in the town centre. The grounds are attractive and there are two bars. There is a bookstall in the foyer. $65/75 HC s/c single/double, or $15/20 for residents.

Equator Hotel   (PO Box 3002, Tel: (057) 3127). This is similar to the New Arusha. It has a bar, a reasonable restaurant, a beer garden, and live music at weekends. $65 HC s/c double.

New Safari Hotel   (PO Box 303, Tel: (057) 8545/7). Although shabbier than the above hotels, this is good value. It has a good restaurant and a pleasant beer garden. $40/50 HC single/double, or $5/9 for residents.

Mt Meru Novatel (PO Box 887, Tel: (057) 2711/7). Arusha's top hotel is 2km from the town centre on the Moshi Road. It is set in landscaped grounds, has a swimming pool and a good restaurant, and offers facilities for businessmen. $110/138 HC s/c single/double, or $59/77 for residents.

Hotel 77 (Saba-saba) (PO Box 187, Tel: (057) 3800). Near the Novatel, this is similar in standard to hotels in the town centre. $40/54 HC s/c single/double, or $7/9 for residents.

Mountain Village Lodge (PO Box 376, Tel: (057) 2699, Fax: 3869). This is the most attractive hotel in the Arusha area, on a coffee farm on the rim of Duluti, a gorgeous forest-fringed crater lake. On a clear day there are views across to Meru and Kilimanjaro. The main building is a converted thatched farmhouse dating to the colonial era; accommodation is in self-contained chalets. Meals at the highly-regarded restaurant cost $10 HC. It is 15km from Arusha, just off the Moshi road. $63/75 HC s/c single/double, or $11/15 for residents.

Hotel Dik Dik (PO Box 1499, Tel: (057) 8110). This Swiss-owned hotel is set in pleasant grounds near Usa River. It has a swimming pool and a restaurant, regarded to be one of the best in the area. $39/78 HC s/c single/double. A five-course dinner costs $11 HC.

Mount Meru Game Lodge (PO Box 659, Tel: (057) 7179). This posh English-type hotel near Usa River has lovely bougainvillaea-draped gardens. The much-publicised game sanctuary is no more than a glorified zoo. $70/88 HC s/c single/double or $52/67 for residents.

MODERATE TO UPPER RANGE

These hotels are cheaper than those listed above, on average around $35 for a room, but could not be called moderately priced.

Golden Rose Hotel (PO Box 361, Tel: (057) 8860). This is about the best value in this price bracket. Rooms are large and have running hot water and mosquito nets, and the restaurant is good. $35 HC s/c double, or $12.50 for residents.

Pallson's Hotel (PO Box 773, Tel: 2485, Fax: (057) 7263). This is a very convenient and comfortable place. Rooms have running hot water and a fan. There is a good restaurant on the ground floor. $30/35 HC s/c single/double.

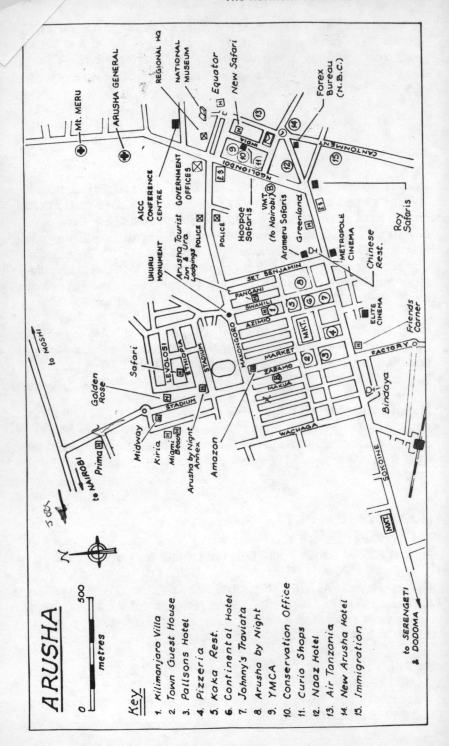

ARUSHA

0 _____ 500

metres

Key

1. Kilimanjaro Villa
2. Town Guest House
3. Pallsons Hotel
4. Pizzeria
5. Kaka Rest.
6. Continental Hotel
7. Johnny's Traviata
8. Arusha by Night
9. YMCA
10. Conservation Office
11. Curio Shops
12. Naaz Hotel
13. Air Tanzania
14. New Arusha Hotel
15. Immigration

Arusha Tourist Inn   (PO Box 1530, Tel: (057) 8863). The rooms here are clean but cramped. Still, there is running hot water and the rooms have fans. The restaurant on the ground floor is good value. $30/35 HC s/c single/double.

Tanzanite Hotel   (PO Box 3063 Arusha, Tel: Usa River 32). This hotel is 400m from the Arusha-Moshi road, near Usa River. Facilities include a swimming pool, a tennis court, and a reasonable restaurant. The campsite has full ablution facilities. $30/40 s/c single/double. $2.50 per person to camp.

MODERATE
Naaz Hotel   (PO Box 1060, Tel: (057) 2087). The Naaz is popular with travellers. All rooms have running hot water, the staff are friendly, and there is a pleasant cafeteria on the ground floor. $15 HC s/c double.

Midway Hotel   This new hotel on a back road near the stadium looks good value. There is a restaurant on the ground floor. $10 double, payable in shillings or hard currency.

Miami Beach Guest House   Near the Midway, the rooms here are clean and comfortable, but it's basically an overpriced guest house. $10 HC double.

YMCA   The YMCA was popular with travellers at one time, but it is a bit overpriced these days. Rooms are large and clean, but not self-contained. Washing facilities amount to a bath tub and cold tap. $7/10 single/double.

Amazon Tourist Hotel   This is conveniently close to the bus station. The rooms are better than you would expect from the outside (which isn't saying much), but they are poor value at $10/12 single/double.

BUDGET
Don't expect much for your money below $5. Most budget hotels in Arusha are basic and could do with a good scrub. In addition to the places mentioned below, there are a few guest houses near the market with rooms for under $2. The **Ura, City and Kiria Guest Houses** are amongst the better, but they are often full.

Safari Guest House   On the backstreets behind the stadium, this is currently popular with budget travellers. It is basic but clean and friendly, and has an OK *hoteli* attached. The owners can organise safaris, and have a reasonable reputation. $2.50 single or double.

Pima Guest House   Also popular with travellers, this is similar in standard and price to the Safari.

Hotel Arusha by Night   (PO Box 360, Tel: (057) 6894). This place apparently makes the rules up as they go along. The first time we asked about a room, we were told it cost $20 HC for a double; a few days later we were told they only accept residents. If you are allowed to pay residents' rates, it is excellent value at $4/5 s/c single/double. The annexe near the stadium is similar.

Continental Hotel   Opposite the Arusha by Night, this extraordinarily run-down hotel is very cheap. $1.25 double.

Friends Corner Hotel   This is basic, friendly and reasonably clean. Rooms are spacious but spartan. $2.50/3.75 single/double.

Greenland Hotel   Scruffy but habitable. The manager is bound to try to get you to organise a safari with him. I have heard nothing that would induce me to take him up on the offer. $2.50/3.50 single/double.

Kilimanjaro Villa Hotel   Despite the ostentatious name, this is very ordinary. Rooms are comfortable but could do with a scrub, and the management is friendly. $4/5 single/double.

CAMPING

Kinyoro Campsite   This is the cheapest and most central campsite, 500m from town on the same road as the New Arusha Hotel. The people who run the travel kiosk in the foyer of the New Arusha can direct you there. $1.25 per person.

Maasai Camp   This well-run site, 3km out of town on the old Moshi road, is popular with overland trucks. Facilities include an ablution block with hot water and a good restaurant. You can get a taxi there (about $2), and it is possible to hitch. $3 per person.

Duluti Club   This lovely campsite is on the edge of forest-fringed Lake Duluti. Facilities include an ablution block and a small cafeteria selling cold drinks and basic meals. Duluti Club is 20 minutes walk from the main Arusha-Moshi road and signposted. If you miss the signpost, you can't fail to see the large wooden giraffe opposite it. $3 per person.

Tanzanite Hotel The campsite at this hotel near Usa River has good facilities. $2.50 per person.

Where to eat

The Pizzeria is the best restaurant in Arusha. It serves pizzas and western dishes for around $4. The dessert menu is outstanding. The food at the nearby **Chinese Restaurant** is average, and the service is painfully slow, but it is popular, cheap, and has a varied menu. The food at the **Safari Grill**, on the ground floor of the New Safari Hotel, is pretty indifferent, but it's popular with travellers. Meals cost around $3. Far better is the rambling beer garden at the back of the hotel, which serves grilled meat at lunch. **Bindaya Restaurant** has the best Indian food in Arusha. Meals cost around $2.50.

For a snack, try **Johnny's Traviata Restaurant**. The vegetarian samosas are excellent. The **Kaka Restaurant** is also good, but ignore the owner if he gets pushy about a safari.

Useful information

Nightlife The most enjoyable place to spend an evening is the bar next to the Chinese Restaurant, where there is live Zairian music most nights from around 9.30pm. The crowd is friendly and relaxed, with a healthy mix of tourists and locals, and food is available. There is also live music most nights at the Equator Hotel. There are discos at the Cave, next to the New Safari, and on the ground floor of the Arusha by Night.

National Parks The National Park Headquarters is in the Arusha International Conference Centre (AICC). This is the best place to buy booklets on various national parks. They cost $2.50 but are sold for three times the price on the streets and at park entrance gates.

Ngorongoro Conservation Authority (PO Box 776, Tel: (057) 3339). The NCA controls the Ngorongoro Conservation Area. Their office is on the corner of Makongoro and Gollondoi roads.

Books and newspapers A few vendors usually hang around the clock tower selling second-hand novels, maps and textbooks. The range of novels is poor, but they may sell maps which are unavailable elsewhere.

Kenyan newspapers are available on the day of publication. You won't need to look for them — the people who sell them will find you quickly enough. The news stand in the foyer of the New Arusha has the best range of new novels in the country, as well as a fair selection of postcards, national park pamphlets, foreign newspapers, maps and non-fiction.

Curio shops   Arusha is one of the best places in East Africa to buy Makonde carvings, batiks, Maasai jewellery and other souvenirs. The curio shops are far cheaper than those in Dar es Salaam, and the quality and variety is excellent. Curio shops are clustered between the clock tower and India Road.

National Museum   This is the worst museum I've seen in my life. Don't waste your time with it.

Excursions

There is not a great deal to do in the immediate vicinity of Arusha. If you have a day to kill you could organise a day safari to Arusha National Park.

Lake Duluti   This attractive forest-fringed crater lake would be a pleasant place to spend a day or two. It is about 2km south of the Arusha-Moshi road. The hotel and campsite on the lake (see *Where to stay* above) are both well-signposted and can be reached by foot or vehicle.

Mount Meru Foothills   The western slopes of Mount Meru are not in a national park, so there is nothing preventing you casually exploring them on foot. The best access point is a dirt road which branches from the main Moshi road opposite the Mount Meru Hotel; a stream next to the junction serves as a carwash. This road continues into the foothills as far as the tree line, passing through bamboo forest on the way. Before you get this far it is possible to divert to a waterfall. About four hours along the road you will reach a plantation of new eucalyptus and pine plantlings. Here you must scramble down to a stream. If you follow the stream for an hour or so, you arrive at the waterfall. There is a shortcut back to the main road, but unless you have a map it is probably more sensible to return the way you came. It may occur to you to attempt to climb Meru from the west in order to save on park fees. As Meru Peak is in Arusha National Park this is illegal. If you attempt it and are caught you are liable to be jailed.

HOOPOE ADVENTURE TOURS TANZANIA LTD.

Hoopoe Adventure Tours Tanzania Ltd will take you anywhere you want to go in Tanzania at a price you can afford. Travel with us and our experienced Driver/Guides by 4 WD Land Rover on an unforgettable safari in the wilds of Africa. Experience the comfort and excellent food of Kirurumu Tented Lodge, our permanent camp overlooking Lake Manyara National Park. Let us arrange your Kilimanjaro and Mount Meru Climbs, your beach holidays and Zanzibar trips. We cater for special interests, and specialise in tailor-made safaris, both Lodging and Camping - the latter being either very simple or luxury-type camps with our own Land Rover support vehicles. Enjoy Tanzania to the full with HOOPOE ADVENTURE TOURS. For brochures, quotations and further information contact Oliver, Stephen or Terri: PO Box 2047 Arusha, Telephone Arusha 7011/7541, Fax (057) 8226.

ARUSHA
India Street
Arusha, Tanzania
PO Box 2047
Tel: (057) 7011/7541
Fax: (057) 8226
Telex: 42103 AFT

LONDON
Suit D2, Kebbell House
Carpenders Park, Watford
WD1 5BE, UK
Tel: +81 428 8221
Fax: +81 421 1396
Telex: 913439 SSINTL G.

ORGANISING A SAFARI

Arusha is the main base for organising safaris, though Mwanza is a possibility if you want to visit the Serengeti only. Over 100 safari companies are based in Arusha, and they cater for all tastes and budgets.

Planning your safari

When you first arrive in Arusha, you feel very popular. Everyone is trying to get you to go on safari with them. This can be overwhelming. Try to decide your priorities before you arrive in Arusha, and don't rush into a decision when you do get there.

If, like many people, your main reason for visiting Tanzania is to go on safari, avoid the trap of looking for the cheapest price. You have already spent a lot of money flying to Tanzania, and no matter how cheap your safari is, it will probably be your greatest expense while you are in the country. It seems silly to spend all this money, then jeopardise your enjoyment trying to save a few extra dollars.

The following are a few factors to think over:

Group size

The individual cost of a safari decreases as the group gets larger. Two people can expect to pay from $55 to $75 per day each for a budget camping safari; four people from $40 to $60.

For this reason, many people form an impromptu group to go on safari. If the people concerned are compatible this can work well; just as often it is a disaster. We did one safari with complete strangers and one on our own. We thought going on our own was well worth the extra cost: we were able to dictate the pace, and the driver responded far more readily to our individual interests and whims.

Four is the largest practical group size. Some companies will take more people, but it really isn't worth it. The difference in price between four, five and six is negligible, and there are only four window seats in most vehicles.

Itinerary

Your itinerary will depend on how much time and money you have, and also the time of year. There are endless options. Most safari companies will put together the package you ask for. They know the ground well and can advise you on what is possible, but tend to assume you will want to cover as many reserves as possible. This is not always the best approach.

A typical five or six-day trip takes in Ngorongoro, Serengeti, Manyara and Tarangire. A typical three-day trip takes in all these reserves except for the Serengeti. In the dry season (March to October) there is little game in the Serengeti; most safari companies will suggest you spend more time in Tarangire.

The distances between these reserves are considerable and the roads are poor; you will have a more relaxed trip if you visit fewer reserves. On a five day safari, I would drop either the Serengeti or Tarangire. To visit all four reserves, six days is just about adequate, seven or more days would be better.

I didn't find three days long enough to get a good feel for Tarangire, Manyara, and Ngorongoro; four days would have been better. The combination of Ngorongoro and Tarangire would make an unhurried three-day safari. If you are limited to two days, you could either visit Tarangire on its own or do a combined trip to Manyara and Ngorongoro. If your budget is really limited, Tarangire can be visited as a day trip from Arusha; it is less than two-hours drive each way.

At the other end of the time scale, there is enough to see and do in the area to warrant a safari of two weeks in duration, or even longer. You could easily spend a few days exploring the Serengeti alone. In a two week package, you could also visit Lake Natron, the Kondoa-Irangi rock art and/or the northern part of the Ngorongoro Conservation Area.

Many budget safari companies use campsites in Mto wa Mbu and Karatu because they are cheaper than those in Manyara and Ngorongoro. Camping in a village dilutes the safari atmosphere; I would prefer to pay extra and camp in the reserves. It's an individual choice, but one worth bearing in mind when you negotiate a package.

Which company

The safari companies in Arusha can be divided into three broad categories: shoestring camping, budget camping, and upper range. Most of them have offices in the Arusha International Conference Centre (AICC).

In all categories, the price you are quoted should include the vehicle and driver/guide, fuel, any camping equipment, food and a cook, and park fees. You are expected to tip the driver and cook. Around $5 per day per party seems to be par, but you should check this with the company. Drivers and cooks are poorly paid; if they have done a good job be generous.

You could put together your own safari by hiring a vehicle and driver, but most budget safari companies operate on a minimal profit margin. You will save little.

There are said to be between 150 and 400 safari companies in Arusha. A few have a particularly high profile, either because they are very cheap, very good value, or offer something out of the ordinary. The companies mentioned below, whether good or bad, are frequently used by travellers. Things change, however; ask around before you decide which company to use.

Shoestring

The going rate at this end of the scale is around $40 per person per day for four people, half of which will be swallowed up by park fees. Any company offering this sort of price is cutting corners; they either run ancient vehicles or do not have their own vehicles and hire the cheapest they can find.

It is tempting to dismiss these companies outright, but they offer a valid service — high-risk, low-price safaris. There is a strong possibility of breakdown, but for many travellers this risk is worth the cost saving. The chance of a trouble-free safari is probably better than even, but if you lose time through breakdown it is unreasonable to expect a refund or time in lieu. The extent of the risk increases with the length of the trip. On a one-day trip to Tarangire or Arusha National Park, it is not great. On the other hand, it would be idiotic to use a shoestring company for a two-week safari to somewhere like Lake Natron.

There are some out-and-out conmen in Arusha who will not even attempt to provide an adequate service. A common trick is to show you a new vehicle before you pay, but take you in an old banger which probably hasn't seen the inside of a garage for ten years. Some companies don't even bother carrying spare tyres.

It is difficult to give hard and fast advice on sorting the cheapies from the conmen; it is a thin line anyway. Ask other travellers which company they used. If you visit Zanzibar or Dar es Salaam before Arusha, you will meet plenty of people who have been on safari already. Leave yourself a couple of days to make your arrangements in Arusha; the longer you spend there the better position you will be in to make a sound judgement.

Shoestring companies attract their clients through flycatchers, the industry name for people who approach tourists in the street (and who net 15% of the money paid by anyone they lure in). These guys have a few standard tricks to get you into an office, such as telling you a safari is leaving the next day when it isn't. Some flycatchers are irritatingly leech-like and best shaken off as quickly as possible; others are reasonably straight and genuinely friendly. Provided you use your judgement and bear in mind they are used to travellers putting price before quality, there's no reason not to use flycatchers to help you fix up a safari.

I cannot recommend any company in this range without strong reservations. The only ones I would even consider are **Amango Safaris** in the AICC, **Arameru Safaris** on Said Barre Street, and the company next to the **Safari Guest House** (and run by the same people).

Budget
If you can afford it, this is the range to look at. The going rate for a camping safari is from $55 per person per day upwards. You can expect a qualified and knowledgable driver/guide, good food, and a newish vehicle. Most companies in this range also organise lodge-based safaris, or a combination of lodges and camping. Three companies stand out, the first two of which I used myself after a lot of asking around and can comfortably recommend.

Roy Safaris (PO Box 50, tel: (057) 2854). This is the cheapest of the reliable companies. They charge around $55 per person per day for four people and $70 per person per day for two. They cut costs by using the campsites at Karatu and Mto wa Mbu, but they have well-maintained vehicles, competent staff and seem to be straight. Roy is popular with travellers, and I have heard no serious criticisms. They have an office in Mwanza, and can also run safaris from there.

Hoopoe Safaris (India St, PO Box 2047, tel: (057) 7011, fax: (057) 8226). Hoopoe is more expensive than Roy, but has an irreproachable reputation and a more flexible approach. The vehicles are new and well-maintained, and our driver/guide was knowledgeable. Their tented camp near Lake Manyara is infinitely preferable to the campsite in the village.

Tropical Tours/Tourinfo (India St; PO Box 727 Arusha, tel: (057) 8353, fax: (057) 8907). This company specialises in personalised camping and foot safaris. Packages within national parks (a three-day hike on Ngorongoro Crater rim; a four-day hike on the Lobo border of the Serengeti; Kilimanjaro climbs on less-used routes) include park fees and are therefore quite pricey. They can arrange hikes outside game reserves for around $40 per person per day. These include hikes through the Monduli and Longido mountains. The Monduli Hills are very scenic, have bamboo forests, and are home to a variety of game including elephant.

Other reputable companies offering camping safaris include **Sengo Safaris** on Sokoine Road (PO Box 180, Arusha, tel: (057) 6982), **Flycatcher Safaris** in the AICC (PO Box 591 Arusha, tel: (057) 3622),

Equatorial Safaris (PO Box 2156 Arusha, tel: (057) 6140) and **Tropical African Trails** (PO Box 6130 Arusha) in the foyer of the New Equator Hotel.

Upper range
Tour operators in this range, mostly branches of UK or US companies, can put together tailor-made safaris based on staying in lodges. Prices start at around $100 to $150 per person per day (more if you fly in to the reserves). Some names and addresses follow:

Abercrombie and Kent, PO Box 427 Arusha, tel: (057) 7803, fax: (057) 7003.

Kingfisher Safaris, PO Box 701 Arusha, tel: (057) 3181.

Ker & Downey, PO Box 2782 Arusha, tel: (057) 7755.

State Travel Service, PO Box 1369 Arusha, tel: (057) 3300, fax: (057) 3113.

Takims Safaris, Suite 421, Ngorongoro Wing, AICC; PO Box 6023 Arusha, tel: (057) 3174, fax: (057) 8211.

United Touring Company, Subzali Building, cnr Ngoliondoi & Sokoine Rd; PO Box 2211 Arusha, tel (057) 7931, fax: (057) 6475.

Wildersun Safaris, Jael Maeda Road; PO Box 930, tel: (057) 3880, fax: (057) 7834.

Hitching and public transport
Hitching into Arusha National Park is a feasible option, but trying to hitch to the other reserves makes little sense. There are few private vehicles, and most safari companies forbid their drivers to pick up hitchhikers. In any case, people who have paid for a safari or are in a private vehicle loaded with supplies are unlikely to want to carry freeloaders. Even if you do get a lift, you may well get stuck in the Serengeti or Ngorongoro and although you will see little game from a campsite or lodge you will still have to pay park fees.

If you cannot afford an organised safari, your best bet is an Arusha-Mwanza bus through the Serengeti. You will get a good look at the scenery and at the right time of year will see plenty of game, but will have to pay $30 in park fees.

There are buses between Arusha and Karatu, passing through Mto wa Mbu. The Ngorongoro Conservation Authority (NCA) plans to introduce a cheap bus service between Arusha and Ngorongoro Crater rim. This will run in opposite directions on alternate days and should be operational by mid-1993. It is primarily for staff, but tourists will be allowed to use it.

ARUSHA NATIONAL PARK

Arusha National Park, which lies between Kilimanjaro and Arusha, only covers an area of 137km², but it protects a remarkable diversity of habitats. The eastern slopes and 4,566m-high peak of Mount Meru, the fifth-highest mountain in Africa, lie within the park and are its main attraction. Arusha is decidedly low-key when compared to Kilimanjaro, and it does not quite match up to the Serengeti or Ngorongoro, but it has plenty to offer those tourists who make the effort to visit it.

Often described as a mini-Ngorongoro, Ngurdoto Crater is in itself worth the entrance fee, a fully intact 3km-wide, 400m-deep volcanic caldera with a forest-fringed rim and lush green floor. Tourists are not permitted to descend into the crater, but points on the rim offer stunning views across it.

Another attraction is the Momella Lakes, a group of shallow alkaline lakes fed by underground streams. They all have different mineral contents and are slightly different in colour. The lakes are some of the best places to see water birds in Tanzania: flamingo, pelican, little grebe and a variety of herons, ducks and waders are common.

Buffalo, elephant, hippo, giraffe, zebra and a variety of antelope are regularly seen. Blue monkey are common in all the forests, and black-and-white colobus can be seen on Mount Meru and on Ngurdoto crater rim. The only large predators are leopard and spotted hyena; we were lucky enough to see both driving between Momella Lodge and the campsite shortly after nightfall. In addition to water birds, Arusha is rich in forest species.

From a vehicle, most of the park can be seen in a day. You can walk anywhere in the park accompanied by an armed ranger, whose services cost $10 per outing. Mount Meru can be climbed in two or three days.

An excellent 52-page booklet *Arusha National Park* is available from the National Parks office in Arusha for $2.50.

A park entrance fee of $15 per 24-hour period is charged.

Geology

The formation of both Meru and Ngurdoto resulted from the same volcanic activity that formed the Great Rift Valley 15 to 20 million years ago. Ngurdoto is long-extinct, but Meru remains dormant; lava last flowed from it 100 years ago. Until about 250,000 years ago Meru was similar in size to Kilimanjaro, but a massive eruption at that time tore out the entire eastern wall.

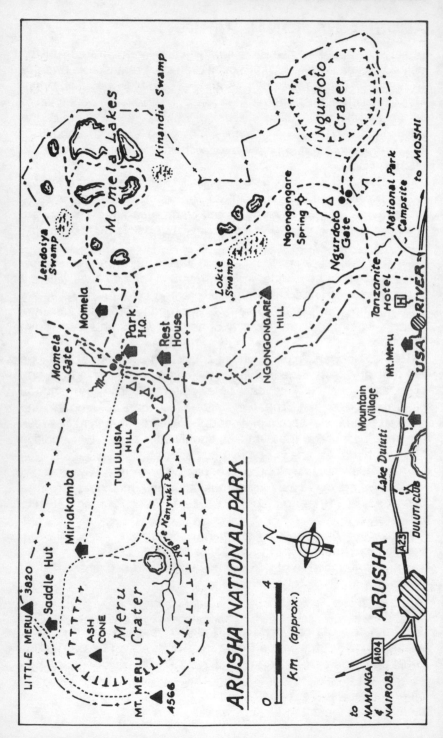

ARUSHA NATIONAL PARK

Getting there and away

Momella gate and camp are 20km from the main Arusha-Moshi road. The turn-off at Usa River is clearly signposted. Ngurdoto gate and campsite are 8km from the turn-off. The approach road is in fair condition and can be driven in an ordinary saloon car.

If you do not have a vehicle, the park can be visited as a day tour from Arusha. Any company can organise this. Most companies can also organise a three-day climb up Meru.

If you want to organise your own climb or spend some time exploring the park on foot you will have to find your own way there. You could hire a taxi in Arusha, but if you are patient you should be able to hitch. Any vehicle heading to Momella Lodge or the village of Ngare Nanyuki will go past the main entrance gate. To get an early start, camp or stay at the Tanzanite Hotel the night before you want to hitch in.

Plenty of locals walk along the main road through the park. It is a long walk from Usa River to Momella gate, but there's nothing stopping you from doing it.

Where to stay

In the upper range, a visit to the park could be based at any of the hotels near Usa River (see *Where to stay* in Arusha). The most convenient place to stay is **Momella Lodge** (PO Box 418 Arusha, Tel: (057) 4648), 3km past Momella Gate, a cosy hotel with an alpine feel enhanced by the log fires in the bar and television lounge. Meals cost $12. Accommodation in chalets costs $51/63 HC s/c single/double, or $10.60/15.35 for residents.

The **National Park Rest House** 2km from Momella Gate sleeps up to five people and costs $10 HC per person per night. You can book it in advance through The Warden, Arusha National Park, PO Box 3134, Arusha, or enquire directly about availability at the gate or the National Parks office in Arusha.

There are four **National Park Campsites**: three at the foot of Tululusia Hill, 2km from Momella Gate, and one in the forest near Ngurdoto Gate. All are scenic and near streams, have drop toilets and firewood, and cost $10 per person. You may not walk between the campsites and the entrance gates without an armed ranger, so unless you have a vehicle it may be more practical to **pitch a tent at Momella Lodge**. This costs $8 per person and entitles you to use the lodge's facilities. The lodge will organise somewhere for you to wash, and can provide firewood.

Climbing Mount Meru

Meru is not the highest mountain in Africa; for the achievement-orientated it is no substitute for Kilimanjaro. On the other hand, those people who climb both invariably enjoy Meru more. It is not as crowded, considerably less expensive, and although it is steeper there are none of the problems associated with Kilimanjaro's altitude.

Meru is just as interesting as Kilimanjaro from a biological point of view and, because comparatively few people climb it, you are more likely see forest animals. A lot of big game can be seen on the lower slopes. Meru can technically be climbed in two days, but three days is more normal, allowing time to explore Meru Crater and to look at wildlife and plants.

Most people arrange a climb through a safari company in Arusha. The going rate for three days is around $150 per person. You can make direct arrangements with park officials at the gate, but won't save much money by doing this. The compulsory armed ranger and guide costs $20 per day ($10 park fee and $10 salary), hut fees are $10 per night, and there is the usual park entrance fee of $15 per day. A rescue fee of $20 per person covers the entire climb. The minimum cost for a three-day climb is therefore $85 per person plus $65 divided between the party. Food and transport must be added to this, and porters are another $5 per day each.

Meru is very cold at night; you will need adequate clothing. In the rainy season, mountain boots are necessary. The rest of the year, good walking shoes are adequate. The best months to climb are between October and February.

If you arrange your own climb, check hut availability at the National Park Office in Arusha before you head off to the gate. At present the huts are rarely full, but Meru is growing in popularity, and this could change.

Day one The trail starts at Momella Gate (1,500m). From there it is a relatively gentle three-hour ascent to Miriakamba Hut (2,600m). On the way you pass through well-developed woodland where there is a good chance of seeing large animals such as giraffe. At an altitude of about 2,000m you enter the forest zone. If you leave Momella early, there will be ample time to explore Meru Crater in the afternoon. The crater is overlooked by the 1,500m cliff rising to Meru Peak. The 3,667m ash cone in the crater is an hour from Miriakamba Hut, and can be climbed.

Day two It is three-hours to Saddle Hut (3,600m), a bit steeper than the previous day's walk. You initially pass through forest, where there is a good chance of seeing black-and-white colobus, then at about 3,000m you will enter a moorland zone similar to that on Kilimanjaro. It is not unusual to see Kilimanjaro peeking above the clouds from Saddle Hut. If you feel energetic, you can climb Little Meru (3,820m) in the afternoon. It takes about an hour each way from Saddle Hut.

Day three You must rise early to ascend the 4,566m peak. This takes four to five hours. It is then an eight to nine hour walk back down the mountain to Momella Gate.

Note Some people prefer to climb from Miriakamba Hut to Saddle Hut *and* do the round trip from Saddle Hut to Meru Peak on the second day (eleven hours altogether), leaving only a five hour walk to Momella on the third. Others climb all the way up to Saddle Hut on the first day (six hours), do the round trip to the peak on the second (eight hours), and return to Momella from the Saddle Hut on the third (five hours).

LAKE MANYARA NATIONAL PARK

Lake Manyara is a shallow, alkaline lake at the base of a cliff-face that is part of the western Rift Valley wall. The northwest of the lake and the land around it are protected in a 330km² national park. In the 1970s, Lake Manyara was famous for its elephant, immortalised by Ian Douglas-Hamilton in his book *Amongst the Elephants*. Poaching has reduced the numbers in recent years; you are unlikely to see a large tusker these days. The park's other claim to fame is its lions, which have a reputation for tree-climbing, behaviour that has also been observed in the Queen Elizabeth National Park (Uganda).

Lake Manyara is worth visiting for the scenery, the plentiful game, and the large flocks of flamingo which gather there when the water level is suitable. Important habitats include the grassy flood plain around the lake and the indigenous fig forest at the base of the rift valley. Blue monkey are common in the forest and elephant, buffalo and — if you are very lucky — leopard may also be seen. The light acacia woodland and grassland around the lake hosts typical plains animals: giraffe, zebra, wildebeest and a variety of antelope. We saw two magnificent male lions strolling along the lake shore.

The shore cannot be approached closely, so it is difficult to get a good look at the flamingo and other water birds. There is, however, an accessible hippo pool. In addition to being the home of dozens of these lumbering beasts, there are plenty of waders and ducks around it. Most people make a trip to the hot springs in the far south of the park.

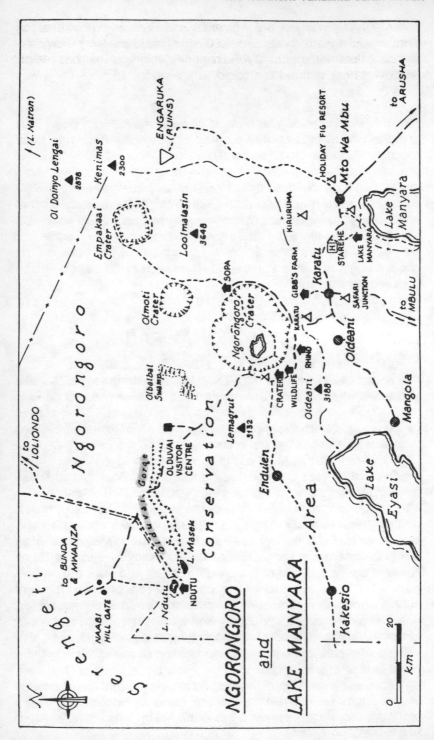

NGORONGORO
and
LAKE MANYARA
Area

A 44-page booklet *Lake Manyara National Park*, published by Tanzania National Parks, costs $2.50 and gives detailed coverage of the park's flora and fauna. Like all national parks, an entrance fee of $15 per 24-hour period is charged.

Mto Wa Mbu

This village near the entrance gate to Lake Manyara sees a lot of tourist traffic and most organised safaris stop at its huge curio market. When you get out of your vehicle expect to be swarmed around by curio dealers. Bear in mind that prices here are double what they would be in Arusha. Mto Wa Mbu means River of Mosquitoes. If you spend a night, you will be in no doubt as to how it got this name.

Where to stay/eat

There is no accommodation in the park, presumably because it is so small. There is plenty of accommodation outside the park.

UPPER RANGE

Lake Manyara Hotel This TTC hotel is perched on top of the Rift Valley wall about 2km from the main road. There are stunning views across Lake Manyara from the verandah, the grounds are pleasant and there is a swimming pool. $86/95 HC s/c single/double. During the off-season there is a 50% discount.

MODERATE, BUDGET & CAMPING

Most people camp at one of the places listed below. The guest houses in Mto wa Mbu are mainly used by drivers, are often full, and cost around $5.00 for a room. The **Starehe and New Flamingo Guest Houses**, along the road to Lake Manyara Hotel, are much cheaper.

National Park Campsites These are near the park entrance gate. Because they are in the forest and are rarely used by safari companies, they are the most pleasant campsites in the area. $10 HC per person.

Holiday Fig Resort This uninteresting, overcrowded site in Mto wa Mbu is popular with safari companies. It has showers, toilets and a cooking area. Basic rooms are available. $5 per person to camp or $15 for a double room.

Kiruruma Tented Camp   This is run by Hoopoe Safaris, but anyone can use it. It is 5km from the main road; the turn-off is opposite the turn-off to Lake Manyara Hotel. Accommodation is in tents set in acacia woodland overlooking the lake. It has a bar and restaurant. $7 HC per person. Recommended.

KARATU

This small, dusty town on the Manyara-Ngorongoro road is often used as a base for visiting the crater. There is a daily bus between it and Arusha.

Where to stay

UPPER RANGE

Gibb's Farm   Built on a coffee farm bordering a patch of indigenous forest, many people rate this hotel the best in the Ngorongoro region. Accommodation is in idiosyncratic bungalows. The restaurant is good. Gibb's Farm is 4km from the main road. $85/105 HC s/c single/double, or $45/65 for residents.

BUDGET & CAMPING

Most people stay at one of the places listed below. There are guest houses in the town which would no doubt be cheaper.

Safari Junction Campsite   This is popular with safari companies, but unlike the Holiday Fig Resort it is some way out of town and has spacious grounds. Facilities include showers, a restaurant and a bar, where we were entertained by two men playing a zeze (a one-stringed instrument similar to a violin) and a bongo. It is 1km out of town and signposted. Camping costs $2.50 per person, hired tents $10 HC per person, and bungalows $35 HC per person.

Karatu Campsite   This is just off the main road towards Ngorongoro, about 10km from Karatu at Njiapanda. Facilities are good. Camping costs $5 per person.

LAKE EYASI

This little-visited and scenic lake lies on the remote southern border of Ngorongoro Conservation Area, at the base of the 1,000m-high Eyasi Escarpment on the western Rift Valley wall. There is plenty of wildlife in the area. Eyasi is notable for the hunter-gatherer Hadza people who live near the shore. The road to Eyasi branches from the Kidatu-Ngorongoro road. There are no tourist facilities, so visitors should be entirely self-sufficient.

NGORONGORO CONSERVATION AREA

The central feature of the 8,300km² Ngorongoro Conservation Area is the crater after which it is named. Ngorongoro Crater is the largest intact caldera in the world and one of the most spectacular sights in Africa. The nearby Olduvai Gorge is the site of some of Africa's most important hominid fossil finds.

Most people are familiar with Ngorongoro's status as a wildlife sanctuary — it has been the subject of countless television documentaries — but the crater is also magnificently scenic. The road from Karatu climbs through densely-forested slopes to the rim where, at Heroes Point, there is a spectacular view over the 260km² crater floor 600m below.

With the notable exception of impala and giraffe — the latter being unable to scale the steep walls — just about every species of African plains mammal lives on the crater floor. The crater has the densest predator population in Africa; because of the plentiful game you'll never see a skinny lion or hyena here. It is normal to see elephant, buffalo, lion and black rhino in the course of one game drive, and there is a fair chance of seeing leopard. Ngorongoro is one of the last remaining rhino strongholds in East Africa. Large herds of grazers, mainly zebra and wildebeest, are resident on the crater floor.

The forested crater rim is worth exploring. There are stunning views back across to the Rift Valley along the road between the main village and Sipa Lodge. Bushbuck and leopard are sometimes seen on this road.

Some people complain Ngorongoro Crater is like a zoo. This is nonsense. The animals are used to vehicles, but they are free to enter and exit as they please. A fairer criticism is that the high tourist traffic robs the crater floor of some of its atmosphere. It is a relatively small area and very open; most animal spotting is done by looking for a group of vehicles clustered together in the distance. Personally I felt the scenery and abundance of animals more than made up for the mild congestion. If crowds put you off there are other places to visit in the Ngorongoro/Serengeti area. Instead of adding to the crowds then moaning about them, give the crater a miss.

An 84-page booklet *Ngorongoro Conservation Area*, similar in style to the national park booklets, is readily available in Arusha and has good information on the crater and Olduvai Gorge. It is especially worth buying if you plan to visit some of the off-the-beaten-track parts of the conservation area.

The crater rim gets very cold at night. Take a jumper or two, especially if you are camping.

An entrance fee of $15 per 24-hour period is charged. This must be payed even if you just pass through between Arusha and the Serengeti.

Geology and history

The mountains in the Ngorongoro region date from two periods. The Gol Mountains, to your left as you descend from Ngorongoro to the Serengeti, are exposed granite blocks over 500 million years old. Ngorongoro and other free-standing mountains are volcanic in origin, formed during the fracturing process that created the Rift Valley 15 to 20 million years ago. When Ngorongoro peaked in size two to three million years ago, it was a similar height to Kilimanjaro today. There are two other volcanic craters in the area: Olmoti and Empakaai. A volcano just north of the conservation area, Oldionyo Lengai (Maasai for *mountain of God*), last erupted in 1983.

Evidence found at Olduvai Gorge and Laetoli (discussed more fully later in the chapter) show hominids have occupied the area for at least three million years. It was occupied by hunter-gatherers until a few thousand years ago, when pastoralists moved in. There are, however, still hunter-gatherers living in the Eyasi Basin south of Ngorongoro. These people, called the Hadza, have strong linguistic links with the San of southern Africa.

The fate of the early pastoralists is not known; a succession of immigrants replaced them. The ancestors of the Cushitic-speaking Mbulu arrived 2,000 years ago. The Nilotic-speaking Datoga arrived 300 years ago. A century later the Maasai drove both groups out in a violent conflict; the Datoga to the Eyasi Basin and the Mbulu to the highlands near Manyara. Most place names in the area are Maasai. I have heard several explanations of the name *Ngorongoro*; the most believable, told to me by a Maasai, is that it is named after a type of Maasai bowl that it resembles.

Europeans settled in the area around the turn of the century. The crater floor was farmed by two German brothers until the outbreak of World War 1. One of their old farmhouses is still used by researchers working in the crater. Tourism began in the 1930s when the Ngorongoro Crater Lodge was built on the crater rim. Ngorongoro was part of the original Serengeti National Park proclaimed in 1951, but it was made a separate conservation area in 1956 in order that the Maasai could graze their cattle there. Ngorongoro Crater was made a World Heritage Site in 1978.

Getting there

The Ngorongoro Conservation Authority's bus service between Arusha and the crater should be operating by the time you read this. This service will be very useful if you have permission to hike in the area (see *Hiking in Ngorongoro Conservation Area* below), but otherwise the value of arriving at Ngorongoro on a bus is questionable. You could hire a park vehicle to take you into the crater, but unless you are part of a large group this is expensive: $140 for a full day, plus $1 per kilometre, plus a $10 crater fee. Add on park fees and you would be better off organising a safari in Arusha.

Where to stay/eat

Except for Sipa Lodge, the lodges and campsite on the crater rim are within a couple of kilometres of the park headquarters. The village near the headquarters has bars and basic shops.

UPPER RANGE

Sipa Lodge The newest and most exclusive lodge is in a magnificent position overlooking the crater. The modern architecture is very impressive. There is a swimming pool, a bar and a restaurant. $106/142 HC s/c single/double or $80/106 for residents. There is a considerable discount from after Easter to the beginning of June: $64/85. Lunch and dinner cost $25 HC each.

Rhino Lodge This is on the opposite side of the road to the crater, so has no view. It describes itself as 'moderate, reasonable and calm', which hardly gets the adrenalin flowing. $55/90 HC single/double (includes dinner).

Ngorongoro Crater Lodge Built in the 1930s, this hotel exudes character — a rustic dining room overlooks the crater while the lawn doubles as a retirement home for aging buffalo. The restaurant is good value; meals cost $8 and afternoon tea and cakes cost $1.25. Bungalows cost $70/88 HC s/c single/double, or $52/67 for residents.

Ngorongoro Wildlife Lodge The TTC lodge has the best position of the lodges near the village, but lacks the character of the Crater Lodge. The balcony overlooks Lekai Forest on the crater floor, and there is a telescope. All rooms face the crater. $67/74 HC s/c single/double (50% discount off-season).

Ndutu Lodge This low-key lodge on the Serengeti border is in the acacia woodland overlooking Lake Ndutu. You can observe animals coming to drink from the bar. Accommodation is in self-contained bungalows. Prices are similar to the Crater Lodge.

BUDGET AND CAMPING

Simba Campsite on the crater rim costs $10 HC per person. The only cheap rooms are at the driver's lodge in the village, but tourists are not normally allowed to stay there. Your best bet for a cheap room is in Kidatu. It used to be possible to camp on the crater floor, and may become so again, but at the time of writing it is forbidden.

Hiking in Ngorongoro Conservation Area

You are permitted to walk in the conservation area providing you have an authorised guide. Tropical Tours in Arusha (see *Organising a safari*) specialise in this kind of thing, but it is possible to make your own arrangements. You could, for instance, hike all the way from Lake Natron to the crater rim, taking in Lengai volcano and other places of interest along the route. This would take at least a week and would probably cost around the same as a Kilimanjaro climb. Another area worth exploring on foot is the Lake Eyasi border.

If you want to do something along these lines, contact the Assistant Conservator of Tourism at the Ngorongoro Conservation Authority in Arusha. At present, few people hike in the area so the chances of getting permission are reasonable, but it is very much at the discretion of the NCA and obviously dependent on what resources are available (guides, porters, transportation within the area etc). If you get permission, you will have to organise food yourself. You should also clarify arrangements for a tent, sleeping bag and other equipment. Remember to take warm clothes; parts of the area become cold at night.

The crater floor

A sheer dirt road descends from Malanja Depression on the crater rim to the crater floor. At the top of the road, Maasai women and children allow you to photograph them for a small fee. The Malanja depression is grassy and open — a good place to spot typical highland antelope such as mountain reedbuck and Kirk's dik-dik, and birds such as the striking auger buzzard and Schalow's wheatear.

The dominant feature of the crater floor is Lake Magadi, a shallow soda lake which supports large flocks of flamingo. Much of the crater floor is open grassland, making animal spotting relatively easy: black rhino, lion, hyena, gazelle, wildebeest and zebra are all commonly seen. The hippo pool near Mandusi Swamp is a popular picnic spot. Lunch is enlivened by to a flock of black kites which have become adept at swooping down on tourists and snatching the food from their hands. Lekai Forest is another attractive spot, made up of yellow fever trees, and the favoured haunt of the crater's elephant.

The ascent back up to the rim passes through patches of forest similar to that on the crater rim.

Olduvai Gorge

The significance of Olduvai Gorge was first recognised by one Professor Katwinkle, an entomologist who stumbled across it in 1911. In 1913, he led an expedition which unearthed a number of animal fossils. The site was abandoned at the start of World War One.

In 1931, Louis Leakey arrived at Olduvai. He thought it an ideal place to uncover traces of early hominids. The gorge cuts through rock beds layered in time sequence from two million years ago to the present and their volcanic origin makes carbon-dating easy. Leakey found ample evidence of human occupation, but without backing his investigations went slowly. It was only in 1959 that his wife, Mary, uncovered a 1.75 million year old *australopithecus* jawbone. This was the first conclusive evidence that hominids had existed for over a million years and that they had evolved in Africa. After this, the Leakeys received proper funding. They unearthed several more fossils, including *homo habilis*, a direct ancestor of modern man. Leakey died in 1972, but Mary continued working in the area until she retired in 1984. In 1976, at the nearby site of Laetoli, she discovered fossil footprints over three million years old, the most ancient hominid footprints yet discovered.

Olduvai gorge is 3km from the main Ngorongoro-Serengeti road. You may only explore the diggings with a guide, and there is an excellent site museum.

Lake Ndutu

This alkaline lake lies south of the B142 on the Ngorongoro-

Serengeti border. When it is full, Maasai use it to water their cattle. In the rainy season it supports large numbers of animals, so Ndutu Lodge (see *Where to stay* above) is a good base for game drives. The acacia woodland around the lake supports different birds to those in surrounding areas. The campsite on the lake shore costs $40 per person.

North of Ngorongoro Crater

Few tourists venture into the northern part of the Ngorongoro Conservation Area, as it does not fit comfortably into the standard three to five-day safari. There are, however, a few places which would be attractive additions to your itinerary if you had time or wanted to head to less touristed spots.

Permission from park headquarters is needed to visit the northern Ngorongoro Conservation Area. The roads in the region are poor and may be impassable after rain. If you plan to explore the area, allocate time generously.

If you visit this area in your own vehicle, treat it as you would any wilderness trip: carry adequate supplies of food, water, and fuel. You should also have essential spares for your vehicle. If you go with a safari company, avoid those on the lower end of the price scale.

Olmoti Crater   This sunken caldera is near the village of Nainokanoka. A track leads from the village to a ranger's post west of it. The crater can only be reached on foot, so at the ranger's post you will have to organise an armed ranger to guide you. From the ranger's post it is a half hour walk to the rim. This is a shallow crater, covered in grass, and it offers good grazing for Maasai cattle and a variety of antelope. From the rim you can walk to a pretty waterfall where the Munge River leaves the crater.

Empakaai Crater   Almost half the floor of this 6km-wide, 300m-high crater is taken up by a deep soda lake. A road circles the forested rim and another leads to the crater floor. Bushbuck, buffalo and blue monkey are likely to be seen on the rim, which also boasts good views across to Lengai Volcano and on clear days, Kilimanjaro and Lake Natron. The crater floor is home to a variety of antelope and water birds. With permission from park headquarters, you may camp wild on the crater rim or sleep in a cabin on the southern shore of the lake.

Engakura Ruins   The ruins of a terraced stone city and complex irrigation system, estimated to be over 500 years old, lie on the eastern side of Empakaai. Nobody knows who built the city — there is no tradition of stone building in this part of Africa — but it was almost certainly occupied by the Mbulu people immediately before the Maasai came into the area. There is a road from Mto wa Mbu to Engakura.

Lake Natron   This spectacular soda lake, north of Lengai Volcano, is set in very harsh surroundings, and has a quality that verges on the primeval. The concentration of sodium carbonate dissolved in the lake is so high that it is often viscous to the touch. As well as being highly scenic, the lake is the only known breeding ground for East Africa's flamingoes.

SERENGETI NATIONAL PARK

There is little I can say about the Serengeti which has not been said already. This is Africa's most famous game reserve, renowned for its dense predator population and annual wildebeest migration. Considering the hype which surrounds it, I half-expected the Serengeti to disappoint, but it didn't. The vastness of the plains and the number of animals which live on them are incredible. I would rate it the best game reserve I have visited anywhere in Africa.

Serengeti National Park covers an area of almost 15,000km², but the Serengeti ecosystem — which includes a number of game reserves bordering the national park as well as Kenya's Maasai Mara Game Reserve — is more than double that size. Most of the national park is open and grassy, broken by isolated granite koppies and patches of acacia woodland. There is little permanent water, so animal migration in the area is strongly linked to rainfall patterns.

The Serengeti was little-known to Europeans until after World War One, when hunters moved in. The national park was created in 1951 and became famous through the work of Professor Bernard Grzimek and his son Michael. At the age of 24, Michael died in an aeroplane crash over the Serengeti. He is buried at Heroes Point on the Ngorongoro Crater rim. Published in the late 1950s, Grzimek's book *Serengeti shall not die* remains worthwhile reading.

Using figures from the 1984/5 census, the Serengeti's most common antelope species are wildebeest (1,300,000), Thomson's gazelle (250,000), impala (70,000) topi (50,000), Grant's gazelle (30,000), kongoni (15,000) and eland (10,000). Other antelope species include Kirk's dik-dik, klipspringer (often seen on koppies) and small numbers of roan, oryx, oribi and waterbuck.

After wildebeest, the most populous large mammal is zebra (200,000), and the two are often seen in mixed herds. There are significant numbers of buffalo, giraffe and warthog. Elephant are relatively scarce, and the few remaining black rhinoceros are restricted to the Moru Koppies area. A few primate species are present, of which baboon are the most common and widespread.

Lion and spotted hyena are the most commonly-seen predators. There are estimated to be over 1,500 lion in the Serengeti. Leopard are common in the Seronera Valley, where they spend much of the day resting in the umbrella-thorn trees which line the Seronera River. Their presence is often given away by a tail dangling below the canopy. Cheetah are also quite common. These solitary animals favour open grassland and are therefore quite easily seen if they are around. The most common canine is black-backed jackal. Side-striped and golden jackal are present, as are African hunting dog and bat-eared fox.

Considering its open nature, I was surprised at how rewarding the Serengeti's bird life is. Ostrich are common, as is the kori Bustard, claimed by some to be the heaviest flying bird in the world. A variety of larks, finches and raptors can be seen, but perhaps the most distinctive small bird is the lilac-breasted roller, an exquisitely-coloured bird often seen perched on trees alongside the road.

Maasai, who traditionally occupied the Serengeti plains from the 17th century, are no longer allowed to graze their cattle in the Serengeti. Evidence of their previous occupation of the area can be seen at Moru Koppies, where there are well-preserved Maasai rock paintings.

A 72-page booklet *Serengeti National Park* is sold at the National Parks office in Arusha for $2.50. Like all the national park booklets, it contains good maps and is an excellent introduction the local ecosystems.

An entrance fee of $15 per 24-hour period is charged.

When to visit

Unlike Ngorongoro, the Serengeti's animal populations are highly seasonal. There is less game in the park during the dry season, although some species (including most predators) are resident and territorial, so do not stray far.

The wildebeest migration

The wildebeest migration follows a fairly predictable pattern, though there are minor variations from year to year. Wildebeest disperse in the southern part of the Serengeti during the rainy season (December to May), calving near the beginning of this period. On game drives around Seronera at this time of year it is not uncommon to see herds of 10,000 animals.

In April or May the animals congregate in preparation for an 800km migration to the western Serengeti and Maasai Mara, which takes place sometime between April and June. During this time, a herd of over a million migrating animals forms a column up to 40km long, one of the most impressive spectacles in the world.

From July to October, the animals spread out into the northern and western Serengeti. The best base is the Lobo area (not really practical for a camping safari). The animals return to the southern plains in November.

Getting there

The only practical way to get to the Serengeti is in your own vehicle or with a safari company.

Where to stay/eat

The main park headquarters are at Seronera, where there is also a small village, a lodge and camping facilities. On a camping safari you will almost certainly be based at Seronera — all the other campsites in the park are so-called special campsites and cost $40 per person per night. Lodge safaris have a wider choice of bases.

UPPER RANGE

Seronera Wildlife Lodge   This lodge is built around a koppie overlooking the surrounding plains. There is a bar (reached by a natural path between two granite boulders) and a restaurant; the former is worth visiting if you are staying at the campsites. $67/74 HC s/c single/double. Lunch and dinner cost $11 HC. Like all TTC hotels, there is a 50% discount off-season.

Lobo Wildlife Lodge   This spectacular building is designed around a koppie, run by the TTC, and has similar facilities to Seronera. Lobo is in the northern part of the park, and the best base for game drives between June and November. $45/55 HC s/c single/double.

Sipa Lodge   The newest and most exclusive lodge in the Serengeti is about 50km south of Seronera. The structure and facilities offered are similar to the Sipa Lodge at Ngorongoro Crater. $106/142 HC s/c single/double or $80/106 for residents. There is a considerable discount from after Easter to the beginning of June: $64/85. Lunch and dinner cost $25 HC each.

Serengeti Springs Lodge   A new lodge due to open in 1993. It is run by the same people as the Ngorongoro Wildlife Lodge and should be similar in price.

MODERATE AND CAMPING

Kijireshi Tented Camp   Near Bunda, on the western border of the Serengeti, this is a good base if you are exploring the area from Mwanza. Furnished tents cost $20 s/c double. It has a bar and restaurant.

Seronera Campsites   There are seven campsites about 5km from Seronera Lodge. The only facilities are long-drop toilets, but you may be able to organise a shower and fill up water containers for a small fee at the lodge. There is a good chance of seeing nocturnal scavengers such as hyena and genet after dark. $10 HC per person.

Special Campsites   There are special campsites at Lobo, Kiwara, Moru Koppies, Lake Ndutu and Naabi Hill. They are little-used, so offer relative solitude, but have no facilities. The most special thing about them is the price. $40 per person.

TARANGIRE NATIONAL PARK

Tarangire is less famous than the other northern reserves, but it is no less rewarding. Like the Serengeti it is part of a wider ecosystem within which there is a great deal of migratory movement. During the wet season, most of its animals disperse to the Maasai Steppe, while wildebeest and zebra move northwest to the Rift Valley floor between Lakes Natron and Manyara.

In direct contrast to the Serengeti, Tarangire comes into its own during the dry season. Between June and November, Tarangire abounds in game attracted to the permanent water of the Tarangire River. During these months it is likely to prove more rewarding than the Serengeti. Vegetation is denser than in the Serengeti, comprising acacia and mixed woodland and, near the Tarangire river, dense elephant grass and the occasional palm tree. Baobab trees are abundant. Tarangire has a wild character, reminiscent of reserves in southern Tanzania.

Tarangire supports similar large mammals to the Serengeti, but the denser vegetation makes predators such as lion and leopard more difficult to see. It is famous for its elephant, with herds of 20-odd animals relatively common. Two localised antelope found in Tarangire are the fringe-eared oryx and gerenuk. According to the 1980 census the greater Tarangire ecosystem supports 25,000 wildebeest, 30,000 zebra, 6,000 buffalo, 3,000 elephant, 2,700 giraffe, 5,500 eland, 30,000 impala and 2,000 warthog. Tarangire is regarded to be the best of the northern parks for birds. It is particularly rich in raptors and acacia-associated species.

Most people spend a day in Tarangire and concentrate on the northern circuit. If you have longer, Lake Burungi circuit offers your best chance of seeing black rhinoceros, bushbuck and lesser kudu, the Kitibong Hill area is home to large herds of buffalo, Lamarkau Swamp supports hippo and numerous water birds during the wet season, the southern plains are favoured by cheetah, and Mkungero Pools is the place to look for waterbuck and gerenuk.

A 56-page booklet *Tarangire National Park* is available from the National Parks Headquarters in Arusha. A park entrance fee of $15 per 24-hour period is charged.

Getting there and away

Tarangire lies off the main Arusha-Dodoma road. Coming from Arusha, this road is tarred as far as the Tarangire turn-off. Most people tag a visit on to the end of a longer safari, but if your time or money is limited, a one or two-day safari to Tarangire is a viable option.

Where to stay

A tented camp, **Tarangire Safari Lodge**, overlooks the Tarangire River. It has a bar, restaurant and swimming pool. $52/65 HC s/c single/double. Two National Park campsites also overlook the river. Neither have water, but this can be obtained from the lodge. Camping costs $10 HC per person.

KONDOA IRANGI ROCK PAINTINGS

Lying off the main Arusha-Dodoma road, the rock paintings found in the Kondoa region of Tanzania are the most numerous in East Africa. There are over 100 known sites, the most accessible and interesting of which are reached from the small centre of Kolo. African rock art is overlooked by many tourists, despite the aesthetic value of many paintings, and the numerous questions the art raises about the artists, their beliefs and their lifestyle.

The paintings of the Kondoa region are between 200 and 4,000 years old. Rock art weathers quickly in African conditions. Many older paintings are badly faded, and the tradition may be more ancient than these dates suggest. Most rock paintings are found in caves or rock overhangs. In the Kondoa region east and west-facing sites were favoured.

Paintings are in a variety of styles and cover a range of subjects. Giraffe and various antelope were favoured subjects and eland seem to have held a special significance. Other paintings depict religious ceremonies. There are also abstract paintings of geometric figures whose significance can only be guessed at. Style changes have been recorded at many sites, with newer paintings superimposed over older ones.

The identity of Kondoa's artists is a mystery. Most southern African rock art is accredited to San hunter-gatherers. San-like people occupied all of East and southern Africa prior to the arrival of Bantu-speakers 2,000 to 3,000 years ago. The Hadza of the Lake Eyasi region and the local Sandawe are thought to be remnant populations of these early hunter-gatherers. Some Sandawe clans claim their forefathers were responsible for the paintings, but there is no tradition relating to them amongst the Hadza. The Wa-Gogo of Dodoma make the improbable claim the paintings were done by the Portuguese!

Whoever the artists were, their decimation was relatively recent. It could be linked to the Maasai invasion north of Kondoa 300 years ago. This caused displacement of the local Bantu-speaking people, and may have had a knock-on effect in Kondoa.

Before you visit the paintings, try to get hold of the National Museums of Tanzania Occasional Paper No. 5, a booklet by Fidelis Masao called *The Rock Art of Kondoa and Singada*. I picked up a copy for $1 at the National Museum in Dar es Salaam.

Getting there and away

Several accessible and highly-rated sites are near the village of Kolo on the Arusha-Dodoma road. The Antiquities Department in Kolo can organise a guide. The paintings are about 10km from the main road. There is no accommodation in Kolo, so a tent would be useful. There are guest houses in Kondoa and Babati, 25km south and 80km north of Kolo respectively. Some Arusha-based companies will include Kondoa in a safari itinerary. The paintings could then be visited as a full day trip from Tarangire.

178

(Uganda) to
KAMPALA
Bukoba
(Rwanda)
BIHARAMULO
Game Res.
Biharamulo
Nyakanazi
329
(Burundi)
MOYOWOSI
Game Res.
GOMBE STREAM
KIGOMA
Ujiji
Uvinza
340
MAHALE
MTNS.
N.P.
Mpanda
KATAVI
Nat. Pk
240
(Zaire)
Sumbawanga
(Zambia)
Kasanga
335

LAKE
VICTORIA
RUBONDO
Is.
MWANZA
KIGOSI
Game Res.
Shinyanga
Nzega
501
TABORA
355
UGALLA
RIVER
Nat. Pk.
Rungwa
UWANDA
Game Res.
LAKE RUKWA
Mbeya

to
KISUMU
Musoma
Bunda
(Kenya)

to
ARUSHA,
NAIROBI

Singida
230
DODOMA
RUNGWA
Game Res.
251
to
MOROGORO,
DAR ES SALAAM
Iringa
350
to LINDI, MTWARA

N

WESTERN TANZANIA
0
200
km

Chapter Nine

Western Tanzania

INTRODUCTION

This chapter covers the vast western part of Tanzania. It is divided into four sections: the Central Railway, Lake Victoria, Lake Tanganyika, and southwest Tanzania.

With international ferry services to Uganda, Burundi and Zambia on its lakes, both of which are also linked to the coast by the central railway line, it is not surprising that large numbers of overland travellers pass through western Tanzania. What is surprising is how few bother to explore it. The region is also rarely visited by short-stay visitors, largely because of the distances involved, and so it is a great destination for travellers with a sense of adventure and few time restrictions.

Africa's largest lakes, Victoria and Tanganyika, dominate western Tanzania. They are totally dissimilar in character. Victoria is vast and amorphous, shallow, muddy and, for the most part, scenically indifferent. The 675km-long Tanganyika is deep and narrow, with a green mountainous shore and crystal clear water. There is good transport on both lakes and plenty of opportunity for imaginative travellers to get well away from the usual tourist beat.

There are four national parks in western Tanzania: Katavi, Gombe Stream, Mahale Mountains, and Rubondo Island. Gombe Stream is well-known for its chimpanzees and for the work done there by Jane Goodall, but the other three are remote and little-visited. All are reasonably accessible, however, provided you are not in a rush and are prepared to rough it a bit.

Climate

Western Tanzania is relatively flat and low-lying. Rain falls between November and May. The vast central plateau between Dodoma and Tabora is hot and dry, while the Lake Tanganyika area is hot and

humid and supports extensive areas of lowland forest. The Lake
Victoria region is more temperate, but can be humid.

Getting around

The main access to the area is via the central railway. This runs from
Dar es Salaam to Tabora before branching to Mwanza, Kigoma or
Mpanda; see *Rail* in Chapter Three for schedules.

A second important link is the Lake Tanganyika steamer, which
does a weekly run between Mpulungu (Zambia), Kigoma and
Bujumbura (Burundi). Boats on Lake Victoria link Mwanza to Port Bell
(Uganda) and various Tanzanian ports. Details of lake ferries are
given under the relevant lake later in the chapter.

Roads are generally in poor condition, and best avoided. I met
someone who took 48 hours to travel between Mwanza and Tabora
by bus. There are exceptions: the Mwanza-Musoma road is tarred
and for the most part in good condition, and the road connecting
Mpanda to Mbeya via Sumbawanga, though not surfaced, is in
reasonable condition — and the only direct way of getting between
these towns.

THE CENTRAL RAILWAY

The 1,238km railway line between Dar es Salaam and Kigoma was
constructed by the Germans between 1905 and 1914. It follows the
old slave caravan route through Dodoma and Tabora, the same
route used by Burton and Speke in their search for the source of the
Nile. The British-built Tabora-Mwanza line was completed in 1928.

The central line is the only sane alternative to flying between the
coast and western Tanzania, and it gives travellers a rare opportunity
to see central Tanzania in something approaching comfort. Between
Dodoma and Tabora, the line passes through the most barren
scenery in the country, a seemingly-endless drought-prone plain of
baked red sand and sparse woodland. It stops at several small
villages, the livelihood of which evidently revolves around selling food
to train passengers.

The scenery becomes more lush as you approach Kigoma. It is
worth waking early to see the patches of indigenous forest, swamp
and dense miombo woodland along the line. Between Tabora and
Mwanza the scenery remains arid until the approach to Lake Victoria,
where strange granite formations break the monotony.

The most important towns along the line, Tabora and Dodoma, are
covered below. See *Rail* in Chapter Three for schedules.

DODOMA

Dodoma was an important village on the 19th-Century caravan route. When the railway reached it, the Germans built a station and administration centre, and planned to make it the capital of German East Africa. During the war the area suffered two famines, killing over 30,000 people, and these plans were shelved.

Dodoma grew steadily between the wars. It was a staging post on the Cape to Cairo flights of the 1930s. Its position on the railway and Trans-Tanzania road before the Iringa-Morogoro stretch was built in the 1950s made it a major internal crossroad. In 1973 Dodoma was again earmarked as the future capital of Tanzania, and it has already taken over some functions from Dar es Salaam.

Whatever its importance in other directions, Dodoma is amongst the most nondescript and unappealing towns I have ever visited.

Getting there and away

Dodoma is linked to Dar es Salaam, Kigoma and Mwanza by rail, and to Dar es Salaam by road. Travellers sometimes cut between the north and south of Tanzania on the Arusha-Dodoma-Iringa route. This looks good on paper, but the roads are awful. You will get where you want as quickly and more comfortably via Chalinze or Dar es Salaam.

Where to stay/eat

Dodoma's only tourist hotel is the ex-railway **Dodoma Hotel** (Tel: (061) 20451), opposite the station. It has a fair restaurant, a bar and a garden. There is a forex bureau in the lobby. $35/45 HC s/c single/double, or $8.75/10.50 for residents.

In the moderate range, I recommend the **Jamboree Hotel** (Tel: (061) 22834), a short taxi-ride from the town centre. It has pleasant gardens, a restaurant and a bar, and costs $4/5 s/c single/double. The similarly-priced **Nam Annexe Hotel**, also a taxi-ride from the town centre, is newer but has less character.

There are plenty of guest houses near the bus station. None is remotely appealing. Instead, try the **CCT Hostel** (Tel: (061) 21258). This is 300m from the railway station next to a domed church. Clean rooms with mosquito nets cost $2-$4. A canteen serves cheap, tasty meals.

TABORA

This hot, dusty town is where the railway lines to Kigoma, Mwanza and Mpanda meet. If you travel around western Tanzania, you are likely to spend a day in Tabora at some point, and may even have to spend a night. Tabora is a friendly place, and quite attractive with its shady roads lined with mango and flame trees.

History

Tabora is the home of the Nyamwezi, Tanzania's second-largest tribe. In the mid-19th Century, under the leadership of Mirambo, they controlled the area between Tabora and Lakes Tanganyika, Rukwa and Victoria. They were actively involved in the slave trade and provided many porters for the central caravan route.

Mirambo, a natural diplomat, kept good relations with Arab traders and European visitors. After his death in 1884, his successor clashed with the Germans, who captured Tabora in 1893. The large fort overlooking the town dates from this period.

The 19th-Century Arab slave-trading post, Kazeh, was a few kilometres from Tabora. Burton and Speke stopped there on their way to becoming the first Europeans to see Lake Tanganyika. In 1872, between his famous meeting with Stanley at Ujiji and his final,

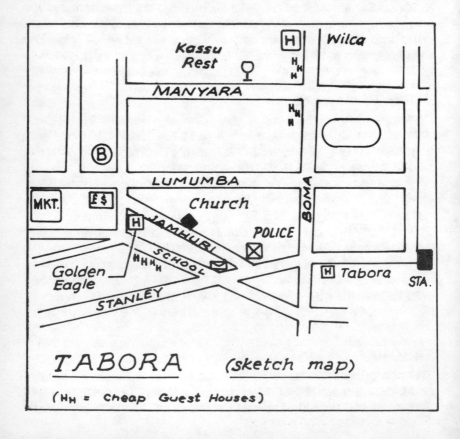

TABORA   (sketch map)

(H H = Cheap Guest Houses)

fatal expedition to Lake Benguela, Livingstone stayed in Kazeh for five months waiting for supplies from the coast. His restored house is now a museum.

Getting there and away

Tabora is an important railway junction; most people who spend time there do so to make a train connection. Buses run between Tabora and most parts of western Tanzania, but they are not a pleasant option. The twice-weekly bus service between Tabora and Mbeya could be useful to travellers. It takes at least 20 hours.

Where to stay/eat

Near the station, the ex-TRC **Tabora Hotel** (PO Box 147, Tel: (062) 2177) has comfortable rooms, a reasonable restaurant and bar, and its verandah is a good place to meet other travellers ($6.25 s/c double with private patio). If you are stuck in Tabora for the day (trains arrive at 6.00am and leave around midnight) you can occupy a room at half-price. The **Wilca Hotel** is on Boma Road, about 1km from the station. It is popular with expats and often full. The restaurant has a good reputation, but the meal we had was very greasy ($5 s/c double). The only proper hotel in the town centre is the overpriced **Golden Eagle Hotel** ($5.75 double). The restaurant here is good. There are several **cheap guest houses** in Tabora, but it can be difficult to find a vacant room. The main clusters of guest houses are on School Street and on Boma Road near the Wilca Hotel. The guest houses near the bus station are very grotty. Expect to pay about $1.50 for a room in a guest house.

   Kassu Restaurant serves inexpensive Indian meals and snacks.

Excursions

Livingstone's House   This museum 6km out of town holds various exhibits relating to Livingstone's stay in Tabora and is worth a look if you have a day to kill. There are no buses, so you will have to negotiate a price for a round trip by taxi.

Rungwa Game Reserve   Rungwa is an extension of the Ruaha ecosystem and protects similar animals to Ruaha National Park. It is 10 hours from Tabora by bus, and there is no guarantee you will be allowed in. To get there, ask a bus to Mbeya to drop you at Rungwa village on the park boundary. At the village, speak to the head ranger for permission to walk in the park and to organise a guide. Bring a tent and food with you.

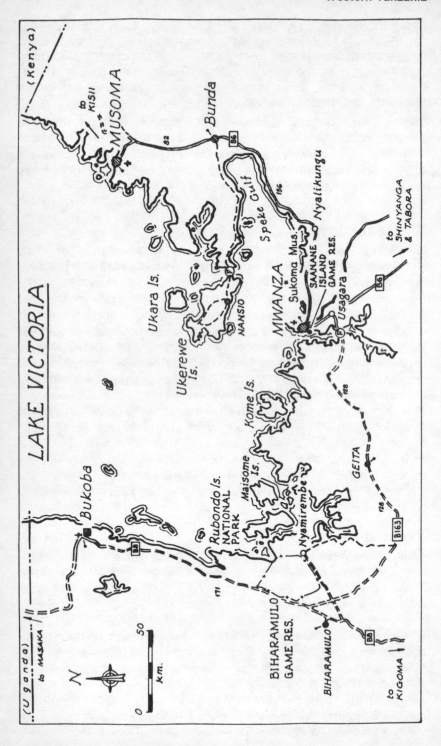

LAKE VICTORIA

Lake Victoria, the largest lake in Africa and the second-largest freshwater lake in the world, is split between Uganda, Kenya and Tanzania, with the lion's share in Tanzania. The lake lies in an elevated basin between the major forks of the Great Rift Valley, and, unlike Lake Tanganyika, it is shallow — only 70m deep on average — and its muddy water is plagued with bilharzia. The most important Tanzanian ports are Mwanza, Musoma and Bukoba.

Most of the people who live around Lake Victoria are fishermen by tradition. The lake's future as a fishery is far from assured. In 1956, Nile perch were introduced to it in order to increase its food yield. These voracious fish have preyed on the cichlid species which naturally occur in the lake. Most Lake Victoria endemics are now extinct or heading that way.

Perch are fished through necessity, but as they are too large to roast on a fire and too fatty to sun-dry, they do not meet local needs. As the number of algae-eating endemics has dropped, the lake's algae level has risen. This is a type of environmental change that perch are known to be sensitive to. Worse still, perch cannibalise their own young when other prey runs out. There is concern that Lake Victoria will become a vast expanse of dead water, leaving a huge gap in the subsistence of lake shore villages and the economy of towns such as Mwanza.

Lake Victoria Ferries

Ferry services from Mwanza are excellent. Those most often used by travellers go to Port Bell (Uganda) and Bukoba. Other ferries go to Ukerewe Island, Nyimirembe and Nkome. Ferries to Musoma were discontinued after the Mwanza-Musoma road was re-surfaced.

Ferries are run by the Tanzania Railway Corporation. Tickets are moderately-priced and can be paid for in local currency. Tickets bought in Uganda must be paid for in US dollars, and cost double what they would in Tanzania. A $5 port tax, levied upon leaving a Tanzanian port, must be paid in US dollars.

Ferries to Bukoba and Uganda have restaurants which serve good meals and all ferries have a bar. There are three classes on most ferries. First class cabins have four bunks; second class cabins have six. Men and women may not share unless they have booked the whole cabin.

First, second and third class fares from Mwanza to Bukoba are $9/6/3, and from Mwanza to Port Bell they are $19/14/8. Mwanza to Nyamirembe costs $5/3 (second sitting/third).

The schedules given below were accurate in December 1992.

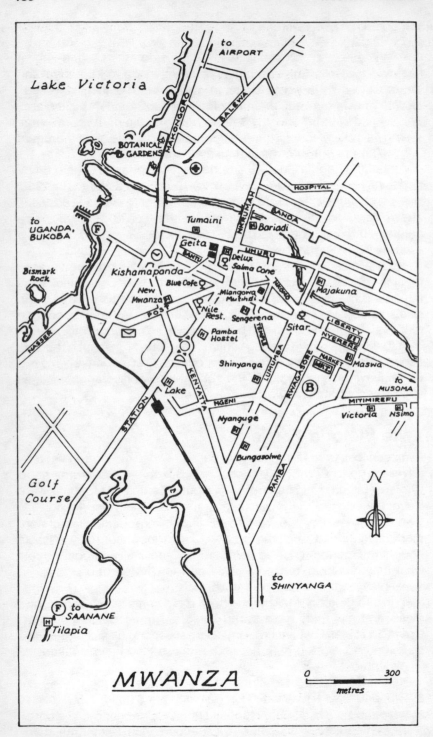

MWANZA

0   300

metres

Timetables on Lake Victoria change frequently; up-to-date details can be obtained at the ferry office in Mwanza.

Mwanza-Port Bell This direct service runs once a week and takes 15 hours. The *MV Bukoba* leaves Mwanza at 3.00pm Sunday and Port Bell in Uganda at 3.00pm Monday. First and second class are normally half full; you should have no problem getting a last minute booking. If you miss this ferry, catch one to Bukoba. You can get from Bukoba to Masaka (Uganda) in a day.

Mwanza-Bukoba There is one ferry in each direction every day except Wednesday (no ferry from Mwanza) and Thursday (no ferry from Bukoba). In both directions, ferries leave at 9.00pm and arrive at 8.00am the following morning.

Mwanza-Nyamirembe/Nkome Ferries run twice-weekly between Mwanza and Nyamirembe. *MV Serengeti* leaves Mwanza at 9.00pm Thursday and Nyamirembe at 7.00pm Friday. *MV Clarius* leaves Mwanza at 8.00am Monday and Nyamirembe at 8.00am Tuesday. *MV Clarius* does an additional weekly run between Mwanza and Nkome, leaving Mwanza at 8.00am Wednesday and Nkome at 8.00am Thursday. All these journeys take approximately 10 hours, and include stops at Kome and Maisome islands.

Mwanza-Nansio(Ukerewe Island) Ferries between Mwanza and Nansio run daily and take three hours each way. They usually leave Mwanza at 9.00am and Nansio at 1.30pm. This varies, so check a day in advance.

MWANZA

According to the 1988 census Mwanza is the second largest town in Tanzania. It is a relaxed place, which, after years of stagnation, seems to have picked up in ecomonic terms far more quickly than in most Tanzanian towns. Mwanza has a reasonably cosmopolitan flavour; it has a large Indian population, good links with Kenya and Uganda, and is a focus for overland travellers and expats. Scenically, Mwanza is notable for the bizarre granite outcrops which surround it, the best known of which is the precariously perched Bismarck Rock at the harbour entrance.

Getting there and away

Mwanza can be reached by rail from Dar es Salaam and other parts of western Tanzania; see *Rail* in Chapter Three. There are daily buses between Mwanza and Kisumu (Kenya). Weekly ferries run between Mwanza and Port Bell (Uganda); see *Lake Victoria Ferries* above.

Travellers wanting to get from Arusha to Mwanza have a few options. A couple of buses go through the Serengeti every week, taking about 15 hours. You should see lots of game at the right time of year, but must pay $30 in park fees. Other buses go via Singida and Shinyanga. In theory this takes 36 hours, but it can take three days. If you are going to Mwanza after a safari, some companies will drop you at Bunda on the Musoma-Mwanza road if arranged in advance. There is a charge, but it will be worth it for a group.

A compromise between time, expense and comfort would be to nip through Kenya. This is only really practical if you don't need a visa for Kenya (which is the case for most Commonwealth and EEC citizens, though you should check this in advance — Australians, for instance, do need a visa) and either don't need a visa for Tanzania or have a multiple-entry visa. With an early start from Arusha, you should make the overnight train from Nairobi to Kisumu. This leaves at 6.00pm and takes around 14 hours. Buses between Kisumu and Mwanza leave in the morning and take about 10 hours.

Where to stay

UPPER RANGE
New Mwanza Hotel   (PO Box 25, tel: (068) 3202). This TTC hotel is the only one in this range in the town centre. Rooms are comfortable and air-conditioned. $50 HC s/c double, or $15 for residents.

Tilapia Hotel   This new hotel is on the lake shore 1km from the town centre. Accommodation is in spacious, comfortably-furnished huts. A restaurant was being built when we visited. $23/32 s/c single/double. Recommended.

MODERATE
Lake Hotel   (PO Box 910, tel: (068) 3263). This is the best hotel in its range. It has a restaurant and a shady outdoor bar. Rooms have fans and mosquito nets. $8.75/10.25 s/c single/double.

Delux Hotel   This is a good compromise between price and comfort, but it often fills up early. The restaurant is good, and there are two bars and a disco. The only drawback is that it can be noisy at night. $4.25/5.00 s/c single/double.

Nsemo Hotel This new hotel near the bus station is convenient and reasonably priced, but it already shows signs of poor maintenance. When we were there the staff were rude and our room was infested with cockroaches. $4 s/c double.

Bungasolwe Hotel This is no more than a glorified and overpriced guest house. $5 s/c double.

BUDGET

A room in a guest house costs from $1.50 to $2.50. Most guest houses in Mwanza are clean and have mosquito nets. Some fill up early, but you shouldn't have to look long to find a room. In addition to those listed, the **Maswa, Tumaini and Sengerema Guest Houses** are all acceptable.

Kishamapanda/Geita Guest House These adjoining guest houses are clean, pleasant and popular. They also fill up early. $2.00/2.50 single/double or $2.50/3.50 s/c single/double.

Panda Hostel This is roughly midway between the bus and rail stations and the ferry terminal. Rooms are clean and pleasant, but the communal toilets and baths leave a bit to be desired. It has a bar and restaurant. $1.75/2.10 single/double.

Victoria Hotel The rooms at this run-down hotel next to the bus station are not particularly clean, but have a mosquito net and fan. $3.00/3.50 s/c single/double.

Mlangowa (Mutindi) Guest House This above-average guest house is freshly decorated and spotlessly clean. $1.50/2.00/2.25 single/double/triple, or $3 s/c doubles.

Shinyanga Hotel The rooms are dingy but seem reasonably clean, and some have balconies. $1.50/2.00 single/double.

Nyanguge Guest House If you can do without electricity, this is a clean, cheap and friendly place. All rooms are single, and cost $1.25 or $1.50 s/c.

Where to eat
The restaurant at the **Delux Hotel** is the best value in Mwanza. It has a varied menu and serves huge portions of tasty food for $1.50. The similarly-priced **Sitar Restaurant** is popular with travellers, but the

meals we were served looked as if they had been cooked in Brylcream and tasted worse. I was impressed by the **Lake Hotel**, where I had a tasty curry for $2.

The outdoor bar at the **New Mwanza Hotel** is reminiscent of the New Africa in Dar es Salaam. It is a good place to meet other travellers, but the food isn't up to much. The **Kidepo Grill** on the second floor is more tempting. An excellent three-course meal costs around $3.50 and there is live Zairian music most nights.

On the lower end of the scale, **Blue Cafe** serves inexpensive, tasty snacks such as samosas, kebabs and fried chicken. **Salma Cone** serves the best ice-cream outside of Dar es Salaam; sundaes cost less than $1. They also sell fresh popcorn. There are plenty of cheap *hotelis* around the market and bus station.

Excursions

Saa Nane Island

This small, rocky island in Lake Victoria has been set aside as a game reserve and zoo. On both accounts it is a bit of a washout; re-introduced buck wander around aimlessly and several listless predators are confined in small cages, as is a decidedly pissed-off looking chimpanzee.

All this detracts from the island's real attraction, the small animals which inhabit it naturally. It is crawling with lizards such as the gaudily-coloured rock agama. We also saw a few water monitors, the largest African lizard, crash gracelessly through the undergrowth. Bird life is profuse. Fish eagle, pied kingfisher and white-bellied cormorant are common near the lake shore. Twitchers will have little difficulty spotting such localised species as swamp flycatcher, yellow-throated leaflove, grey kestrel and slender-billed weaver. Rock hyrax are the most visible mammal.

The motorboat to Saa Nane leaves from a jetty 15 minutes walk from Mwanza town centre. It departs at 8.00am, 11.00am, 1.00pm, 3.00pm and 5.00pm, and returns an hour later. You can spend as long as you like on the island for an admission fee of $0.50. At present, you may not stay overnight. We were told there are plans to build a campsite, but these seemed very vague.

Sukoma Museum

Tanzania's largest tribe, the Sukoma, live in and around Mwanza. The Sukoma Museum, 20km out of town, displays exhibits relating to their lifestyle. Try to visit it on a Saturday, when the Sukoma Snake Dance is performed in tandem with a live python. If you visit the museum on weekdays it may well be deserted. You can camp for free if you have a tent, but facilities are limited and there is not always water.

The Sukoma Museum is a short walk from Kissesa on the Mwanza-Musoma road. Any bus to Musoma can drop you off there.

Ukerewe Island

Ukerewe Island is two to three hours from Mwanza by ferry; see *Lake Victoria Ferries* for details. The island's largest town, Nansio, is also the ferry terminal. The round trip to Nansio is a good way to see some of Africa's largest lake.

Nansio is a scruffy little town. You will have an hour to wander around while you wait to re-embark the ferry, which is more than adequate. The island itself is very pretty, however, and the sandy beaches west of Nansio are said to be bilharzia-free. If you have a couple of days spare in the Mwanza area, you could do worse than spend them exploring Ukerewe using Nansio as a base.

Of the basic lodges in Nansio, the **Panda Hostel** and **Island Inn** are the most appealing. Rooms cost around $1.50. The Island Inn has a restaurant.

There are occasional vehicles between Nansio and Bunda on the main Mwanza-Musoma road.

Kome and Maisome Islands

Adventurous travellers may be intrigued by these two large islands on Lake Victoria, both of which can be reached by ferry from Mwanza. According to maps, both islands have substantial areas of forest; it seems likely they will harbour similar animal species to those which occur naturally on Rubondo Island National Park. It's less likely there will be any formal accommodation; assume you'll need a tent. A survey map might also be handy. Depending on who you speak to, the staff at the ferry office in Mwanza can be very helpful with information about places where ferries stop.

Ferries from Mwanza to Nyamirembe/Nkome stop at both islands on Mondays, Wednesdays and Thursdays; ferries returning to Mwanza stop at both islands on Tuesdays, Thursdays and Fridays (see *Lake Victoria Ferries* for details).

BUNDA

Bunda, the largest town on the Mwanza-Musoma road, is a route focus of sorts. It is where Arusha-based safari companies drop off passengers heading to Mwanza, and the best place to catch a pick-up to Ukerewe Island.

The scenic road between Mwanza and Bunda is in good condition. It passes first through dry, flat country dotted with small koppies and Sukoma homesteads and offers regular glimpses of Lake Victoria.

Before reaching Bunda it skirts the Serengeti; at the right time of year there is some wildlife to be seen.

Bunda is no more than moderately intriguing. More substantial than maps suggest, it has a scenic position at the foot of a range of steep granite hills. If you have the inclination to climb one of these, you would have a superb vantage point over Lake Victoria and the Serengeti plains.

There are several guest houses and *hotelis* in Bunda. Rooms cost less than $2.

MUSOMA

Musoma lies on a pretty part of the Lake Victoria shore, but apart from strolling around town or lazing at the Silver Sands Inn, there is little to do there. Travellers coming from Kisumu (Kenya) used to stop in Musoma to pick up a ferry to Mwanza, but since the Musoma-Mwanza road was re-surfaced the ferry service has been discontinued. Musoma now sees few tourists.

Where to stay/eat

The colonial-style Railway Hotel, on the lake shore about 3km from the town centre, costs $12 s/c double. In the town centre, the Orange Tree Hotel is clean, has a bar and restaurant, and charges $7/9 s/c single/double.

The best budget hotel is Silver Sands Inn, overlooking the lake

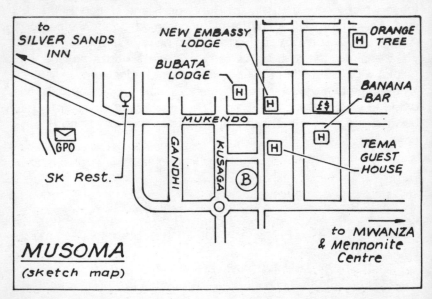

1km from the town centre. Meals are served on request and soft drinks are available ($2/3 s/c single/double). The Mennonite Centre is clean, friendly and popular with travellers, and it has a canteen, but it is often full ($2 double).

There are several guest houses with rooms for under $2. Butata Lodge is basic, but it is clean and friendly, and rooms have mosquito nets. The livelier Banana Bar Lodge has a bar, a restaurant, and video shows in the evening; not the place to stay if you want an early night, but fun if you don't.

The restaurant at the Orange Tree Hotel is fair. SK Restaurant serves western and Indian meals for under $2. Several bars and *hotelis* line Mukendo Road; the Banana Bar and Embassy Lodge look reasonable.

RUBONDO ISLAND NATIONAL PARK

This national park protects the 240km² Rubondo Island. The predominant vegetation type is rain forest, but there are also patches of grassland and papyrus swamp. Several large mammal species are present: sitatunga, bushbuck, vervet monkey and hippopotamus are indigenous, elephant, chimpanzee, roan antelope and black rhino have been introduced. Rubondo is rich in forest and water-associated birds.

Game viewing is done either on foot or from a boat, which makes the island attractive to budget travellers. A round trip from Mwanza takes the best part of a week, so few people visit it. If you do, you could well have it to yourself.

An entrance fee of $15 per 24-hour period must be paid in hard currency.

Getting there

If you can afford it, the simplest way to get to Rubondo is to charter a flight from Dar es Salaam or Arusha.

Coming by boat or by road, the normal base for reaching Rubondo is Nyamirembe Port. Ferries from Mwanza to Nyamirembe run twice a week; see *Lake Victoria Ferries* for details. Getting to Nyamirembe by road is only feasible with your own 4x4. There is no public transport beyond Geita. Some Arusha-based safari companies will include Rubondo in a safari itinerary.

At Nyamirembe, you will have to organise a boat across to the island. The best place to do this is at the Fishery Department. The ride across takes about two hours.

If you are using the ferries, you will spend four nights in the area. There are guest houses in Nyamirembe, so you could spend a

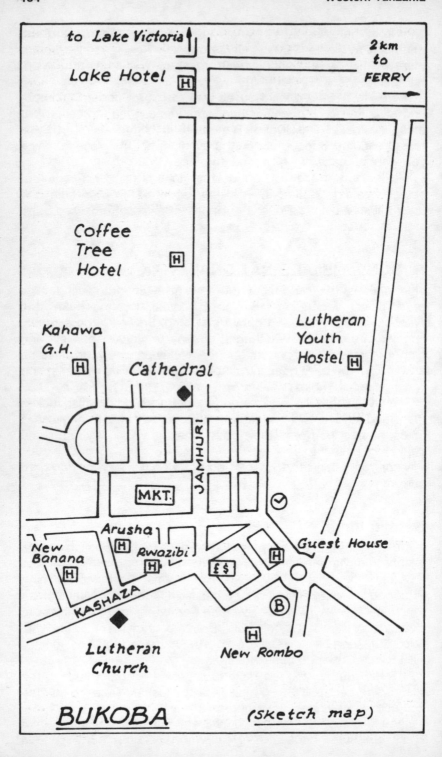

to Lake Victoria

2 km
to
FERRY

Lake Hotel   H

Coffee
Tree
Hotel   H

Kahawa
G.H.   H

Cathedral   ◆

Lutheran
Youth
Hostel   H

JAMHURI

MKT.

Arusha   H
Rwazibi   H
New
Banana   H

Guest House

£$ H

KASHAZA   ◆

B

New Rombo   H

Lutheran
Church

BUKOBA   (sketch map)

couple of nights there to save on park fees. Exploring the roads around Nyamirembe could well pay dividends. The port borders Biharamulo Game Reserve, which provides sanctuary for 30 large mammal species including elephant, zebra, buffalo and hippopotamus. Biharamulo is the northern extreme of the miombo woodland belt. Two antelope species — roan and common reedbuck — also reach the northernmost extent of their range there.

Where to stay
The basic camp on the island has bandas and a campsite. Both cost $10 per person. All food should be brought from Mwanza.

BUKOBA
This quiet, attractive port is situated on green hills which roll down to the Lake Victoria shore. It is the centre of a thriving coffee industry, but otherwise has a distinct air of decline. There are a number of impressive Indian-style buildings in the town centre, but most are in poor condition. Bukoba is said to have been founded by the Emin Pasha in 1890.

There is no sightseeing in Bukoba, but it is an agreeable place. We arrived after two-months in Uganda, and enjoyed the town simply for the relaxed air that is so typical of Tanzania. To wander around a town and not have *Mzungu!* yelled at us from every direction was indescribably pleasant.

If you have time to kill, take a walk along the marshy area between the town and the lake. A surprisingly large variety of water birds can be seen.

Getting there and away
Travellers who visit Bukoba generally do so on their way to or from Uganda. Details of this route are in Chapter Three. Details of ferries between Bukoba and Mwanza are given under *Lake Victoria Ferries* in this chapter. Occasional buses connect Bukoba to Mwanza and Kigoma. Personally, I think you would be crazy to contemplate using them.

Where to stay
Moderate
Lake Hotel This faded colonial hotel is the best value in its range. Its balcony overlooks the lake, and it has a restaurant and bar. $2.50/3.75 single/double or $4 s/c double. Rooms in the annexe cost $9/10 s/c double/suite. I have heard you can camp in the grounds

for a negotiable fee.

Coffee Tree Inn   This is not as pleasant as the Lake Hotel. It has a
restaurant and bar. $2.50/3.75 single/double.

New Banana Hotel   This is the best hotel in the town centre, with
efficient staff, comfortable rooms and a good restaurant. $4/5 s/c
single/double.

Kwa Bizi Hotel   This is friendly, clean and convenient, but the
rooms are cramped and the restaurant had no food when we were
there. $4.25 s/c double.

Budget
Bukoba's guest houses are decidedly grotty. I can recommend the
Kahawa Guest House and its adjoining annexe; both are well above
average and cost $1.50/2.00 single/double, or $3.25 s/c double. A
dormitory bed at the **Lutheran Church Hostel** costs $1.

LAKE TANGANYIKA

Africa's deepest and second-largest lake is 675km long, an average
of 50km wide, over 1,400m deep, and holds a volume of water seven
times greater than that of Lake Victoria. It follows the western arm of
the rift valley and is very attractive, with green, hilly shores and
crystal clear water.

   Due to its age and isolation, Lake Tanganyika is one of the richest
aqueous habitats in the world. It supports at least 250 fish species,
of which 200 are cichlids, most of them endemic. The most important
fish economically is the *dagaa*, a plankton-eater which lives in large
shoals. It is sun-dried on the lake shore for sale throughout western
Tanzania.

Lake Tanganyika Ferries

The legendary *MV Liemba*, originally called the *Graf Van Goetzen*,
was transported to Kigoma by rail and assembled during World War
One. Before its maiden voyage, the Germans sank it to prevent it
from falling into British hands. The boat was salvaged and re-named
in 1924 and has steamed up and down the lake almost continually
since then. The oft-repeated story that *Liemba* was used in the
filming of *The African Queen* is to the best of my knowledge a myth.

   Liemba does a round trip every week between Kigoma, Bujumbura
(Burundi) and Mpulungu (Zambia). It departs from Kigoma at 4.00pm

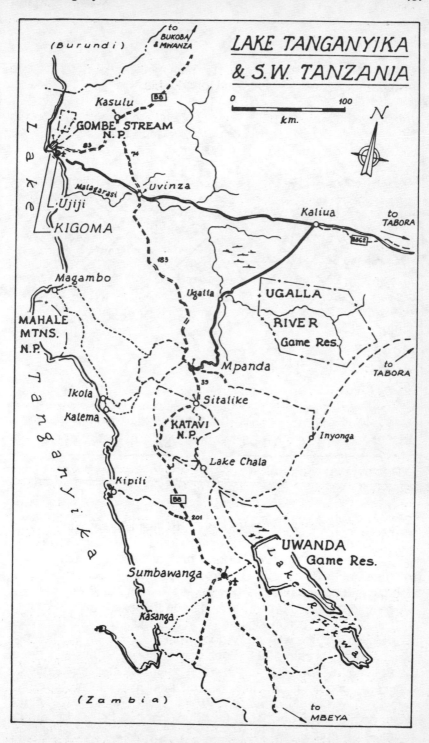

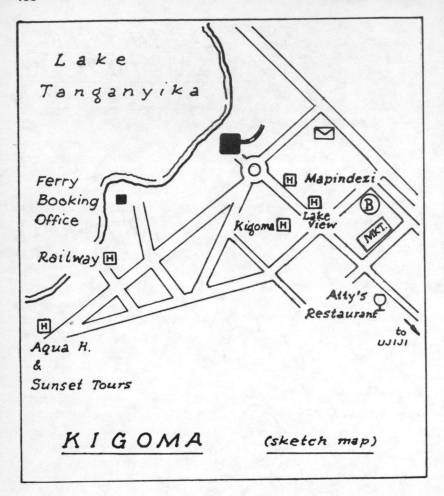

Lake
Tanganyika

Ferry
Booking
Office

Railway [H]

[H] Mapindezi
[H]
Lake
Kigoma [H] View
(B)
MKT.

[H]

Ally's
Restaurant

to
UJIJI

Aqua H.
&
Sunset Tours

KIGOMA   (sketch map)

Wednesday and arrives in Mpulungu at 10.00am Friday. It then turns
back at 4.00pm Friday and arrives in Kigoma at 10.00am Sunday. It
leaves Kigoma at 4.00pm Sunday and arrives in Bujumbura at
10.00am Monday. The return trip from Bujumbura departs at 4.00pm
Monday and arrives back in Kigoma at 10.00am Tuesday.

A second boat, *MV Umoja*, operates on the lake within Tanzania.
Both times I have been in Kigoma (1988 and 1992) only one boat was
in operation. *Liemba* was in dry-dock when I last visited, and is likely
to remain so until early 1994. When only one boat is running, it does
the Bujumbura-Mpulungu run and the other service is suspended.

Tickets bought in Tanzania can be paid for in local currency.
Kigoma to Mpulungu costs $22.50 first class and $18.25 second
class. Both classes consist of four-bunk cabins. Tickets bought in
Zambia or Burundi must be paid for in US dollars and cost double

what they would in Tanzania. Both boats have a restaurant. Meals cost $1.25. A bar serves beer and sodas.

The ferry stops at lake-shore villages such as Mugambo, Ikola, Kalema and Kasanga. If you don't want to go into Zambia, Kasanga is the place to get off. There is road transport from Kasanga to Sumbawanga and on to Mbeya. The ferry arrives at Kasanga in the early morning, so there is plenty of time to find a lift.

There is nowhere for ships to dock at these villages. When the ferry arrives it is greeted by a floating market selling dried fish and other foodstuffs, while passengers are ferried to and from the shore on rickety fishing boats. Viewed from the upper decks this is richly comic; if you are embarking or disembarking it is a nightmare. The hold seethes with passengers climbing over each other to get in and out; the ticket officer frantically tries to identify and extract a fare from the newcomers; at the exit, the smaller boats ram each other trying to get the best position.

If you have the inclination to explore Lake Tanganyika slowly, small boats do run between minor ports. I cannot vouch for their regularity or reliability. Most settlements along the lake shore have no formal accommodation, so you are advised to carry a tent.

KIGOMA

Kigoma, the largest town on Lake Tanganyika, was founded in 1915 when the railway line reached the lake. Kigoma is an easy-going and cosmopolitan town, built around a mango tree-lined avenue that climbs uphill from the lake. When I last visited Kigoma it was crawling with overland trucks, travellers and African businessmen, all waiting for transport connections.

Getting there and away

The only realistic ways to get to Kigoma are by air, rail or water. You could come by road from Mwanza, but you would measure the journey in days. For details of rail services, see *Rail* in Chapter Three. Details of the lake ferry are given above. Air Tanzania flies from Dar es Salaam to Kigoma once a week.

Where to stay

There are two tourist hotels in Kigoma, both on the lake shore 10 minute's walk from the town centre. The newer **Aqua Hotel** has comfortable rooms and good facilities, and costs $18.75/22.50 s/c single/double. I prefer the older, cheaper and cosier **Railway Hotel**, which costs $10/13 s/c single/double. Two hotels in the town centre are geared to travellers. The friendly **Lakeview Hotel** has clean, comfortable rooms with mosquito nets for $2.00/2.50 single/double. The similarly-priced **Kigoma Hotel** is scruffier, but just as friendly. There are several guest houses on the main road towards Ujiji.

Where to eat

The best place to eat is **Ally's**, where a remarkable variety of meals are served, all for less than $1. Ally's has an amazing snack menu: fresh bread and pastries, pizzas, samosas etc. The **Lakeview and Kigoma Hotels** have fair restaurants. The **Railway Hotel** is more expensive, but the food is good.

UJIJI

Most people who pass through Kigoma make a trip to Ujiji, 10km away. Said to be one of Africa's oldest market villages — whatever that means — Ujiji was a 19th-Century Arab trading post, and still shows Swahili influences you would not expect in this part of the country. Stanley and Livingstone met in Ujiji in 1872; it is where the famous phrase 'Doctor Livingstone, I presume?' was first uttered. A plaque marks where the meeting took place; the adjoining museum displays some inept and absurdly-captioned paintings of Livingstone.

People who visit Ujiji expecting it to be a thriving, vibrant market town are invariably disappointed. These days it is no more than a large fishing village. It is quite interesting to watch the fishermen and boat builders practise their trades.

There is regular transport between Ujiji and Kigoma. Should you want to overnight in Ujiji, there is a basic guest house.

GOMBE STREAM NATIONAL PARK

Gombe Stream is renowned for its chimpanzees and the research done into their behaviour by Jane Goodall. It was gazetted as a game reserve in 1943 and made a national park in 1968. Goodall arrived there in 1960 sponsored by Louis Leakey, who felt her lack of scientific training would allow her to observe chimpanzee behaviour without preconceptions. After initial difficulties trying to locate them, Goodall overcame the chimps' shyness through the combination of a banana-feeding machine and sheer persistence.

Since the late 1960s Goodall's work has achieved both popular and scientific recognition. Her painstaking studies of individual chimps and the day-to-day social behaviour of troops has been supplemented by a series of observations confronting conventional scientific wisdom. Observations which initially caused controversy —

tool-making, inter-troop warfare and even cannibalism — have since been confirmed and accepted. Much of Goodall's work is described in her books *In the Shadow of Man* and *Through a Window*. The study of Gombe's chimpanzees is now the longest-running study of an individual wild animal population in the world.

Gombe Stream supports a significant baboon population, the subject of research since 1967. Other common primates are vervet, blue, redtail and red colobus monkeys. Most other mammals found there are secretive or nocturnal, so are rarely seen by visitors. Over 200 bird species have been recorded.

To see the chimpanzees you will need to go on a guided walk. They are most frequently observed at a feeding station near the main camp. If they are not there, you will have to go deeper into the forest. The only part of the park where you may walk unguided is along the lake shore. The forest reaches down to the beach, so you should see plenty of birds, butterflies and primates in this area, especially towards dusk when many nocturnal animals come to drink at the lake.

Because they are genetically similar to humans, chimpanzees are susceptible to the same diseases. If you are unwell, do not visit the park. Even a cold has the potential to kill chimpanzees who may not have your immunity.

Gombe is popular and its capacity is limited. Park fees are regularly increased, presumably whenever numbers threaten to become unmanageable. At present the entrance fee is $50 per 24-hour period, and a further $30 to stay overnight. Fees must be paid in hard currency, and are likely to have increased by the time you read this. Before you head off to the park, check up-to-date fees at the Railway Hotel.

A 72-page booklet, *Gombe Stream National Park*, is the most comprehensive in the series published by Tanzania National Parks. It's an essential purchase if you plan you visit the park, and includes checklists and detailed coverage of chimpanzee behaviour. It may be difficult to buy a copy outside of Arusha.

Getting there and away

Gombe Stream is 16km from Kigoma and can be reached by lake-taxi. These are uncovered and can become uncomfortably hot in the sun. If you have an umbrella, take it along. Lake-taxis leave from a village 3km from Kigoma at roughly 11.00am. They take four hours to get to Gombe, and cost $2. From Kigoma, you can hire a taxi to take you to the village from which the lake-taxis leave. Lake-taxis returning to Kigoma pass Gombe Stream at around 5.45am.

Sunset Tours (next to the Aqua Hotel) can organise day trips to

Gombe on a private boat. The use of a boat for a day costs $120. For a group of three or more, this is worth thinking about, bearing in mind it will save you paying the overnight fee charged at Gombe.

Where to stay

The camp is not far from the lake shore. Accommodation is in bandas, and there is a communal kitchen. The camp is plagued by baboons, which are likely to attack you if you carry food openly between your banda and the kitchen. You can pitch a tent on the lake shore. Again, baboons are a problem. They may knock down your tent if there is fruit in it. All food must be brought from Kigoma. Avoid bringing fruit.

MAHALE MOUNTAINS NATIONAL PARK

Mahale Mountains was gazetted in 1985 to protect a 1,613km^2 knuckle of land jutting into Lake Tanganyika. The Mahale range, the highest peak of which, Nkungwe, rises to 2,462m, is the park's dominant physical feature. The lake shore west of the mountains is very scenic. The western foothills receive an annual rainfall of 2,000mm, and are covered in lush lowland forest. The drier eastern slopes are covered in miombo woodland. At altitudes above 2,000m there is both bamboo and montane forest.

Over 700 chimpanzees live in Mahale's lowland forest. A group of 100 has been habituated and studied by Japanese researchers since 1961.

Other lowland forest species found at Mahale are similar to those found at Gombe, with the addition of typical west African species such as brush-tailed porcupine and giant forest squirrel. An endemic black-and-white colobus subspecies is found in the park's montane forests. The eastern slopes of Mahale support woodland species: elephant, lion, roan antelope, buffalo and giraffe. These often stray into the forest; lions have killed several chimps, and African hunting dogs have been seen on the beach.

Chimps are less readily seen than at Gombe Stream, but most people feel that Mahale's scenery and wilderness atmosphere make up for this. It is also a lot cheaper to visit than Gombe. All game viewing is on foot, but you may not walk without a guide. Guides can be organised when you arrive at Kasiha. If you want to hike into the mountains or to climb Nkungwe peak, arrangements should be made in advance.

An entrance fee of $15 per 24-hour period must be paid in hard currency. It is not recommended that you visit the park during the rainy season (November to April). Much of the information in the

National Parks booklet *Gombe Stream National Park* will be useful to visitors to Mahale.

Getting there and away

One of the attractions of Mahale is its remoteness. It can only be reached by plane or boat. Any tour operator in Arusha or Dar es Salaam will be able to organise a chartered plane. It is possible to charter a boat from Kigoma to Mahale. Contact Sunset Tours in Kigoma. A three-day trip will cost around $800.

The only way for budget travellers to get to and from Mahale is on the Lake Tanganyika ferry. This stops at Mugambo, the village 15km north of the park boundary, seven hours after it leaves Kigoma. On the return trip, the ferry stops at Mugambo at 4.00am and arrives at Kigoma seven hours later.

From Mugambo, most people hire a private boat to the headquarters at Kasiha. We did, however, receive a letter from someone who walked the 15km to the boundary. He says you are unlikely to get lost as the mountains are in front of you the whole way and the path is flat. You will pass through several villages, where you must exchange greetings with the village chairman, who can usually be found at the school. Unfortunately, he did not say what he did once he got to the boundary. It is another 15km from there to Kasiha.

Where to stay

There is a guest house and campsite at Kasiha. Both cost $10 per person. Bring all the food you need from Kigoma. There is also a privately-run luxury tented camp in the park, which can be booked through Ngare Sero (PO Box 425 Arusha Tel: (057) 3629 Fax: (057) 2123). It is open between May and October.

SOUTHWEST TANZANIA

This section follows the little-used B8 from northwestern Tanzania to the southern town of Mbeya. The B8 passes through Katavi National Park and the towns of Mpanda and Sumbawanga.

MPANDA

This small town is the terminus of the southern branch of the central railway line. It is unremarkable but, presumably because so few tourists pass through, people are helpful and friendly.

Getting there and away

The obvious way to get to Mpanda is by rail. Three trains run weekly between Mpanda and Tabora; see *Rail* in Chapter Three. The odd truck uses the road connecting Kigoma and Mpanda.

A more interesting but less reliable way to reach Mpanda is via Ikola or Kalema. The Lake Tanganyika ferry passes both villages in the mid-morning. There is no regular transport on to Mpanda and nowhere to stay in either village. Carry a tent. Except after rain when the road becomes impassable, a truck runs between Ikola and Mpanda most days. The trip takes five hours.

Where to stay/eat

City Guest House, on the Sumbawanga road, is convenient, clean and friendly. It has a restaurant and bar. Rooms cost $1.25. Most truckies use this guest house, so it's a good place to ask around for lifts to Katavi. We stayed at the **Stima Guest House** in the town centre, which is also basic but fine. Rooms cost $1.00/1.30 single/double. There are other guest houses around the market.

Katavi National Park

In *Ivory Knights*, Nicholas Gordon describes Katavi as 'isolated and unloved, and in need of support'. He does not exaggerate — when we arrived in November 1992 we were only the 18th party of tourists to visit it in over two years, and the first to arrive without a vehicle. Katavi may be Tanzania's most obscure national park, but it offers excellent game viewing and has a real wilderness atmosphere. It is also surprisingly easy to visit independently.

The dominant vegetation type is miombo woodland, broken by the grassy Katavi flood plain and palm-fringed Lake Chala in the south. Most large African mammals are present, including significant populations of elephant (over 4,000), hippopotamus and buffalo, predators such as lion, leopard and spotted hyena, and herbivores such as sable and roan antelope, zebra, giraffe, eland and waterbuck. Over 400 bird species have been recorded.

If you arrive without your own vehicle, a park vehicle can run you from the entrance gate to a cement hut overlooking Katavi flood plain. Game viewing from the hut is fantastic: we saw more than 100 hippo grazing one evening, and herds of 200 buffalo and 50 elephant. There is a good chance of spotting predators as they cross the plain. If you take an armed ranger to stay with you, you can walk onto the plain — an invigorating experience.

There is a fair road network in Katavi. If you have a vehicle, the

Lake Chala region is rewarding. A detailed map is pinned up in the ranger's office. Plenty of game can be seen from the Mpanda-Sumbawanga road which bisects the park. No fee is charged for just passing through.

An entrance fee of $15 per 24-hours must be paid in hard currency, as must a camping/hut fee of $10 per person. A park vehicle costs $0.50/km (about $20 to the flood plain and back). An armed ranger costs $10/day. A two-night stay cost us $70 each, all-inclusive.

Getting there and away

There is said to be the odd bus between Mpanda and Sumbawanga, but you will probably have to rely on lifts with trucks, for which you should expect to pay. Ask at the City Guest House or Agip Garage in Mpanda. The entrance gate is just off the main road, 1km south of Sitalike village. Sitalike is 35km from Mpanda and 200km from Sumbawanga.

Heading south from Katavi may involve a long wait at Sitalike. By the time you get there from the hut at Katavi, most traffic to Sumbawanga will have already come past. There is nowhere to stay at Sitalike, so if nothing comes towards mid-afternoon try to get back to Mpanda. If you got stuck, you could probably camp at the entrance gate and try again the next morning.

If you are heading to Katavi in your own vehicle, make sure you have enough petrol. There is nowhere to fill up between Mpanda and Sumbawanga.

No tour operators yet run regular trips to Katavi, but a recent (July 1993) letter from a friend in Kigoma suggests this is likely to change in the near future. I don't have details, but it's reasonable to assume these will be fly-in packages tied in with visits to Mahale. Ngare Sero in Arusha do bookings for the private camp in Mahale and should be familiar with the latest developments (PO Box 425 Arusha Tel: (057) 3629 Fax: (057) 2123).

Where to stay

The only accommodation is in an unfurnished two-room concrete hut overlooking Katavi flood plain 15km from the entrance gate. Bring your own sleeping bag. Firewood is available, but drinking water must be brought from a spring near the entrance gate. The rangers will fill up a jerry-can on request. Bring all provisions from Mpanda or Sumbawanga.

You may camp at a number of places in the park. The best site is at Lake Chala. Campsites are basic, with firewood but no drinking water.

UWANDA GAME RESERVE/LAKE RUKWA

Uwanda lies 20km southeast of Katavi. Together, they make for one of the most alluring wilderness destinations in East Africa. Uwanda's dominant feature is Lake Rukwa, a shallow alkaline lake with an extensive floodplain which attracts large ungulate herds after the November rains.

Rukwa is subject to seasonal fluctuations. Often it is split into two expanses of open water separated by a marsh. Mammals found are similar to those in Katavi, but one antelope species, the localised puku, is rarely seen anywhere but Uwanda. Rukwa is notable for albino giraffes, unusually-striped zebra, and a high crocodile density. Over 400 bird species have been recorded.

It is only feasible to visit Uwanda in your own vehicle. You must carry adequate spares, fuel, food, water, and camping equipment. Roads are rough and may become impassable after rain. The safest time to visit is between March and October, but there is more game in the wet months. Rukwa can be approached from either Mbeya, Sumbawanga or Katavi.

Sumbawanga

Due to its name, which sounds like the chorus for a Hollywood musical about Africa, I approached Sumbawanga with some curiosity. Sadly, it turned out to be a dusty, unloveable place. You will probably only want to spend a night before you move on.

Getting there and away

There is a fair amount of traffic from Mpanda, but what you get is pot luck. Fate dealt us a truck filled a metre deep with timber, which exaggerated the roughness of the road — as did the absence of suspension. Be very, very kind to fate the day before you head out this way.

There are several buses every morning between Sumbawanga and Mbeya. In both directions they leave at 7.00am. Book a seat in advance. It is an eight-hour trip on a fair road which passes through Tundumu.

If you are heading to Kasanga on Lake Tanganyika, there are a couple of buses a week. If you ask at the market before midday, you should find a pick-up truck heading that way.

Where to stay/eat

The only proper hotel is the **Upenda View Inn**, a pleasant place with newly-furnished rooms, a good restaurant and a bar and garden. When we visited, the staff were irritatingly dopey, but this could easily change. $8.25 s/c double.

There is no shortage of guest houses, and most look perfectly adequate. Two of the best are the **Kisumu and New Nakuru Guest Houses**, opposite each other about 50m from the bus station ($1.50/1.75 single/double and $2.00/2.50 s/c single/double).

The food at the Upenda View is good and not prohibitively expensive, but there are plenty of cheaper *hotelis* around if you prefer.

Excursions

Between Sumbawanga and Lake Rukwa lie the Mbizi Mountains. The little I know about this range whet my appetite, but we didn't have time to explore. According to a ranger at Katavi, you can get from Sumbawanga to the village of Kijiji on the back of a pick-up truck and from there walk to another village called Mpondo, where there are spectacular views over Lake Rukwa. The implication was that this could be done as a day trip, but I wouldn't bank on it. Take a tent.

Maps of the area suggest a road continues on to Rukwa, passing through patches of forest on the way. My feeling is that if you have the appropriate maps and equipment the area could be well worth exploring on foot, but I would suggest you get permission from the district headquarters in Sumbawanga before you attempt it.

SOUTHERN
HIGHLANDS
and
LAKE NYASA

Chapter Ten

The southern highlands and Lake Nyasa

INTRODUCTION

This chapter covers an area bounded by the Tanzam Highway to the west, Songea to the east, Makambako to the north, and Zambia and Malawi to the south. Southern Tanzania is easy to get around and exceptionally pretty, a combination which should make it particularly attractive to budget travellers. Despite this, the only tourists it sees are overlanders dashing between Dar es Salaam and Malawi. At the turn-off to the Malawi border near Kyela, we were virtually forced off the bus: no-one could believe tourists wanted to continue to the Tanzanian part of Lake Nyasa!

The principal town is Mbeya. Other major towns include Tukuyu, Songea, Njombe and Kyela. The most significant physical features are Lake Nyasa and the mountains either side of the lake. The Poroto and Kipengere ranges lie north and east of Nyasa; the Livingstone Mountains rise dramatically to its immediate west.

Climate

With altitudes ranging from under 500m to over 2,500m this region has a varied climate. Lake Nyasa (478m) is hot and humid, but the rest of the region is temperate. A sweater will come in useful at night. Tukuyu has the highest rainfall in Tanzania, and is best visited during the dry season between May and October.

Getting around

Mbeya, the main gateway to the region, can be approached by rail or road from Dar es Salaam or by road from western Tanzania. See *Mbeya* for details. Songea can be approached from Mtwara on the south coast, on a road passing through some very wild and spectacular scenery.

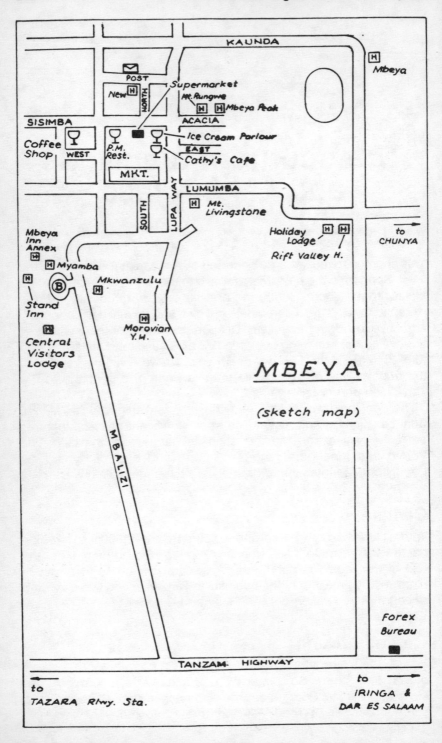

MBEYA

(sketch map)

Within the region there is plenty of transport along the Mbeya-Kyela road, the Songea-Makumbako road and the Tanzam Highway. Two ferries a week run between Itungi and Mbamba Bay on Lake Nyasa. Transport on side roads is less erratic than in most parts of the country.

MBEYA

Mbeya was established in 1927 to service the Lupa gold fields near Chunya, which closed in the 1950s. Surrounded by rich agricultural lands and in a strategic position along the Tanzam Highway and Tazara Railway, Mbeya has continued to prosper.

Mbeya is an appealing town. Its skyline is dominated by the impressive — and climbable — Mbeya range. It has an unusually westernised, bustling feel and shows few of the signs of neglect that characterise most Tanzanian towns. Mbeya is mainly used by travellers as a stop-off point on the way to Zambia or Malawi, but it is a good base for exploring the southern highlands.

Getting there and away

Most people travel between Mbeya and Dar es Salaam by rail. There are five trains a week on the Tazara line; see *Rail* in Chapter Three for details. There are regular buses between Dar es Salaam and Mbeya. This 893km trip takes around 20 hours. Overnight buses on this route have a bad reputation for theft; it is advisable to split the trip at, for instance, Iringa.

From Arusha or Moshi, you can either go via Chalinze/Dar es Salaam or Dodoma. For reasons discussed elsewhere, the Dodoma route is not recommended.

From western Tanzania, the most comfortable option is to get to Dar es Salaam by train and proceed to Mbeya from there. A more adventurous route goes via Mpanda and Sumbawanga; see Chapter Nine. There are two buses a week along the little-used Tabora-Mbeya road, passing through one of the most remote parts of Tanzania. They take at least 20 hours.

Buses to local destinations such as Kyela, Tukuyu, Njombe and Tundumu leave regularly on a fill-up-and-go basis. Buses to more distant destinations should be booked in advance.

Where to stay

There is plenty of accommodation in Mbeya, but places tend to fill up early. Almost everywhere we looked at was clean and good value.

UPPER RANGE

In addition to the hotels listed below, a tourist hotel was being built opposite the post office when we were in town. It should be functional in 1994.

Mbeya Peak Hotel   (Tel: (065) 3471). The most central and popular hotel in its range, this has a pleasant, busy bar and a fair restaurant. $9.50 s/c double.

Rift Valley Hotel   (Tel: (065) 3756). This is similar in price and quality to Mbeya Peak. It has the best restaurant in Mbeya. $8/10 s/c single/double.

Mount Livingstone Hotel   (Tel: (065) 3331). Except for price, there is little to choose between this and the above hotels. $40/60 HC s/c single/double, or $12/20 for residents.

MODERATE

Mbeya Hotel   (Tel: (065) 2504). Presumably because it has no restaurant and is a bit run-down, this TRC-run hotel was empty when we stayed at it. It is a good place to head for if you arrive late in the day. Rooms are spacious and reasonable value. $4.75/7.25 s/c single/double. Rooms using communal baths are cheaper.

Holiday Lodge   (Tel: (065) 2821/3375). This is the best value in its range, but it fills up early. Rooms are clean and large, but spartanly furnished. The restaurant is good value. $6.25 s/c double.

Central Visitors Lodge   (Tel: (065) 2507). This conspicuous brown-and-blue double-storey building behind the bus station seems good value. $3.75 s/c single (with double bed).

BUDGET

Two places stand out in this range. The **Moravian Youth Centre Hostel**, a couple of minutes walk out of town, is clean, secure and popular with travellers ($2 double). Even better is the cosy and friendly **Mount Rungwe Guest House**, next to the Mbeya Peak Hotel. There are wash basins in the rooms and the communal showers have hot water ($1.75/2.00 single/double). There are also several clean, cheap guest houses behind the bus station. Try the **Mbeya Inn Annexe Guest House** ($1.75/2.50 single/double) or the similar **Myambo and Stand Guest Houses**.

Where to Eat

Cathy's Cafe near the market serves dishes such as whole fried tilapia & chips for around $1. It is only open for lunch. The **ice cream parlour** alongside it is worth a try. The restaurant at the **Holiday Lodge** is outstanding; a tasty chicken stew cost us $1.50.

Going up in price, there is nothing wrong with the restaurants at any of the upper range hotels. The **Rift Valley Hotel**, however, is special, with a varied menu, world-class food, enormous helpings, and good service. Main courses cost around $4.

Useful Information

Foreign Exchange When we were there, the only forex bureau was Ndigo's, 2km out of town on the Dar es Salaam road. It is likely there will be a forex bureau in the town centre by the time you read this.

Tazara Railway Station This is a few kilometres from Mbeya on the Tanzam highway towards Zambia. The booking office is at the station. Your best bet is to either get a taxi or take a bus towards the Zambian border and ask to be dropped off.

Shopping Mbeya is the place in which to stock up if you are planning a few days hiking or camping in the surrounding area. The supermarkets on Market Square sell a fair variety of imported goods. Fruit and vegetables are best bought at the market. Plenty of small *dukas* surround the market.

Excursions

Chunya

This intriguing small town, 70km north of Mbeya, was the centre of the 1920s/1930s gold rush. Mining stopped in the 1950s when it ceased to be profitable. Chunya then enjoyed a short-lived tobacco boom before degenerating into something approaching a ghost town. Many of the grander buildings are now boarded up and there is a general air of faded prosperity. You can still see local prospectors panning the river which runs through the town. There is talk of working the gold again using modern methods.

A few pick-up trucks, leaving from near the Mbeya Peak Hotel, ply the scenic road from Mbeya to Chunya every day. You can normally get to Chunya and back in a day, but there are two guest houses there: the Moonlight and Night Queen.

World's End Viewpoint, just off the Chunya road 21km from Mbeya, offers excellent views across the Rift Valley escarpment to the Usunga Flats.

If you have your own vehicle, it is possible to continue past Chunya to Lake Rukwa (see Chapter Nine).

Mbeya Range

The mountains which tower over Mbeya are of less biological interest than the more extensive ranges covered later in the chapter, but there are good views over the Rukwa region from the peaks and wild flowers are abundant in the wet season. The most accessible peak, Kaluwe (2,656m), can be climbed in a few hours from Mbeya by following a path which starts behind the hospital.

The highest point in the range is Mbeya peak (2,834m). This is most easily climbed from Luiji, a village about 20km from Mbeya town. The climb takes six hours and is steep in parts, so it should only be attempted if you are reasonably fit. To get to Luiji, ask any bus heading south from Mbeya to drop you at the turn-off near Mbalizi. It is 9km from Mbalizi to Luiji. I am not aware of any public transport, so expect to walk.

The only accommodation in Luiji is at Utengule Country Resort, built on a coffee farm ($20 s/c double). A cheaper campsite should be operating at the resort by the time you read this.

If you want to do a longer hike in the area, you can cross from Mbeya Peak to Pungulume (2,230m) at the western extreme of the range. Utengule Country Resort can give you details.

Mbozi Meteorite

This 15-ton meteorite, discovered in 1942, is believed to be the third-largest in the world. It lies 10km off the Tanzam Highway southwest of Mbeya. The turn-off is signposted. It is difficult to get to without transport.

TUKUYU

Tukuyu is a shapeless small town salvaged from anonymity by having one of the most appealing settings in Tanzania. It is ringed by the Poroto Mountains and lies at the base of Mount Rungwe, a dormant volcano which at 2,957m is the second-highest point in the southern highlands. Tukuyu is the obvious base for exploring the Poroto, a range dotted with waterfalls, crater lakes, and patches of forest — all capped by stirring views to Lake Nyasa more than 1,000m below.

The area between Tukuyu and Nyasa is home to the Nyakyusa people, whose neatly painted homes were described by the explorer Joseph Thomson as 'perfect arcadia'. It is a fertile region, with rich volcanic soils and an annual rainfall of over 1,500mm. The dirt roads that criss-cross the area are lined with small subsistence farms growing bananas, mangos, tea and coffee.

Tukuyu was founded as a German administration centre in the late 19th Century, and originally called Nieu Langenberg. The old Langenberg, on Lake Nyasa near Ikombe, was abandoned due to the high incidence of malaria and is now a mission.

If you plan on hiking, the area is best between May and October. At other times there is rain most afternoons. Tukuyu is cold at night.

Getting there and away

Tukuyu is on the tarred Mbeya-Kyela road. Regular buses run in both directions on a fill-up-and-go basis.

Where to stay/eat

The **Langiboss Hotel** is all a traveller could wish for. Rooms are clean and comfortable, the manager speaks English and is well-informed about hikes in the area, and there are even hot showers. It is 1km out of town and has a marvellous view of Mount Rungwe. There is a bar and restaurant (meals must be ordered in advance). If you are hiking, you can leave excess gear at the hotel. $1.50/2.00 single/double. If it is full there are plenty of scruffy guest houses dotted around the town.

There is a campsite on the grounds of the **Pentecostal Holiness Association Mission**, the turn-off to which is signposted 10km from Tukuyu on the Mbeya road. The priest in charge is helpful and knows the surrounding area well. It is a half-hour walk from the turn-off to the mission.

Excursions

This area is ideal for casual rambling. Wander along any of its winding dirt roads and you will be rewarded with lovely views and scenery, varied bird life and vegetation, and regular glimpses into rural African life. Even on by-roads there is a fair amount of traffic (expect to pay for lifts, though), so exploring the area over a few days from one base is possible.

The following are some of the more accessible spots, most of which are easily visited as a day trip from Tukuyu. With time, initiative and

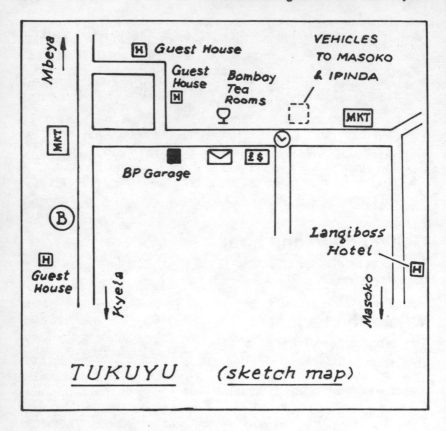

TUKUYU   (sketch map)

some 1:50,000 maps from the Department of Lands and Surveys in Dar es Salaam, you can explore further.

Ngozi Crater Lake The most spectacular crater lake in the Poroto mountains is over 2km long and circled by 200m-high cliffs. To get to the rim you walk up the forested southeastern slopes, rich in plant and bird life. Ngozi is attributed with magical powers locally. A faded signpost marks the turn-off to Ngozi a few kilometres from Isongole village. From there a driveable dirt track continues for 5km before it reaches the footpath to the rim. From Isongole, the trip takes two to three hours each way by foot. It is advisable to organise a guide; the path is not always clear, particularly during the rainy season.

Kiwira Natural Bridge A natural rock bridge, formed 400 years ago by water-cooled lava from Mount Rungwe, spans the Kiwira River further along the same road as the Pentecostal Holiness Association Mission (see *Where to stay*). To walk there from the mission takes a couple of hours. Trucks run most days from the main road to an

army base near the bridge, and may give tourists a lift. Ask for
details at the mission.

Mount Rungwe   If you are reasonably fit, Rungwe can be climbed
and descended in about 10 hours. Alternatively, if you have a tent
and are adequately prepared, you could spend a couple of days
exploring the slopes. The most popular route starts at Isongole,
bypasses Shiwaga Crater, then takes you through extensive patches
of forest. A 1:50,000 map of Rungwe is available from the
Department of Lands and Surveys in Dar es Salaam.

Masoko Crater Lake   This pretty spot was once the German's
regional headquarters (the old boma is now a courthouse). At the
end of World War One, retreating German forces are rumoured to
have dumped a fortune in gold bars, money and military vehicles
into the lake. As Masoko is said to be 3km deep, it's not surprising
that — except for the odd coin — no trace of the fortune has ever
been found. Masoko is 15km from Tukuyu on the Ipinda/Matema
road. A fair amount of traffic goes this way (mainly overcrowded
pick-up trucks), leaving Tukuyu from near the clock tower. You may
prefer to walk: it's a pretty road, gently downhill most of the way, and
there are some wonderful views of Lake Nyasa. If you leave Tukuyu
early, you should get a lift back easily enough.

Kapalogwe Falls   The main attraction of this waterfall is that you
can wade through the river to a large cave behind it. Without a
vehicle, it's a bit far from the main road to make for a viable day trip
(12-15km each way). The turn-off is 10km from Tukuyu on the Kyela
road.

Hiking in the Tukuyu area

The Poroto Mountains extend westwards into the Kipengere Range
almost as far as Njombe, creating an extensive highland area with
a number of possible access points. I have not heard of anyone who
has attempted to hike in this area, but there are some interesting
possibilities.

   The foremost of these is the Kitulo Plateau connecting the two
ranges, on which lie the highest peak in the southern highlands,
Mtorwi (2,961m), and the 2,929m Chaluhangi Dome. The plateau is
noted for the wild flowers which blanket it after the November rains,
and the pastoral Nji people who inhabit it. If you have a vehicle, the
approach from Chimala on the Tanzam Highway climbs a
succession of dizzying hairpin bends and is said to be very
dramatic. There is little in the way of public transport in the region,

so access could be a problem for backpackers.

I know of people who have hiked in the Livingstone Mountains near Matema. The manager of the Langiboss Hotel in Tukuyu may be able to advise you on this.

The Department of Lands and Surveys in Dar es Salaam stocks 1:50,000 maps of the region. You would be foolish to think of hiking without them. You should carry proper equipment and be self-sufficient in terms of food. It might be an idea to speak to the police or some other authority in Tukuyu about your plans and try to get some form of written permission, just in case.

If any readers do hike in this area, I would be interested to hear about it so information can be included in the next edition.

LAKE NYASA

Broadly speaking, Lake Nyasa is the Tanzanian part of Lake Malawi (as explained on page 12, calling it Lake Malawi will not get you very far in Tanzania). Whatever you call it, it is without a doubt the most scenic of Africa's three great lakes, and although most travellers visit the Malawian part, the Tanzanian portion is equally attractive. Lake Nyasa contains 30% of the world's cichlid species. These colourful fish can easily be observed in the lake's clear water.

Lake Nyasa has a bad reputation for cerebral malaria. Take your pills and continue to take them for four weeks after you leave the area. If you show any signs of malaria, get to a doctor quickly.

Getting there and away

The gateway to Nyasa is Kyela, 10km from Itungi Port on the lake shore. Regular buses between Mbeya and Kyela take about four hours and stop at Tukuyu. The 1,000m descent from Tukuyu to Kyela is breathtaking; make sure you get a window seat. The contrast between the pleasantly cool highlands around Tukuyu and the cloying heat of the lake shore may come as something of a shock.

The Lake Nyasa Ferry

Few travellers are aware of the ferry service between Itungi Port and Mbamba Bay, the best way to see the northern part of Nyasa. The scenery is dominated by the Livingstone Mountains rising sharply on the east shore. The ferry stops at several fishing villages where the locals approach in dugouts, selling fish, fruit and other goods to passengers.

The ferry to Mbamba Bay runs twice a week. It leaves Itungi at 7.00am on Monday and Friday and arrives at Mbamba Bay at around midnight the same day. It turns around more-or-less immediately and arrives back at Itungi at 5.00pm the next day. These times are *very* approximate. The ferry stops at Lupingu, Manda, Lundu, Nindai and Liuli.

A third ferry leaves Itungi at 7.00am on Wednesday and arrives back on Thursday afternoon. This stops at most lakeside villages, including Matema, but doesn't go as far as Mbamba Bay. It is about an hour from Itungi to Matema, so you could use the ferry to get there and back if the timing was suitable.

In theory *MV Songea* does the Monday and Friday run and the smaller *MV Iringa* does the Wednesday run. We went on a Friday and *MV Iringa* was used, so this may not always be the case. Lake Malawi can get very choppy, and the smaller boat is not much fun in rough weather. *MV Songea* is said to be much smoother.

There is no accommodation in Itungi. You will have to spend the night in Kyela and get a vehicle to Itungi at around 5:30am on the morning of departure. Vehicles leave from in front of the TRC office, 1km out of town. There is a booking office at the TRC building, but as the ticket officer travels with the ferry it serves no practical function. You can buy a ticket at Itungi while you wait for the ferry to be loaded up.

There is one class, and it is not overcrowded. Tickets cost $4. Meals are available on board, as are sodas and beers.

Kyela

Kyela is not my favourite town. It is sweaty and scruffy, and has more than its fair share of people who feel an uncontrollable need to yell *Mzungu!* at any passing European. The town centre is a small grid of roads around a central market. The TRC office is 1km from the market in the same direction as Itungi.

Where to stay/eat

There are loads of indifferent guest houses in Kyela. Rooms cost under $2. If you are catching the ferry, try either the **nameless lodge opposite the TRC office** or the **New Vatican City Lodge** 300m towards town.

In the centre, the **nameless guest house opposite the Ram Hotel** is acceptable. So is **Kyombo Guest House** on the main road 200m towards Tukuyu. **Mkoko's Restaurant**, behind the market, has a shady verandah and a fridge stocked with beer and sodas.

Matema Beach

This beach on the northern tip of Lake Nyasa is rated the best anywhere on the lake. With the Livingstone Mountains rising sharply to the east and the Poroto Range on the western horizon, it is difficult to imagine a more visually attractive setting. Matema is the kind of place you could settle into for a while: swimming in the warm bilharzia-free water, taking short walks, chatting to the locals — or just waiting for the sun to set behind the Poroto.

Getting there and away

The daily bus between Mbeya and Matema passes Tukuyu, Kyela and Ipinda on the way. It arrives at Matema after dark, and leaves at 5.00am, so is not that convenient.

It is easier to get to Matema in hops. There is regular transport from Kyela to Ipinda, a large village 27km from Matema, and even the odd pick-up truck from Tukuyu (via Masoko Crater Lake). The daily bus aside, you can find private transport between Ipinda and Matema, especially on Saturdays. There is a basic but adequate guest house in Ipinda, behind the bank ($1/2 single/double). I have heard you can walk between Ipinda and Matema along a river which comes out at Lake Nyasa 3km west of the mission. I have no idea how long this would take.

The day before you plan to leave Matema, ask the mission if any of their vehicles are heading to Ipinda the next morning.

The ferry which leaves Itungi at 7.00am Wednesday arrives at Matema an hour later. It also stops at Matema on Thursday afternoon on its way back to Itungi. Ferries to Mbamba Bay *do not* stop at Matema.

Where to stay

The **Lutheran Mission Resort** on the shore has spotless *bandas* with comfortable beds and mosquito nets. A kiosk sells cold sodas and coffee/tea, and a canteen serves enormous buffet-style meals. These must be ordered in advance and cost $2.50 per head. The home-made bread served at breakfast is wonderful. Double *bandas* cost $3.50, *bandas* sleeping four cost $7. You can camp for $2.50 per tent.

Excursions

In the stifling heat of the lake shore even the shortest stroll feels like a major excursion. The time to explore is the early morning. One warning: if you head further afield, ask before you swim. There are no crocodiles at Matema, but they are common on nearby parts of the shore, where they kill villagers with a frequency that suggests caution is advisable.

There are a few local spots worth looking at. The best-known is Matema Pottery Market, held every Saturday at the village 1km east of the resort. The pots are crafted by the Kisi who live on the northwestern lake shore and are sold as far afield as Dar es Salaam. On weekdays, you could try to arrange for a fisherman to row you to the peninsula where the pottery is made.

About 500m past the village, the shore becomes rockier. This is a good place to see colourful cichlids. Crocodile are common at the river mouth 3km west of Matema and hippo have been seen a short way upriver.

Mbamba Bay

The southernmost town on the Tanzanian part of Lake Nyasa lies on a pretty coconut-lined beach. The only accommodation is the basic but friendly **New Mbamba Guest House**, where single rooms cost $1. If you are waiting for the ferry to Itungi (which can arrive at any time of night) there are palm-leaf shelters on the beach. It is said to be safe to sleep under these if you arrive late with the ferry, but we didn't try it.

Mbinga

From Mbamba Bay, a 60km dirt road winds its way up the valley wall through well-developed miombo woodland to a grassy plateau and Mbinga. This is a thrilling route, the road clinging to the mountainside and offering dramatic views back to the lake.

There is an erratic bus service along this road. If the bus doesn't show up, you will have to take what you get (a crowded pick-up in all probability). It normally takes three hours, but we did it in light rain and it took closer to seven. Most of this time we spent trudging through mud while the driver tried to free his vehicle; the rest of it we clung terrified and dripping to the sides of the overloaded vehicle while it skidded uncertainly around the precipitous road. I imagine this road is impassable after heavy rain.

Mbinga is an oasis. You can get hot tea there. Had I arrived in a more rational state, I would probably call it a typically-dull small African town, but... Whatever else, once you hit Mbinga there is plenty of transport along a well-maintained dirt road to Songea. There is even a 'Special Video Bus' to Dar es Salaam three days a week. There are a few guest houses and *hotelis* around Mbinga's bus station.

SONGEA

Songea is a large, lively town at the junction of the road to Mbamba Bay and the road connecting the Tanzam Highway to the south coast. If you arrive in Songea from the south coast or Lake Nyasa, its busy market, well-stocked supermarkets and general state of good repair are a welcome re-connection with the modern world. Until the ivory moratorium in 1989, Songea was a major centre for poachers smuggling ivory out of the Selous. This may well account for the town's comparative prosperity.

Getting there and away

A recently-built tar road connects Songea to Njombe and the Tanzam Highway. Regular buses run along it. Buses to Njombe and Mbeya go when they are full; buses to Dar es Salaam should be booked in advance.

There are buses along the wild, scenic road connecting Songea to the south coast. If you are heading this way, you may well end up spending a night in Tunduru, a one-street town about halfway between Songea and Masasi. Between 1985 and 1988, according to Nicholas Gordon's *Ivory Knights*, the streets of Tunduru were plagued by man-eating lions. Almost 50 people were killed, including the game warden sent to sort the problem out, and a further 28 wounded. The offending cats have since been shot. There are a few guest houses and *hotelis* in Tunduru.

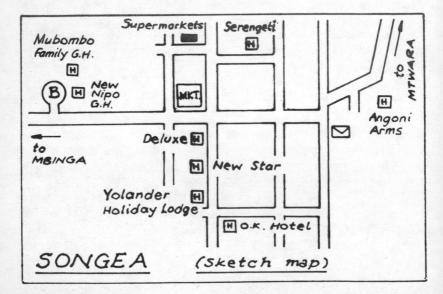

Where to stay

In the moderate range, **Hotel Angoni Arms** on the Tunduru road is idiosyncratic and likeable, but a bit run-down. The rooms are spacious, there is an attractive view from the balcony, and it has a restaurant and bar ($3 s/c double).

In the town centre, try the **OK Hotel**, which has a lively bar and the best restaurant in town, or the quieter but similarly-priced **Yulander Holiday Lodge**. They are opposite each other and both cost $5 s/c double.

As usual there are plenty of guest houses at the bus station and in the town centre. Two deserve a special mention. Rooms at the **Deluxe Guest House**, a two-storey hotel in the town centre, are clean and have mosquito nets ($1.25/1.50 single/double). Around the corner, the **New Star Guest House** is clean and friendly, and its rooms have mosquito nets ($1.50 single).

NJOMBE

There is not much of interest in this quiet, pleasantly-situated small town. If you have a spare afternoon it could be a pretty area in which to do some walking. There is an attractive waterfall on the Ruhidji River, next to the main road 2km north of the town centre. Njombe is cold at night.

Getting there

Njombe is 237km from Songea (the distance is marked incorrectly on some maps). They are connected by a good tar road, so the bus ride between them takes less than five hours. There are regular buses in all directions from Njombe. In fact, for such a sleepy-looking town, it has one of the most chaotic bus stations I have seen. Watch your belongings.

Where to stay

The two-storey **Milimani Hotel**, 250m from the bus station towards Songea, has a good bar and restaurant (meals around $2.50). Rooms are clean, comfortable and spacious, and the showers are hot ($4 s/c double). The **Lutheran Centre Hostel** offers beds in clean recently-furnished dormitories for less than $1 per person and it has a canteen. It is 50m and signposted from the main road, just before the Milimani. Of the several guest houses around the bus station, the best is the **Shamba Guest House** ($2/3 single/double).

MAKAMBAKO

This important junction town is a good place to hitch a lift from in any direction. If you get stuck there is a Lutheran Hostel, and also a couple of private lodges.

226

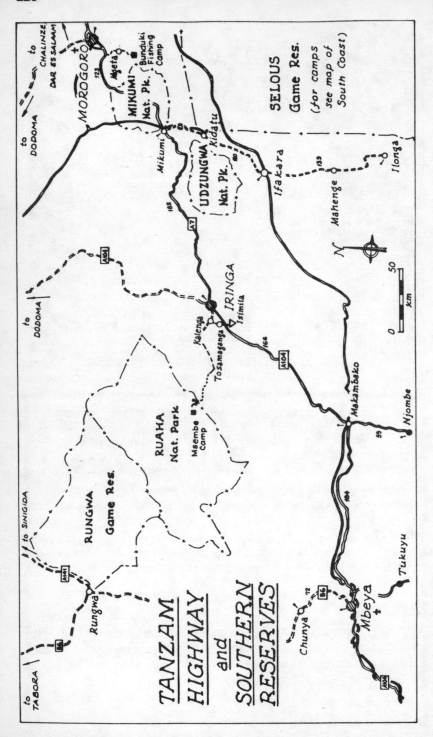

Chapter Eleven

The Tanzam Highway and the southern reserves

INTRODUCTION

The Tanzam Highway, so-named because it links Tanzania to Zambia, is the main road through southern Tanzania. It starts at Tunduma on the Zambian border, passes through Mbeya, Iringa, Mikumi and Morogoro, then connects with the Dar es Salaam-Arusha road at Chalinze. This chapter picks the road up at Iringa and follows it northwards to Chalinze.

The region's most significant physical features are the Uluguru Mountains near Morogoro and the Udzungwa Mountains near Mikumi. It is passed through by Tanzania's largest river, the Rufiji, and its main tributary, the Great Ruaha. The stretch of road from Iringa to Morogoro is very scenic, first following the Ruaha River through the baobab-clad foothills of the Udzungwa Mountains, then passing through Mikumi National Park.

Some of Tanzania's most alluring conservation areas flank the highway. The Selous, the largest game reserve in Africa, covers a vast area of miombo woodland lying between the Tanzam Highway and the south coast. Ruaha National Park lies west of the highway near Iringa. Mikumi National Park is bisected by the highway between Iringa and Morogoro. The newly-proclaimed Udzungwa Mountains National Park lies south of Mikumi towards Ifakara.

Climate

Much of the area covered in this chapter is low-lying and hot. The Udzungwa and Uluguru Mountains and, to a lesser extent, Iringa are cooler. The rainfall pattern is typical of Tanzania, with the bulk of the rain falling between November and March.

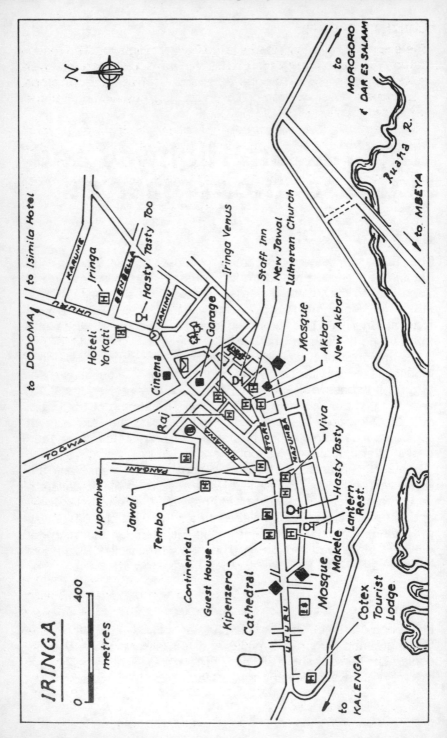

IRINGA

0   400
metres

N

to DODOMA
to Isimila Hotel

KARUME
BENBELLA
UHURU
HAKIMU

Iringa
Hasty Tasty Too

Hoteli
Ya Kati
Cinema

Raj

Garage
Iringa Venus

Staff Inn
New Jawal
Lutheran Church
Mosque
Akbar
New Akbar

MKWAWA
STOCK
MAZUMBA

Viva
Hasty Tasty

Lupombwe
PANGANI
Jawal
Tembo
Continental
Guest House
Kipenzero
Cathedral

UHURU

Makele
Lantern Rest.

Mosque
Cotex
Tourist
Lodge

to
KALENGA

to
MOROGORO
& DAR ES SALAAM

Ruaha R.

to MBEYA

Getting around

There is plenty of transport along the Tanzam Highway. The road is tarred and, even though it is potholed in parts, buses are relatively quick. Expect to cover around 50km per hour allowing for stops. Hitching is a possibility; the only time we tried, however, near Iringa, we waited two hours without any luck.

The Tazara Railway runs roughly parallel to the highway for most of its length. They split at Makumbako and re-connect at Dar es Salaam, so the line is of little use to travellers wanting to explore the area. The Tazara Railway does stop at Ifakara, and is a good way of getting to Udzungwa National Park.

IRINGA

It would be misleading to describe Iringa as exciting, but the town is both interesting and agreeable. There are several period buildings in the old German quarter near the market, while Majumba Street, the main trading road, is very colourful and lively. Iringa is situated on a hill from which there are good views over the Ruaha valley.

The area around Iringa is not without interest. Day trips can be made to the nearby Isimila Stone-Age Site and to Mkwawa's capital at Kalenga (see *History*. Iringa is the jumping-off point for visits to Ruaha National Park.

History

Iringa is the home of the Hehe, a relatively modern grouping forged in the 1850s under the leadership of Munyigumba. His son and successor, Mkwawa, achieved a legendary status amongst both his own people and his enemies. Mkwawa was a cunning warrior who expanded his territory to include large parts of the caravan route between Tabora and the coast. The name *Hehe* is believed to derive from the battle-cry he initiated, a loud *hee-hee*.

Mkwawa refused to acknowledge the German administration. When they attempted to treatise with him, he responded by blocking caravans from passing through his territory. In 1891 Emil Zelewski and 1,000 German troops were dispatched to quell the Hehe. After a few skirmishes, Mkwawa ambushed Zelewsky, killing half his men and making off with over 300 rifles and all their ammunition. Over the next three years Mkwawa set about fortifying his capital at Kalenga. Iringa, incidentally, is a European corruption of the Hehe word *lilinga*, which means fort.

In October 1894, Kalenga was attacked and demolished by the

Germans, who stood a battery of cannons along the ridge of a hill which overlooks it. Amongst other blows, a direct hit was scored on the arsenal holding the gunpowder Mkwawa had borrowed in 1891. Mkwawa went on the run; for the next four years he fought the Germans using guerilla tactics. When faced with capture in 1898, he shot himself through the skull rather than be taken alive. His skull, originally taken to Germany, was returned to Tanzania in 1954. It now rests in the Mkwawa Museum in Kalenga.

Getting there and away

You can get to Iringa easily from anywhere on the Tanzam Highway. Getting away from Iringa is less simple. The apparent busyness of Iringa bus station is deceptive; few buses actually start their journey there and although plenty will be going in your direction it may be difficult to find a seat. It is advisable to book a seat in advance. Iringa is about nine hours from Dar es Salaam by bus.

Seats for Dodoma-bound buses should also be booked in advance. The road is terrible; the trip takes up to 12 hours.

Where to stay

Moderate

Iringa Hotel (PO Box 48, Tel: (064) 2039). The ex-Railway Hotel is a pleasant old colonial building. The lounge and bar are spacious, the food is good value, and the staff is efficient and friendly. The rooms are tired-looking but comfortable. $7 s/c double.

Isimila Hotel (PO Box 216, Tel: (064) 2605). More modern than the Iringa Hotel, the Isimila has pretensions it doesn't really live up to. Rooms are small but clean, and have hot water. There is a bar and restaurant. $7 s/c double.

Cotex Tourist Lodge This is in an excellent position with views to the Ruaha Valley, but seems to be permanently closed. If it were to be renovated, it would be worth checking out.

Raj Hotel This new place, close to the bus station, has an excellent restaurant and a helpful owner. Rooms are pleasantly furnished, but a bit cramped. $4.50/6.25 single/double.

Budget

There are dozens of cheap guest houses, but it can be difficult to find a vacant room. The best are around the bus station and market: **Lupombwe** ($1.75/2.00 single/double), **Tembo** ($1.75/2.00), **Iringa Venus** ($1.00/1.75) and **New Akbar** ($1.25/2.00). Avoid the guest houses on Uhuru Avenue towards the stadium. All those I looked at were scruffy, unfriendly and full.

Sambula Lodge   This is the best value in its range, but rather inconvenient as it is 1km past the Isimilia Hotel on the Dodoma road. Rooms are clean and have mosquito nets, and there is a bar, restaurant and garden. $1.25 single, or $2.50/3.75 s/c single/double.

Hoteli Ya Kati   This place seemed a bit grubby, but the gardens are attractive and the restaurant is good. $2/4 s/c single/double.

Lutheran Centre   (Karume Rd, Tel: 30175). I have been told the Lutheran Centre Guest House accepts travellers.

Where to eat
There is a good choice of restaurants in Iringa. For lunch, **Hasty Tasty** and **Hasty Tasty Too** serve a variety of tasty and inexpensive stews, juices, and Indian snacks. The **Raj Hotel**, Iringa's top restaurant, has a varied menu and is open long hours. Main courses cost about $3. The **Iringa Hotel** serves three-course set menus for $2.50. Its bar is well-stocked and cheap; a sociable place to linger for the evening. **Hoteli ya Kati** is also good. Main courses costs around $1.50.

The **Lantern Restaurant** has great views over Majumba Street and across to the hills surrounding Iringa. The menu lacks surprises but the food is good. After you eat, you can relax and enjoy the view at the attached bar. Main courses cost $2.

Excursions

Kalenga
This small village on the banks of the Ruaha was the site of Mkwawa's fortified capital (see *History* above). A small museum houses Mkwawa's bullet-shattered skull and several of his artefacts. The well-informed and enthusiastic caretaker speaks good English and will happily take you around the village.

To the untrained eye Kalenga is an unremarkable African village, but the caretaker can point out several remnants of Mkwawa's capital: the remains of fortified walls, the mound used by the chief to address his people, and the foundations of his home. He will also point out the ridge from where the Germans unleashed the barrage of cannon fire which destroyed the capital. This hill has since become known as Tosamaganga (throwing stones), and is now the site of a quaint 1930s Italian mission.

Pick-up trucks to Tosamaganga and Kalenga leave Iringa every hour or so. They wait for passengers at the end of the surfaced road 200m past Samora Stadium. At Kalenga you will be dropped off next to the market; it is a five-minute meander through the village from there to the museum. Keep asking for directions. If your Swahili is limited, asking for Mkwawa will get you further than asking for a museum.

Isimila Stone Age Site

In a dry river bed 22km south of Iringa lies one of East Africa's richest stone age sites. Its significance was recognised in 1951 by a schoolboy who collected two rucksacks full of stone implements, amongst them a 40cm-long, 4kg hand-axe. Isimila was first excavated by Professor Howell of Chicago University in 1957.

Isimila was inhabited by stone age people of the Late Achulean culture about 60,000 years ago, at which time it was a shallow lake. A small museum houses a number of their tools, including cleavers and hand axes. You can also see fossilised bones and teeth of the extinct *hippopotamus gorgops*. In another gulley, 10 minutes walk away, a group of striking 10m-high sandstone pillars, carved by a river which dried up years ago, look like the set for a Lilliputian western.

The turn-off to Isimila is signposted on the Tanzam Highway south of Iringa, a few metres past the 20km marker — any bus heading that way can drop you there. It is a 20-minute walk from the road to the site. On the way you pass through a small group of huts where the caretaker lives. Ask for him on your way past.

You can negotiate with a taxi driver to do a round trip to Isimila. This cost us about $15. The caretaker at the site speaks little-to-no English — if your Swahili is limited an English-speaking taxi driver will be a definite asset.

RUAHA NATIONAL PARK

Ruaha is Tanzania's second-largest national park, and one of its wildest. Only the area around the Great Ruaha River has been developed for tourism, and even this sees relatively few visitors. There are plans to extend the internal road system from the present 400km to 1,500km.

Ruaha protects a wide variety of habitats, including evergreen forest and swamp. Much of the park is covered in miombo woodland. There are also significant areas of grassland dotted with acacia and baobab trees. The roads following the Ruaha River are said to be the best for game viewing.

Ruaha boasts the largest elephant population of any Tanzanian national park. Despite heavy losses due to poaching, there are still over 12,000 in the greater Ruaha ecosystem, which incorporates two neighbouring reserves.

Other common mammals include buffalo (over 30,000 in 1990), zebra (over 20,000), giraffe and warthog. Impala are the most numerous antelope; waterbuck, eland, roan, sable, bushbuck and both types of kudu are also likely to be seen. Predators include lion, leopard and cheetah. African hunting dogs are often seen in the Mwanyangi area. Over 400 bird species have been recorded.

A 64-page booklet *Ruaha National Park* is available from the National Park headquarters in Arusha and sometimes from the entrance gate of Ruaha. It contains maps, animal descriptions and checklists, and details of where to look for localised species.

Ruaha is best visited between July and November, when animals concentrate around the river. Internal roads may be impassable during the rainy season (December to May).

An entrance fee of $15 per 24-hour period must be paid in hard currency.

Getting there and away

The park headquarters at Msembe are 120km from Iringa by road and can only be reached using a 4x4 vehicle. If organised in advance through Ruaha River Camp or the park authorities, you can charter a flight to Msembe and hire a vehicle to use in the park.

A number of Dar es Salaam-based companies run safaris to Ruaha. These are pricey, and unless you fly you will use up the best part of two days just getting there and back.

It is possible to arrange a safari in Iringa at a price comparable to that of a camping safari in the northern reserves. Only one company in Iringa offers 4x4 hire: Iringa Safari Tours (PO Box 107, Tel: (064) 2718/2291). Their office is on Uhuru Avenue between Benbella Street and Karume Road; the owner can also be contacted at the Iringa Hotel. The price will depend on how long you want the vehicle for. You will be looking at around $250 for up to four people for three days. This covers vehicle hire, a driver and fuel. Park entrance fees, food and accommodation costs must be added to this.

Hitching to Ruaha is for incurable optimists only.

Where to stay

Ruaha River Camp (bookings through Valji and Alhibai, PO Box 786, Dar es Salaam, tel: (051) 20522/26537, fax: (051) 37561). This highly-regarded private camp is on a koppie above the rapids on the Ruaha River. Accommodation is in bandas or fixed tents. There is a restaurant and bar. $60 per person full board.

Msembe Camp This basic camp is near the headquarters and the river. There are nine double bandas and two family bandas. All are self-contained, with bedding, firewood and water provided. There is a basic campsite with pit toilets but no water. Campsites and bandas cost $10 HC per person.

MIKUMI

This village on the southern border of Mikumi National Park has grown rapidly in the last few years. It is a service town to the national park and an important stopover along the Tanzam Highway. It is also on the junction with the B127 to Ifakara (and Udzungwa National Park). There are several guest houses and you can get a reasonable meal at the *hoteli* with the covered verandah at the junction with the B127.

UDZUNGWA NATIONAL PARK

Tanzania's newest national park opened to the public in October 1992. It protects the remote Udzungwa Mountains and an extensive montane forest community. Altitudes within the national park range from around 250m to over 2,500m. Facilities were limited when we visited in December 1992, but with publicity Udzungwa seems likely to become a major draw for hikers and nature lovers.

There are many similarities between the forests of west Africa, Madagascar and the eastern Tanzania mountains. Madagascar was once part of the African mainland, so these forests may once have been linked physically. The dispersal of seeds during cyclones may also be a factor. Madagascar split from the mainland about 165 million years ago and the eastern Tanzanian forests have been isolated from those in west Africa for over five million years. Forests such as those of the Udzungwa and Usambara are separated by large distances and thus have a high level of endemism. More than 25% of Udzungwa's plant species are not present elsewhere.

Two monkeys are endemic to the Udzungwa: Uhehe red colobus

and Sanje crested mangabey. Blue, red-tailed, and black-and-white colobus monkey are also present. Udzungwa is part of the Mikumi-Selous ecosystem, so it harbours large game species such as lion, elephant, leopard, buffalo and sable antelope.

Udzungwa is one of the best bird-watching sites in Tanzania, with numerous localised species recorded. Three endemics were first described in the last decade: rufous-winged sunbird, a weaver and a cisticola. Udzungwa's forests are still relatively little-known scientifically; there may yet be species awaiting discovery.

An entrance fee of $15 per person per 24-hour period must be paid in hard currency.

Getting there and away

The entrance gate to Udzungwa is 100m from the main Ifakara road, at the village of Mangula 20km south of Kidatu. A few pick-ups do the Kidatu-Ifakara run every day and will drop you off there.

The best way to reach Ifakara is by rail. All trains on the Tazara line stop there; see *Rail* in Chapter Three. They arrive in the evening, so plan on a night at one of Ifakara's basic guest houses.

Kidatu is reached by road. Any bus between Iringa and Morogoro can drop you at Mikumi. A daily bus from Morogoro passes through Mikumi at about 4.00pm and reaches Kidatu at nightfall. The odd private vehicle goes through to Kidatu. There is accommodation in Kidatu; see *Where to Stay* below.

If you visit Udzungwa as a round trip from Dar es Salaam, the ideal would be to come by rail and return by road. Slow trains to Ifakara pass through Selous Game Reserve in daylight. By road, you will pass through Mikumi National Park.

Where to stay

There is no accommodation in the park. If you have a tent you might be allowed to camp at the entrance gate, but there are no facilities. **Twiga Guest House**, in Mangula 200m from the entrance gate, is an attractive base for exploring the Udzungwa. The canteen serves cheap, filling meals, the bar has a fridge, and the grounds look across to the mountains. $4 s/c double.

You could also stay at Kidatu, a hot, mosquito-ridden town dominated by the Udzungwa's craggy peaks. Surrounded by sugar plantations and the site of a major hydro-electric plant, Kidatu is considerably larger and busier than maps suggest.

A basic room in Kidatu costs under $2. **Mkanga Guest House** and **Stop Over Lodge** are both adequate. **Maryland Lodge**, 200m from the main road, has spotless rooms with mosquito nets and fans. A limited range of meals is served and there is a beer garden with a fridge. $1.50/2.50 single/double, or $4 s/c double.

What to do

A short trail leads from the entrance gate to a small waterfall in the forest. We saw plenty of monkeys along this, including red colobus. If you sit quietly at the waterfall in the early morning or evening, you might see monkeys come to drink. The roads around Mangula are pleasant to walk on.

Two longer trails are planned: a seven-hour round trip to the nearest peak and an overnight hike to the 2,111m Mwanihana peak. Guides and porters will be available, but you should bring all food etc with you. Contact the National Parks office in Arusha for up-to-date information.

If any readers hike in the Udzungwa (or in the Mahenge range 80km south of Ifakara), I would like to hear about it so details can be included in the next edition.

MIKUMI NATIONAL PARK

Mikumi is Tanzania's third-largest national park, covering 3,230km². It is relatively flat, but flanked by the Uluguru and Udzungwa mountains to the north and south respectively. Mikumi was gazetted in 1964, when the large herds which gathered on the Mkata flood plain were threatened by hunters after the area was opened up by the construction of the Morogoro-Iringa road. It was extended to share a border with the Selous in 1975.

Mikumi's main vegetation type is open grassland interspersed with patches of miombo and acacia woodland and the odd solitary baobab. The area becomes marshy after rain. A wide variety of mammal species is present; amongst the more commonly-seen are elephant, buffalo, wildebeest, impala, warthog, zebra and giraffe. There are significant populations of three antelope species which are rare in the northern Tanzanian reserves: greater kudu, roan and sable antelope. Predators include lion, leopard, African hunting dog, and black-backed jackal.

A park entrance fee of $15 per person per 24-hour period must be payed in hard currency. A 44-page booklet *Mikumi National Park*, available at the National Park headquarters in Arusha for $2.50, contains a wealth of background information, a good map, and details of the animals and birds found in the park.

Getting there and away

Mikumi is bisected by the Tanzam Highway. It can be reached in an ordinary saloon car, but a 4x4 is needed to drive within the park. You can see plenty of game from a bus passing through the reserve; we saw 10 mammal species, including a herd of 20-odd eland and four herds of elephant.

Safaris to Mikumi run from Dar es Salaam, four hours away by road. A two-day, one-night trip is normal. It is the cheapest of the southern reserves to visit, but lacks the wild character which makes the others so attractive.

As it is only an hour from Mikumi by road, I expected people in Morogoro to organise safaris there. It seems not, but this could change. If you hired a vehicle in Morogoro, a day trip would a feasible option. The Morogoro or Savoy Hotels or the New Green Restaurant would be the best places to enquire.

Where to stay

Mikumi is a popular weekend trip for residents of Dar es Salaam. It is advisable to book over weekends and public holidays.

UPPER RANGE

Mikumi Wildlife Lodge   (PO Box 14 Mikumi, tel: Mikumi 27). This attractive TTC lodge, 3km from the main road, sits on a ridge above a waterhole. It has a swimming pool, a restaurant and a bar. $44/53 HC s/c single/double or $11/14 for residents. Lunch and dinner cost $11 each.

Mikumi Wildlife Camp   (Book through the Oyster Bay Hotel in Dar es Salaam). Accommodation here is in s/c bandas. It has a restaurant and bar. $40 HC per person, or $29 for residents on weekdays. Meals cost $11 each.

BUDGET AND CAMPING

The three campsites near the main gate cost $10 per person. They have long drop toilets and firewood, but water is not available. Special campsites cost $40 per person. The cheapest option is to stay at one of the guest houses in Mikumi village.

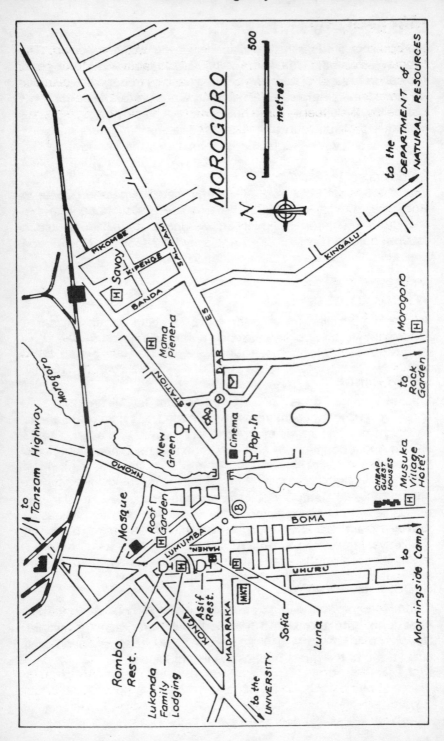

MOROGORO

Morogoro is a likeable town, spacious and well-maintained. The Uluguru Mountains tower attractively 2,000m above it. Morogoro is the centre of a major agricultural region and its fruit market is known countrywide. There are few tourist attractions around Morogoro, but its healthy, lively feel — three hotels had live music playing when we visited — makes it worth a minor diversion.

Getting there and away

Buses between Dar es Salaam and Morogoro leave every hour or so and take about four hours. There is regular transport between Morogoro and Iringa. A bus leaves Morogoro for Kidatu at around 2.00pm daily.

Where to stay

UPPER RANGE

Morogoro Hotel (PO Box 1144, Tel: (056) 3270). Morogoro's only tourist hotel lies on the slopes of the Uluguru 2km out of town. It has pleasant grounds and the usual facilities. $45/50 HC s/c single/double or $12/16 for residents.

MODERATE

Masuka Village Hotel (PO Box 930, Tel: (056) 4774/4430). This well laid-out hotel is on Boma Road, 1km from the bus station. It has a bar and restaurant, and live music in the evenings. Rooms are comfortable and good value at $9 s/c double.

Savoy Hotel (PO Box 35, Tel: (056) 2345). Near the station, this TTC hotel is a bit run-down, but its rooms are spacious and clean and they have private verandas. There is a bar and restaurant, and live music most evenings. $7 s/c double.

Luna Hotel Near the bus station, this has a lively bar, with a disco and/or live music at night. It has seen better days, but rooms are spacious, clean and have mosquito nets and a fan. $5 s/c double.

Roof Garden Hotel This hotel is basically a jumped-up guest house. It has a well-stocked bar and a restaurant (meals cost under $2). Unless you want an early start, the nearby mosque is a drawback. $9 s/c double. The nearby Sofia Hotel is similar.

Mama Pienera Hotel This seems a very quiet, homely place, and it has a good bar and restaurant. $7.25 s/c double.

BUDGET

Guest houses are dotted all around Morogoro. At least six are clustered on Boma Road near the Masuka Village Hotel, and there are more along the University road. **Lukumba Family Guest House** near the bus station merits a special mention. It has clean rooms, with mosquito nets and fans. $2 double or $3 s/c double.

Where to eat

Most of the moderate hotels have restaurants, and there are several *hotelis* around the bus station and on Uhuru Street. There is an **ice-cream parlour** next to the Luna Hotel. The best food is at the **New Green Restaurant**, which serves a variety of Indian and western dishes for around $3.

Excursions

Rock Garden Resort

This is a sort of botanical garden on the lower slopes of the Uluguru Mountain. It is 1km past the Morogoro Hotel, and worth a look if you have an afternoon to spend.

Uluguru Mountains

This range lies directly east of Morogoro. It rises to 2,646m. Like most eastern Tanzanian mountains, it contains extensive areas of forest. The Uluguru are less accessible than the Usambara or Udzungwa, but there is no reason why a determined hiker should be put off. Maps are available from the Department of Lands and Surveys in Dar es Salaam.

A possible base for hiking into the Uluguru is the disused **Morning View Camp** near a patch of natural forest halfway up the mountain. Though originally a research centre for Sokoine University, permission to camp there must now be obtained from the Department of Natural Resources, 2km out of town on Kingalu Road. Check the water situation before heading out. To get to Morning View, head out on Boma Road past Masuka Village Hotel for about 8km. You might get a lift some of the way, but don't bank on it.

If you have a vehicle and are self-sufficient, you could also try the **abandoned fishing camp at Bunduki**. I spoke to the man who ran it in the mid-70s, and it sounds a lovely spot, on a river in an area rich in game. The camp itself is dilapidated, but it is unlikely anyone would stop you from pitching a tent. To get there from Morogoro follow the Tanzam Highway south for 20km then turn off for Mgeta. Bunduki is about 10km past Mgeta.

CHALINZE

Just over 100km west of Dar es Salaam, Chalinze is one of the most important junction towns in Tanzania, where the Tanzam and Northern Highways split. If you are travelling between the north and south of the country, and want to bypass Dar es Salaam, you will find a vehicle heading in your direction at Chalinze.

Its strategic position aside, Chalinze is enlivened only by the numerous vendors and stalls which sell food and curios to passing bus passengers. There are a couple of basic guest houses.

SELOUS GAME RESERVE

Because of its size and remoteness, a definite mystique surrounds the Selous. The reserve is difficult to describe without resorting to hyperbole: it is the largest in Africa (and the second largest in the world); 50,000 square kilometres of archetypal wilderness; home to 30,000 elephant, 200,000 buffalo, 80,000 wildebeest and significant populations of almost every other species of African mammal, including the rare African hunting dog and black rhinoceros.

Before you rush off and book a safari to the Selous, you should be aware of its drawbacks. The reserve is divided into two unequal sections by the mud-brown Rufiji River. The remote expanse of African bush described above lies south of the river; unless you have your own 4x4 and are thoroughly self-reliant, or are prepared to pay a fortune to make individual arrangements with a tour operator, this area is totally inaccessible.

The Selous most people see is the relatively small area north of the Rufiji. There is less tourism here than in the northern reserves, but it is nevertheless well-developed in tourist terms. The area is not as scenic as the northern reserves, nor are you likely to see as many animals or as much variety as you would in, for instance, the Serengeti. When we were there all the camps seemed intent on showing their visitors a particular pride of lions which had been resident in one area for a week. Spot-the-lion-along-with-three-other-vehicles is a game you can play in any large African reserve, and in theory is the type of thing people go to Selous to avoid.

That's not to say Selous isn't worth visiting. The walking and boat safaris offered by all the camps are a real bonus. The Rufiji teems with hippo and massive crocodiles which can be approached closely in a boat, and the bird and animal life along the shore is amazing. A variety of antelope are likely to be seen, as are buffalo and elephant. Of the birds, African skimmer is often seen on the sand banks exposed during the dry season, fish eagle perch on the *borassus* palms which line the river, and waders, herons, kingfishers and weavers are all well-represented.

Game walks allow you to look at smaller animals and birds, and there is a real sense of excitement attached to wandering around in the bush, especially if the group is small. You will go with an armed ranger. The highlight of our trip was a family of elephant shrews feeding at dusk next to our tent.

The accessible part of the Selous is covered in miombo woodland and animals can be quite difficult to spot from a vehicle. Game drives consequently centre around a series of small lakes between the camps. Animals likely to be seen in this area include lion, elephant, impala, greater kudu, eland, giraffe, zebra, wildebeest and buffalo.

Not only does the Rufiji divide the reserve from a tourist's viewpoint, but it acts as a natural barrier between the ranges of two wildebeest subspecies (eastern white-bearded wildebeest north of the river and Nyasa wildebeest to the south). The Rufiji also forms the southern limit of the range of the Maasai giraffe, though this is in part due to the absence of acacia trees south of the river.

Roads within the Selous become impassable after heavy rain. As a consequence camps close towards the end of the wet season, in April, and re-open in July. An entrance fee of $15 per person per day is charged.

You'll hear a few different pronunciations of Selous; to the best of my knowledge *Selloo* is correct.

History

Because of tsetse fly, much of the area that is now the Selous has never been densely-populated. People who lived in the area suffered badly at the hands of the slave caravans in the 19th Century. Better-populated areas such as the Mutumbi Hills were virtually cleared of human habitation by the famine induced by the Germans after the Maji-Maji uprising.

The Selous is named after Frederick Courteney Selous, an English elephant hunter, explorer, naturalist and writer (his best-known book is *A Hunter's Wanderings in Africa*). Selous spent most of his life in East and southern Africa; amongst his many exploits, he was a white hunter for Theodore Roosevelt and the trailblazer for the troop of settlers sent by Rhodes to take over the area that became Rhodesia (now Zimbabwe). In World War One, Selous volunteered for service and was made a captain in the 25th Royal Fusiliers. He died in battle in 1917 at the age of 64, of wounds inflicted while advancing on a German encampment on the Beho river. His grave is on the north of the river near Selous Safari Camp.

The part of the reserve north of the Rufiji was proclaimed in 1905. Kaiser Wilhelm gave part of it to his wife as a present, which earned it the nickname of *Shamba la Bibi* (The Woman's Field). Selous received its current name in 1922 and reached its present size and shape in the 1940s, when the government moved the remaining tribes out of the area to combat a sleeping sickness epidemic. It has been declared a World Heritage Site, one of three in Tanzania.

Getting there

The ideal way to visit the Selous is to organise your own safari starting in Dar es Salaam. This involves either hiring a vehicle and driver and making your own bookings, or getting one of the camps to put together a drive-down package. The advantage of doing it yourself is that it gives you the autonomy to explore away from the roads favoured by the camps. The drive from Dar es Salaam to Selous is along poor roads and takes about 10 hours. All the camps have access to an air-strip and can charter a flight to take you down.

Four days is the minimum realistic length for a drive-down safari. Prices vary widely depending on the camp, your length of stay and the size of your group. Four people going for four days can expect to pay a minimum of $100 per person per day.

You can get to the Selous by train, but must make advance arrangements with the camp you plan to visit. Take the Tazara rail and disembark at either Fuga Halt, Kinyanguru or Kisaka, depending on the camp's instructions. Rail is the most practical way of getting to Selous Safari Camp or Stiegler's Gorge cheaply.

The cheapest way of visiting Selous to go to Impala Camp using the bus between Dar es Salaam and Mloka, about 25km from the camp. If arranged in advance, a vehicle will meet your bus. A three-night safari done like this would give you two full days in the park and cost around $250 per person all inclusive. Impala Tours can give you details of where to book onto the bus.

Where to stay

There are five camps, all privately run, and all over $70 per person per night, inclusive of meals. All camps can organise game drives and boat safaris for around $25 per person and walking safaris for about $10 per person. The camps are all shown on the map of the South Coast (page 248).

Impala Camp   (PO Box 4783 Dar es Salaam, Tel: (051) 25779). The most basic and cheapest of the camps. Accommodation is in standing tents, with showers and long drops attached, overlooking the river. The owner has a positive attitude to budget travellers (there are vague plans to build a campsite). $70 per person full board, inclusive of park fees.

Stiegler's Gorge Camp   (PO Box 348 Dar es Salaam, Tel: (051) 32855). Built for a hydroelectric project in 1977, this camp is situated on a hill overlooking the sheer 100m-deep gorge after which it is named and into which the Rufiji bottlenecks in a spectacular fashion. Accommodation is in self-contained cabins. Stiegler's Gorge is some distance from the other camps, so it's a bit more exclusive.

Rufiji River Camp   (PO Box 20058 Dar es Salaam, Tel: (051) 63546). This is the oldest camp in the Selous, built on a bank overlooking the Rufiji. Accommodation is in standing tents with communal toilets. The owner is a German ex-hunter whose knowledge of the Selous is said to be unrivalled.

Mbuyu Camp   (PO Box 1192 Dar es Salaam, Tel: (051) 34535, Fax: (051) 28486). This camp is built around a large baobab tree. Accommodation is in luxury self-contained tents on the banks of the Rufiji, near the lakes. Plenty of animals can be seen from the bar overlooking the river.

Selous Safari Camp (book through Oyster Bay Hotel in Dar es Salaam). Situated on a hill overlooking the plains around the lakes, accommodation here is in self-contained cabins. It is possible to swim in the nearby hot springs. Full board costs $90 per person. Park fees are not included.

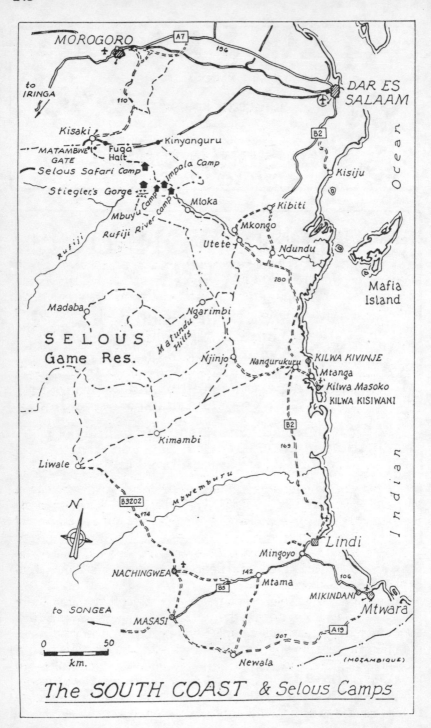

The SOUTH COAST & Selous Camps

Chapter Twelve

The South Coast

INTRODUCTION

This chapter covers the coast south of Dar es Salaam, which stretches for over 500km to the Ruvuma River on the Mozambique border. The only towns of any size on the south coast are Kilwa Masoko, Lindi and Mtwara. This chapter also includes coverage of the Makonde Plateau, the area immediately inland of Lindi and Mtwara. The major towns on the plateau are Masasi and Newala.

Lack of reliable transport and the long distances involved in getting there have left the south coast one of the most isolated parts of East Africa. The area offers little to those who value their creature comforts: only in Mtwara is there anything resembling a tourist hotel, few people anywhere speak even rudimentary English, there are no organised tourist attractions and buses are overcrowded, uncomfortable and painfully slow.

Despite all this, the south coast is a fascinating, thought-provoking and often enchanting area, endlessly rewarding to those with a sense of adventure and curiosity. The older towns are profoundly Swahili; crumbling German and Arab buildings create the air of being in a time-warp. The people, too, retain a gracious, slow pace of life into which it is easy to slip. Scenically the area is typical of the East African coast: palm-lined beaches, mangrove swamps and dense baobab-studded scrub.

The south coast's isolation can easily be romanticised, but there is a depressing reality behind the picturesque images. I was struck by the number of beggars, cripples and blind people in the towns, the malnourished children in roadside villages and the total lack of industry. This situation should be partly remedied when plans to extend the Mtwara-Lindi tar road to Dar es Salaam come into fruition.

If you visit the south coast, bear in mind the conservative nature of Swahili culture. Dress and behave accordingly.

Climate

Like the rest of the Tanzanian coast, this region is hot and humid at all times. The ideal time to visit is in the drier, cooler months between April and October.

Getting around

During the dry season there are daily buses between Dar es Salaam and all the large towns covered in this chapter. During the rainy season the road is often impassable. Buses to Lindi and Mtwara leave Dar es Salaam from Morogoro Road bus station. Buses to Kilwa leave from in front of Kariakoo Market. There are good local services on the tar roads connecting Lindi, Mtwara and Masasi. The south coast can be reached by road from the southern highlands; see *Songea* in Chapter Ten.

The ideal way to visit the south coast is to take a boat down to Mtwara and work your way back by bus. The only regular boat service is the *Canadian Spirit*, which sails from Dar es Salaam to Mafia Island and Mtwara every other week during the dry season, and every week during the rainy season. The trip takes about 24 hours. When we used the boat, it sailed from Dar es Salaam on Thursday morning and from Mtwara on Friday, but the schedule changes from time to time. There are three classes: first class costs around $15 and second class $10. Meals and drinks are served on board. The first class lounge is in immaculate condition, but it is at the front of the boat and hell in rough weather. For this reason, second class is preferable.

MAFIA ISLAND

This island opposite the Rufiji Delta has a near-legendary status amongst travellers, largely because so few ever get to it. It was an important Shirazi settlement between the 12th and 15th Centuries, with strong links to Kilwa. It is now mainly known for its excellent deep-sea fishing. I have not met anyone who has been to Mafia, but if what we saw from the *Canadian Spirit* is anything to go by, it is pretty much what you would expect a remote, densely-vegetated and thinly-populated Indian Ocean island to be. We were sorely tempted to get off the boat and, had we not had a schedule to stick to, we probably would have.

If you visit Mafia, it will probably be to fish or to laze around. There are, however, several sightseeing possibilities — Shirazi ruins at Ras Kisimani, Omani ruins on the nearby island of Juani and a turtle colony on another nearby island — but I have no idea how accessible they are. If any enterprising traveller does get to Mafia, it would be interesting to include more information in the next edition.

Getting there and away

Mafia is relatively straightforward to get to, but getting away could involve a certain amount of improvisation. Budget travellers should only think about visiting Mafia if they are very flexible time-wise.

The weekly Air Tanzania flights between Dar es Salaam and Mafia are said to be unreliable. People do charter flights to the island. Presumably spare seats are sometimes available.

The only regular boat service is the *Canadian Spirit* (see *Getting around* earlier in the chapter). This always stops at Mafia on its way to Mtwara, but does not always stop on the return trip to Dar es Salaam. If you only want to spend a night on the island, speak to the captain in advance to clarify what the boat is doing. If you don't mind spending a week there (or two in the dry season), you can pick up the boat when it next goes to Mtwara. There may be other boats between mainland towns and Mafia, but I have not heard of any. There are certainly none on a regular basis.

Where to stay

The TTC-run **Mafia Island Lodge** has air-conditioned rooms and costs $32/41 HC s/c single/double or $6.50 for residents. The only other option is to pitch a tent. It is said to be safe to camp anywhere on Mafia. You can buy basic foodstuffs such as fish locally, but it would be sensible to do some stocking up In Dar es Salaam.

KILWA

There are three settlements called Kilwa. The oldest, Kilwa Kisiwani — Kilwa on the island — lies on a small island 2km offshore. It is the site of the most impressive ruins on the East African coast, those of the medieval city of Kilwa — the *Quiloa* of Milton's *Paradise Lost* and once thought to be the site of King Solomon's mythical mines.

The other settlements are both on the mainland. Kilwa Kivinje (Kilwa of the Casuarina Trees) was a major 19th-Century slave trading centre, only rivalled in importance on the mainland by Bagamoyo. Kilwa Masoko (Kilwa of the market) is a more modern town, and is now the regional headquarters.

Although the Kilwa area is primarily of historical interest, the surrounding coast is lovely. The seas around Kilwa have the world's densest dugong population. Dugong are large, bizarre-looking marine mammals, believed to have been the origin of the mermaid myth. Common as they are, you would be lucky to see one.

History

It is a reflection of the widespread ignorance regarding Africa's past that while tourists flock to Tanzania's game reserves only a handful pass through Kilwa every year. Even more disturbing is the fact we were told by a number of people in Kilwa (including the caretaker) that the Husuni Kubwa — the island's most impressive building and the apex of Swahili architectural aspirations — was Portuguese-built. With the above in mind, the following history is as detailed as space and the known facts will allow.

As with all African history, many details of Kilwa's past are open to conjecture. There have been extensive archaeological diggings on the site and some contemporary descriptions have survived. The primary historical source is the *Kilwa Chronicle*, written in 1520 under the supervision of the then-exiled Sultan of Kilwa. Two versions of this exist, one dating from 1565 and the other from the 19th Century. Discrepancies exist, but the broad history of Kilwa is well-understood.

Kilwa was occupied by precursors of the Swahili in the 9th Century. In about 1150 the island was bought by a trader called Ali bin Al-Hasan, generally regarded to be the founder of the Shirazi Dynasty which dominated coastal trade until the Portuguese invasion. His importance can be gauged by the fact that coins bearing his name — probably minted long after his death — have been found as far afield as Pemba and Mafia islands.

Although Kilwa's importance grew under Al-Hasan and his successors, its eventual dominance of the gold trade is linked to the arrival of Abu-Al-Mahawib, a trader from Sofala in modern-day Mozambique, and is most plausibly explained by a simple accident of geography. Gold arrived at the coast from the interior at Sofala, but until the mid-13th Century it was sold to the Arabs at Mogadishu, in modern-day Somalia. The normal explanation for this is that Arab vessels could not reach Sofala within the annual monsoon cycle, and that the gold was transported up the coast by a succession of local middlemen.

As the volume of coastal trade increased, improvements in Arab navigation and ship design allowed them to penetrate steadily further south. Sofala would have been beyond their reach whatever they did — winds south of Kilwa are notoriously fickle — but it seems likely to have suited Sofalan traders to cut out the middlemen by bringing the centre of trade closer to home. In this scenario, Kilwa would have been the ideal compromise — by the mid-13th Century it was evidently within reach of Arab vessels, yet it was near enough to Sofala for traders there to control the trade from top to bottom.

The source of Kilwa's gold, shrouded in mystery for centuries, gave rise to such myths as Queen Sheba and King Solomon's Mines. It is now thought that the gold was mined in the Zimbabwean interior and arrived at Sofala via the Zambezi valley. There are strong parallels between the timing of the rise and fall of Kilwa and that of Great Zimbabwe. Furthermore, a coin minted at Kilwa was found at Great Zimbabwe in 1971. There are, however, no cultural parallels between the cities or their architecture. Assuming they were linked, it is uncertain what the mechanisms of trade were. No evidence suggests coastal traders ever visited Great Zimbabwe.

Kilwa prospered throughout the golden age of Swahili (1250 to 1450). It was the dominant town on the coast, considered by the medieval traveller, Ibn Battuta, who visited it in 1331, to be 'among the finest and most substantially built in the world'. It had a population exceeding 10,000, the first coin mint in sub-Saharan Africa, and an extensive system of wells which is still in use today. The Friday Mosque and *Husuni Kubwa*, the most impressive buildings on the island, if not the entire coast, date to this period. In addition to gold, Kilwa exported ivory and ebony, and it imported such fineries as eastern cloth and Chinese porcelain.

Kilwa's wealthy traders lived in houses of coral and had small private mosques. Ordinary townsmen lived in mud-and-wattle huts. Even though some Arab traders settled on Kilwa, the vast majority of its occupants were local Swahili. The island was too small to be self-sufficient in food, so had extensive agricultural interests on the mainland.

In 1498, the Portuguese explorer, Vasco Da Gama, rounded the Cape and sailed up the east coast on his way to establishing trade links with India. He described Kilwa in detail, but as he never visited the city, his oft-quoted report is probably pure fabrication. In fact, though it was still a trading centre of note, Kilwa was well past its peak by this time. For reasons that are unclear, Mombasa dominated coastal trade from about 1450 onwards. Da Gama met with a hostile reception in Mombasa; perhaps the Sultan there exaggerated Kilwa's strength in order to frighten the Portuguese away from the coast.

Da Gama's description of Kilwa might explain why it was so heavily targeted when the Portuguese took over the coast in 1505. Three-quarters of its residents were either killed or forced to flee. A Portuguese fort was built, the gold trade moved to Mozambique and the Sultan exiled to the mainland. By 1512 the town was virtually abandoned; even the Portuguese had moved on. In 1589, those residents who had remained were attacked and eaten by a tribe

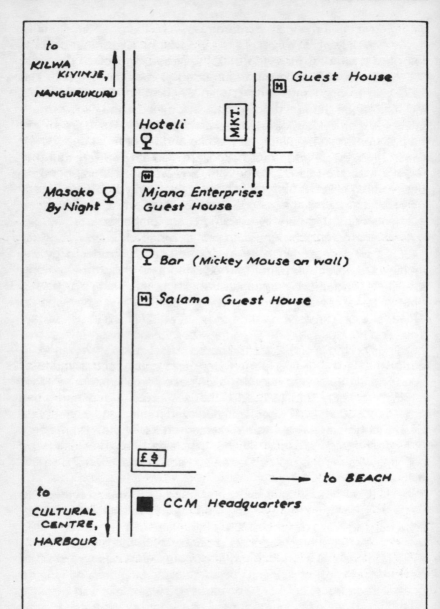

to
KILWA
KIVINJE,
NANGURUKURU

Guest House

Hoteli

MKT.

Masoko
By Night

Mjana Enterprises
Guest House

Bar (Mickey Mouse on wall)

Salama Guest House

→ to BEACH

to
CULTURAL
CENTRE,
HARBOUR

CCM Headquarters

£$

KILWA MASOKO   (sketch map)

called the Zimba. The city was left to crumble.

The island came briefly to life in the late 18th Century, after the Omani captured the coast from the Portuguese. Omani Arabs occupied Kilwa for a period, which is when they built the large fort which is visible from the mainland. They seem to have relocated to the mainland town of Kilwa Kivinje in the early 19th Century.

Kilwa Kivinje became the centre of the southern slave trade. By the mid-19th Century it was a very wealthy town, with up to 20,000 slaves passing through annually. In 1873, the Sultan of Zanzibar outlawed the slave trade. It survived at Kilwa longer than anywhere else, but had been stopped entirely by the end of the 1870s. Many of Kilwa's slave traders established rubber plantations and business continued to prosper. In 1886, Kilwa Kivinje become a German administrative centre.

Kilwa Kivinje remained a town of regional importance during the first half of this century, but since the end of the Second World War it has gradually been reduced to backwater status. The more modern town of Kilwa Masoko is now the regional headquarters.

Getting there and away

A good tar road connects Kilwa Masoko to Nangurukuru on the main Dar es Salaam-Mtwara road. Vehicles from Nangurukuru to Kilwa Masoko run every hour or so and take 20 minutes. Nangurukuru has a guest house, should you get stuck there.

Daily buses between Dar es Salaam and Kilwa Masoko leave at 5.00am in either direction. In Dar es Salaam they leave from Kariakoo Market, not the best place to wander around in the dark. Instead, catch a bus to Mtwara or Lindi (from the Morogoro Road bus station), get off at Nangurukuru, and make your way to Kilwa from there. The road between Dar es Salaam and Nangurukuru is very rough; the journey takes about 12 hours.

There are no direct buses to Kilwa from other towns on the south coast. You will have to catch a bus to Dar es Salaam and get off at Nangurukuru.

Kilwa Masoko

There is little of interest in Kilwa Masoko itself, but it is the best base for exploring the Kilwa area. It is a friendly place and sees few tourists; anyone who speaks English is likely to grab you for a chat. Kilwa Masoko's town centre — a small grid of dirt roads around a central market — is 1km inland of the harbour; a long tar road connects the two. All accommodation is in the town centre; government buildings and banks lie along the main tar road.

Kilwa Masoko's one attraction is the sandy baobab-lined beach east of the harbour. To get there from the town centre, walk down the main tar road for about 300m, then turn left at the CCM buildings (just past the bank — look out for a statue of a man running). The beach is 100m further.

Where to stay/eat

There are three basic guest houses in Kilwa Masoko, all clustered around the market and easy to find. A room costs around $1.50. We stayed at **Mjana Enterprises Guest House**, a friendly, clean place with single rooms only, all of which have a mosquito net and fan. **Salama Guest House** seems similarly pleasant and it has double rooms. The third guest house, behind the market, is scruffier. It is popular with bus drivers, so a good place to stay if you want to be woken for the 5.00am bus to Dar es Salaam.

You can fill up for under $1 at the excellent *hoteli* opposite Mjana Enterprises. The **Masoko by Night** bar is a pleasant place to drink; it serves food grilled on a coal fire. Another, better, bar — which I enjoyed so much I was in no state to write its name down — is covered with paintings of Mickey Mouse.

Kilwa Kisiwani

The modern settlement of Kilwa Kisiwani is little more than a mud and thatch village, unremarkable in itself, but surrounded by some of the most compelling ruins in East Africa. The island is separated from the mainland by a 2km channel; the only way to reach it is in one of the small fishing dhows moored in Kilwa Masoko's harbour.

Permission to visit the island must be obtained from the Kilwa Cultural Centre in Kilwa Masoko. This is a straightforward process and there is no charge attached, but expect it to take some time; you will probably be asked to complete several forms and have to spend a while making small talk with the rather bleak immigration officer (bring your passport). If possible, get the formalities over with the day before you plan to go.

The Cultural Centre can organise a fishing dhow to take you to the island. The price is negotiable and depends on how long you plan to spend there. Expect to pay around $10 per party for a half-day return trip. If you want to spend a night on the island, the Cultural Centre has restored a **small cottage for the use of tourists**. The Cultural Centre is opposite the post office, on the main tar road halfway between the town centre and the harbour.

There is a caretaker/guide on Kilwa Kisiwani. Although he is helpful, he speaks little English, has a minor obsession with medieval toilets (perhaps it's the only English word he knows) and is less than fully-conversant with the island's history. He will expect a tip.

Before you visit Kilwa, don't miss the excellent display in the National Museum in Dar es Salaam.

Around the island

The *Gereza* is the squarish, partially-collapsed building which draws the eye as you sail across to the island. *Gereza* is a Swahili word meaning prison; it in turn is derived from a Portuguese word meaning church. The *Gereza* on Kilwa, however, is a fort. It was built by Omani Arabs in about 1800 and incorporates the walls of a smaller Portuguese fort built in 1505. It has thick coral walls and an impressive arched door.

Walking uphill from the *Gereza*, you pass first through the small modern village before coming to the main ruins. There are a number of interesting buildings here; an ornate *Domed Mosque* and the so-called *Great House* stand out. West of these is the triangular *Mukatini Palace*, parts of which are very well-preserved. The palace was built in the 15th Century after the *Husuni Kubwa* fell into disuse (see below), and is enclosed by a crumbling 18th-Century wall built by the Omani. Also of interest are the remains of the ancient well system, still used by the villagers today.

The most impressive building in the main ruins is the *Great Mosque*, also known as the *Friday Mosque*. This multi-domed building is the largest mosque of its period on the coast, and was built during the 14th-Century gold boom as an extension of an earlier 11th-Century mosque. Most of its magnificent arches and domes are still intact, but many of the outbuildings are crumbling. In the 14th Century the Great Mosque would have been the focal point of community life in Kilwa, where Friday prayers were held. A few hundred metres south of the mosque, a graveyard houses the tombs of many of Kilwa's sultans.

The most remarkable building on Kilwa lies about 1km east of the main ruins, on a low cliff overlooking the sea. Known locally as the *Husuni Kubwa*, it was described by the archaeologist Neville Chittick as 'the only attempt to go beyond the merely practical and approach the grand' in pre-colonial Africa.

The word *Husuni* derives from an Arab word meaning fort, but there is no evidence to suggest the building ever was one. The name was probably acquired centuries after the building fell into disuse. The *Husuni Kubwa* was the Sultan of Kilwa's palace, used both as a dwelling place and a store house. The name *Husuni* has been attached to it by virtue of a nearby smaller, square building, the *Husuni Ndogo*, which superficially resembles a fort (*kubwa* and *ndogo* are KiSwahili for large and small). The purpose of the *Husuni Ndogo* is something of a mystery — there is no comparable building elsewhere in East Africa — but it may have been a fortified market place.

The *Husuni Kubwa* was built by al-Hasan ibn Talut, the first ruler of the Abu-al-Mahawib dynasty, in the early 14th Century, and was probably lived in for three generations. In some aspects — its geometrical design, for instance — it is a typical Swahili building, but its scale and complexity are unprecedented and many of its features are unique. The building includes domestic quarters, an audience court, a staircase leading down the cliff to the sea, large ornamental balconies and a swimming pool. The *Husuni Kubwa* is in poor condition, but the main features are clearly discernable.

Kilwa Kivinje

This small, run-down town is a living memorial to its more prosperous past. The overall impression is of a once important town gradually returning to its fishing village roots — much of the main street consists of boarded-up shops, while mud huts have been built using the walls of old Omani fortifications. I knew little about Kilwa Kivinje when I arrived there, but was able to piece together much of its history just by walking around.

The town came to prominence as an Omani slave-trading centre in the early 19th century. The crumbling remains of Omani dwellings and fortifications are dotted all around, and while none is habitable, many are in good enough condition to allow you to imagine what they must have looked like 150 years ago. There is an interesting mosque and, to the east of the town, an old Muslim graveyard.

The whitewashed German Boma overlooks the waterfront. It is the town's largest building, used as an administrative centre into the 1950s, but it serves no apparent purpose now. A cannon, presumably dating to World War One, stands on the common (complete with park benches) between the Boma and a stone sea wall. Behind the Boma a small monument commemorates two Germans who died in 1888.

Along the main street lie glimpses of Kilwa Kivinje in the 1940s and 1950s: double-storey buildings with ornate balconies, small homes with Zanzibar-style doors, and shops still carrying steel advertising boards which must date to the 1950s. The main covered market, still in use today, is said to have been built by the Germans.

As well as being historical, Kilwa Kivinje is a pretty town. It lies on an attractive stretch of coast surrounded by mangroves, and has a peaceful Muslim atmosphere. I could think of worse places to settle into for a few days. The **Savoy Guest House**, on the beachfront near the German Boma, may not live up to its name, but it is clean and cheap: double rooms with fans and mosquito nets cost $1. A couple of *hotelis* near the market serve cheap, basic meals.

LINDI

Like Kilwa Kivinje, Lindi was a 19th-Century slave-caravan terminus. A chimney-like stone tower opposite the NBC club, said to have been used to hold prisoners, is the only obvious relic of this era.

There is every indication Lindi was a prosperous town at one time. The sprawling town centre contains numerous posh colonial-era buildings, many of which are now ruined or heading that way. On the beachfront, a building marked on a 1970 map as the Area Commissioner's Residence houses nothing but trees. A cyclone which hit the town in the 1950s may go some way to explaining this general state of disrepair.

With one eye closed you can imagine that Lindi's beachfront was a resort of sorts, possibly used by farmers living upcountry. Today, however, the benches are all broken, the Beach Hotel exudes squalor, and the town probably goes months at a stretch without seeing a tourist.

Whatever its history — and even that seems to have been lost or forgotten — Lindi is something of a backwater now. It is a pleasant and interesting place to visit, but ultimately a depressing reminder of what much of Tanzania was like in the mid-1980s. The only part of town which seems to escape the general air of torpor is the busy bus station, which — when the electricity is working — rings with the chimes of Zairian guitars and the pumping bass of reggae late into the night. Here the town's unemployed youth and orphaned children hang around all day, breaking into unselfconscious dances, while vendors scrape a living selling fried chicken and dried fish, melting sweets and single cigarettes to passing bus passengers.

Lindi lies on a glorious stretch of coast. Its sandy, palm-lined beach stretches for a couple of kilometres. The wooded hills on the opposite side of the bay provide a scenic backdrop. If you swim, dress modestly; this is a Muslim town.

Ferries run regularly from the pier next to the Beach Hotel to a small settlement on the opposite side of the bay. I didn't check them out, but if you want to explore further...

Getting there and away

There are buses between Dar es Salaam and Lindi most days. They leave Dar es Salaam at the Morogoro Road bus station and should

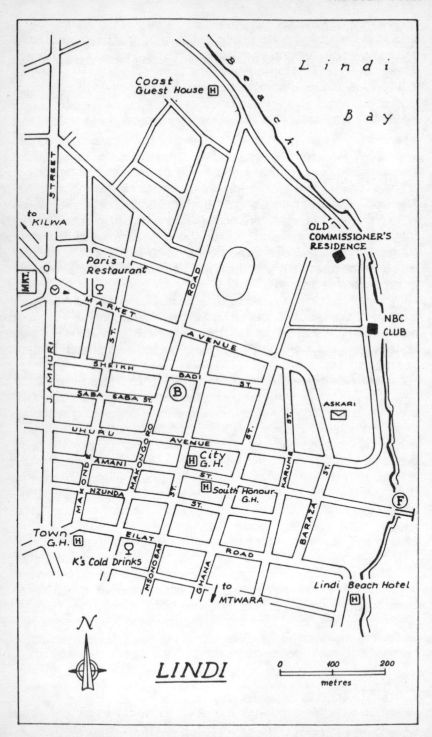

LINDI

N

0   100   200
metres

be booked in advance.

Lindi is connected to Mtwara and Masasi by good tar roads. A few buses run daily to and from Mtwara, leaving when they are full. There are no direct buses between Lindi and Masasi; buses to Masasi leave from Mtwara and bypass Lindi at Mingoyo.

A small, very crowded bus does a daily run between Lindi and Newala. It leaves Newala at 5.00am, gets to Lindi at midday, and then turns back.

Where to stay

There are guest houses dotted all around the bus station. Two of the best are the **South Honour and Town Guest Houses**. Both are friendly and offer clean rooms with mosquito nets and fans for less than $2. The less-central **Lindi Beach Hotel** is in a lovely position but, barring complete renovation, it is of interest to masochists and entomologists only. If you want a room on the beach, try the **Coast Guest House** instead. It is a bit scruffy and the rooms lack mosquito nets, but it's cheap, pleasant and has the beach on its doorstep.

Where to eat

The most pleasant place for a cold beer is the **NBC Club** on the beachfront. Non-members are charged a nominal entrance fee ($0.50). Meals such as chicken and chips are served on request.

Otherwise try **K's Cold Drinks**, where you can get chicken or eggs and chips for less than $1. There are a few *hotelis* around the market and vendors sell snacks all day at the bus station.

MINGOYO

This village is on the junction of the roads to Lindi, Mtwara and Masasi. If you are heading from Lindi to Masasi, you must head to Mingoyo to pick up a vehicle. Mingoyo apparently thrives on its position. The vendors here offer an array of roadside snacks second to none: fried and stewed chicken, fish, prawns, meat kebabs, cakes and fruit. There doesn't appear to be any accommodation in Mingoyo.

MTWARA

Mtwara is a relatively modern and rather bland town, sprawling in a manner that suggests someone once intended greater things for it.

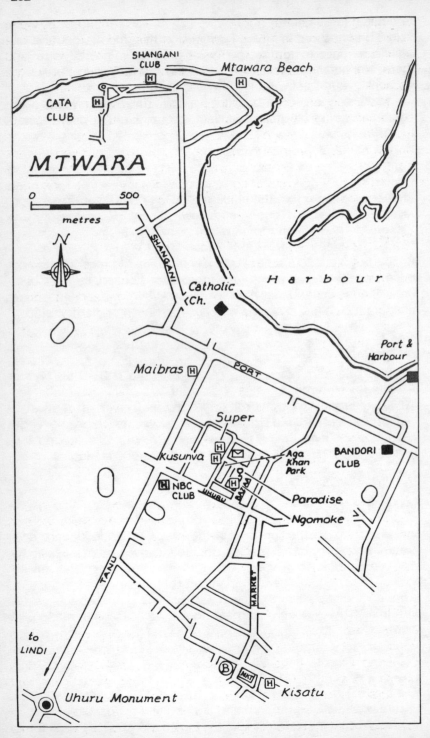

The small town centre, about 1km inland, is surrounded by open fields. The harbour is 1.5km northeast of this, the market and bus station are about 1km south, the beach is about 2km north, and there is what appears to be a small industrial area east of the harbour.

If Mtwara is less than scintillating, the surrounding coast offers some consolation. A good swimming beach is within easy reach of the town, near the Beach Hotel. Local expats raved about the beach on the sandbar protecting the harbour entrance, but you need a boat to get there. Otherwise, much of the coastline immediately around Mtwara consists of coral flats; interesting for the rock pools that form on them and the wading birds that visit.

Getting there and away
Buses between Dar es Salaam and Mtwara leave daily from the Morogoro Road bus station and should be booked in advance. A boat, the *Canadian Spirit*, runs between the towns at least once a fortnight; see *Getting around* at the beginning of the chapter.

There are several buses daily between Mtwara and Masasi, and Mtwara and Lindi. These leave when they are full.

Where to stay
The most attractive places to stay are on the beach, 3km from the bus station. You can walk out or hire a taxi. The cheaper guest houses are in and around the town centre.

UPPER RANGE
Mtwara Beach Hotel If you have read *Ivory Knights*, you will be pleased to know this was closed for renovation when we were in town. It should be open by now. There is no indication of what prices will be like, but it's unlikely to be more than $20/double in this part of the country.

MODERATE
TCMB Club This is run by the Cashew Marketing Board, which used to have another name, the initials of which were CATA. Everyone still calls it the CATA Club (pronounced like Carter). It is a pleasant place, not far from the beach, and has a bar and restaurant. Rooms have a fan and mosquito net. $4 double.

Shangani Club This overlooks the beach, but is rather dear and a bit disorganised. The food is excellent (worth trying if you are staying at CATA club), and there is a well-stocked bar. A good second choice if CATA club is full. $8 per person full-board (negotiable if you eat elsewhere).

BUDGET

NBC Club   On the Lindi road about 500m from the town centre, this is the best of the guest houses, and often full. Meals and drinks are served in the garden. $2.50 double.

Ngomeke Guest House   There are four guest houses in the town centre, of which this is the most appealing. It's still no great shakes. $1.50 double.

Maibras Guest House   This is the closest guest house to the beach, but I thought it scruffy and unfriendly. $1.50 double.

Kisutu Guest House   Near the bus station, this is basic, but clean and friendly. Rooms have mosquito nets and fans. $1.25 single.

Where to eat

There are reasonable *hotelis* in the town centre and around the market. The only proper restaurant in the town centre is the **Paradise Hotel**, where western-style meals cost around $1.50. The **Shangani Club** does excellent meals for around $2.50; these must be ordered in advance. The **Beach Hotel** should have a restaurant attached when it re-opens.

Excursions

The village of Mikindani, 10km north of Mtwara, is far older than its larger neighbour and has considerably more character. Little more than a fishing village now, Mikindani was an important port in the 19th Century. It is where Livingstone set off for his last expedition into the interior, an event commemorated by the predictable plaque, and it has several dilapidated Zanzibar-style buildings, as well as ruins dating back to the slave trade and what appears to be a disused German fort alongside the main road.

Mikindani lies on the main Mtwara/Lindi road, on an attractive stretch of coast. It can be visited as a day trip from Mtwara, but could also be quite an interesting place to stay over. A small hotel was being built on a beach about 2km away when we visited; ask at the Paradise Hotel in Mtwara for details.

THE MAKONDE PLATEAU

The Makonde Plateau lies immediately inland of Mtwara and Lindi. It is the home of East Africa's most renowned craftsmen, the Makonde carvers. The Makonde originated in what is now northern Mozambique and have been practising their craft for at least 300 years. In its purest form, the intricate ebony carvings relate to the Makonde cult of womanhood; they are traditionally carried by the (male) carver as a good luck charm. This custom started when the first carver, who according to folklore was a person but not yet a man, carved a piece of wood into the shape of a woman and left it outside his home overnight. Overnight, the carving was transformed into a real woman. Twice the woman conceived, but both times the child died after three days. Each time, the pair moved higher onto the plateau, believing this would bring them luck. The third child lived and became the first true Makonde.

Typically, Makonde Carvings consist of one or more people in a highly stylised and distorted form. Traditional carvings often depict a female figure surrounded by children. But, like any dynamic art form, Makonde is responsive to external influences and subject to changes in fashion; in recent years, carvings have become increasingly abstract and have incorporated wider moral and social themes. Recent innovations include *Ujamaa* sculptures, which relate to Tanzania's collective social policy, and *Sheteni*, grotesque but evocative figures modelled on Makonde ancestral spirits. Makonde carvings have become highly collectable in the West and are regarded as amongst the best and most imaginative produced anywhere in Africa.

Many of the carvings you see elsewhere in Tanzania come from the Makonde Plateau (many, too, are carved by Makonde who have settled in Arusha or Dar es Salaam), but you will need contacts to see any on the plateau itself. Most are bought by dealers for distribution in the more touristy parts of the country. In fact, the only carvings we saw in Mtwara were not made of ebony, but of ordinary wood covered in black boot polish. If you can buy directly from the carvers, however, you will get a far better price than you would in Arusha or Dar es Salaam. By cutting out the middleman, the carver will also get a fair price.

Another intriguing aspect of traditional Makonde culture is *sindimba* dancing, performed by men and women together using stilts and masks, but in the ordinary course of things, you are unlikely to come across this.

The two main towns on the plateau are Newala and Masasi. The road to Newala is interesting, climbing the plateau through dense *miombo* woodland and passing numerous Makonde villages. These villages are immaculately neat and orderly, and apparently rarely visited by tourists — every time the bus stopped a crowd of curious children gathered around us and stared in amazement.

There is a strong missionary presence in the area. Most schools and hospitals are run by missions. Some missions insist on importing western luxury goods for local distribution. As a consequence, all sorts of unlikely items are offered for sale at the roadside, ranging from lace petticoats to name-brand chocolates and toiletries.

Getting there and away

There are regular buses between Mtwara and Masasi. The tar road between Mingoyo and Masasi is in a good state of repair.

There is a bus every other day in each direction between Masasi and Dar es Salaam. This leaves from in front of the Masasi Hotel, not from the regular bus station. Seats should be booked in advance at the Masasi Hotel.

A daily bus runs between Newala and Masasi, leaving Newala at 5.00am and arriving at Masasi at around 11.00am. It then returns to Newala. See Lindi for details of buses from Newala to Lindi.

Newala

Newala is mainly of interest for the drive there, described above. There are a few indifferent guest houses if you need to spend the night.

Masasi

The principal town on the Makonde Plateau is an attractive place, surrounded by large granite koppies which reminded me of parts of Zimbabwe. Masasi has a modern atmosphere — it feels remarkably healthy after the lazy degeneracy which characterises many of the coastal towns — but there is nothing much to do there. Unless you arrive late, you will probably want to move on.

If you do stay over, the **Masasi Hotel** is good value. Clean, spacious rooms with fans and mosquito nets cost $2.00/3.50 s/c single/double, and a bar and restaurant are attached. It is 10 minutes walk from the bus station along the main tar road to Lindi. There are also plenty of **cheap guest houses** along the road between the bus station and the Masasi Hotel. You can eat at the hotel or the nearby **Top Spot Restaurant**, which serves cheap meals and cold beers and sodas in a garden.

MATCHLESS TANZANIA

Contrasting landscapes and an unsurpassed richness of wildlife make Tanzania matchless for a big game safari. Long distances are eaten up by light aircraft as you are transported between the spectacular game parks of the Serengeti, Nrorongoro Crater and Tarangire.

African wildlife does not, however, end on the plains. Under the waters of the Indian Ocean there is a brilliant marine world waiting to be explored. Liveaboard and lodge based holidays are available for divers and non divers with land safari options.

TWICKERS WORLD 081 892 7606
22 Church Street, Twickenham, TW1 3 NW
Fax 081 892 8061 ABTA 60340 ATOL 1996

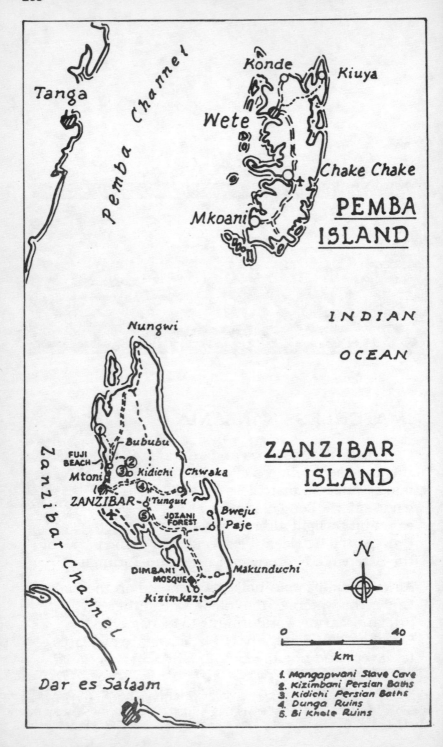

Chapter Thirteen

Zanzibar

By David Else

INTRODUCTION

Zanzibar, a separate state within Tanzania, consists of two large islands, Unguja (Zanzibar Island) and Pemba, plus several smaller islets. Zanzibar Island is about 85km long and between 20km and 30km wide; Pemba is about 75km long and between 15km and 20km wide. Both are flat and low lying, surrounded by coasts of rocky inlets or sandy beaches, with lagoons and mangrove swamps, and coral reefs beyond the shoreline.

Zanzibar used to be hard to reach, and it had a reputation for being expensive and unfriendly. This has changed: the island now positively welcomes tourists. Most visitors come to see the fascinating buildings in the old Stone Town and the many ruined palaces dotted around the island. Other attractions are the clove and coconut plantations and the seemingly endless, palm-fringed tropical beaches.

Farming and fishing are the main occupations on Zanzibar. Most people live in small villages. Cloves are a major export, along with coconut products and other spices. The capital, and by far the largest settlement, is Zanzibar Town or City, on the island's west coast.

Like other coastal areas, Zanzibar is predominantly Muslim. Away from the beaches you should dress modestly.

Accommodation in Zanzibar *must* be paid for in hard currency, preferably US dollars. Public transport and food can normally be paid for in local currency.

Climate

Zanzibar has a typical coastal climate, warm to hot all year round and often very humid. It receives more rainfall and is windier than the mainland.

History

Zanzibar has been trading with ships from Persia, Arabia and India for about 2,000 years. From about the 10th Century AD, groups of immigrants from Shiraz (Persia) settled in Zanzibar and mingled with the local Swahili. The Portuguese established a trading station on the site of Zanzibar Town in the early 16th Century. At the end of the 17th Century they were ousted by Omani Arabs.

In 1840, Sultan Said moved his capital from Muscat to Zanzibar. Many Omani Arabs settled on Zanzibar as rulers and landowners, forming an elite group, while Indian settlers formed a merchant-class. The island became an Arab state, an important centre of regional politics, and the focus of a booming slave trade. Britain had interests in Zanzibar throughout the 19th Century; explorers such as Livingstone, Speke and Burton began their expeditions into the African interior from there. In 1890 Zanzibar became a British protectorate.

Zanzibar gained independence from Britain in December 1963. In 1964, the Sultan was overthrown in a revolution. Nearly all Arabs and Indians were expelled. Later the same year, Zanzibar and Tanganyika combined to form the United Republic of Tanzania.

Today, the distinctions between Shirazi or Swahili are often blurred. The islanders fall into three groups: the Hadimu of southern and central Zanzibar, the Tumbatu of Tumbatu Island and northern Zanzibar, and the Pemba of Pemba Island. Many people of mainland origin live on Zanzibar; some the descendants of freed slaves, others more recent immigrants. Many of the Arab, Asian and Goan people expelled in 1964 have since returned.

Getting there and away

To/from Dar es Salaam   Air Tanzania flies between Dar es Salaam and Zanzibar every day. Tickets cost $43 one-way. The service is not very reliable, but is improving. If you can track it down, it may be possible to fly to Zanzibar on the small aeroplane which delivers newspapers there every morning. Try enquiring at the Daily News Circulation Office on Maktaba Street, or at Tanzanair next to the New Africa Hotel. It is easier to find a seat on the return flight, as it flies empty.

The easiest way to go between Dar es Salaam and Zanzibar is by ship. There are three regular services. Sea Express, a hydrofoil, costs $30/$20 for a first/second class seat, as does Flying Horse, a large catamaran, which also sells deck space for $10. Zanzship, an old steamer, costs $10 wherever you sit. Schedules are chalked up at the booking offices near the main passenger port in Dar es

Salaam. Tickets can be bought on the spot.

The two Zanzibar Shipping Corporation ships which run between Dar es Salaam and Zanzibar are old and unreliable, but only cost $3. Their office is in the CCM Youth Building, next to a large temple on Morogoro Rd.

It is illegal to go between Dar es Salaam and Zanzibar by dhow.

To/from Mombasa Kenya Airways flies three times per week each way between Mombasa and Zanzibar. This service is reliable and costs around $40 one-way. Motorised dhows between Mombasa and Zanzibar cost about $15. They can take over two days and are uncomfortable and dangerously overloaded. Departure days vary; ask around at the old port. Bring your own food and water. The Flying Horse and Sea Express should start going between Mombasa and Zanzibar in 1993.

To/from Tanga Unscheduled dhows run between Tanga, Pemba and Zanzibar about once a week. These take up to two days and are both uncomfortable and dangerous. We have heard stories of shipwrecks.

Arrival and departure

As Zanzibar is a separate state, you must complete an immigration card and show your visa on arrival, even if you have come from mainland Tanzania. Customs officials may check your bag, but a detailed search is unlikely.

Non-Tanzanians must pay a departure tax of $20 in hard currency when flying out of Zanzibar Airport on international flights (eg to Mombasa). The tax for flights within Tanzania is $0.75.

ZANZIBAR TOWN

Zanzibar's old quarter, usually called the Stone Town, is a fascinating maze of narrow streets and alleyways which lead the visitor past numerous old houses and mosques, ornate palaces, and shops and bazaars. Many buildings in the Stone Town date from the 19th-Century slave boom. Houses reflect their builder's wealth: Arab houses have plain outer walls and large front doors leading to an inner courtyard; Indian houses have a more open facade and large balconies decorated with railings and balustrades. Most are still occupied.

A striking feature of many houses are the brass studded doors and elaborately-carved frames. The size of a door and intricacy of its

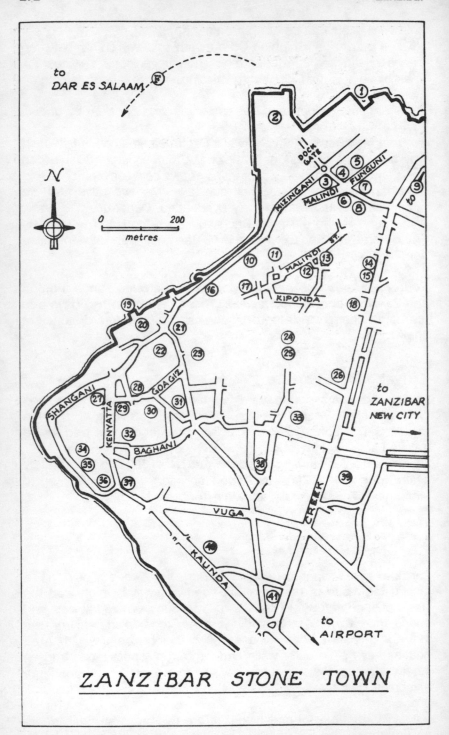

to
DAR ES SALAAM

N

0   200
metres

DOCK GATE

to ZANZIBAR NEW CITY

to AIRPORT

ZANZIBAR STONE TOWN

1   Old Dhow Harbour
2   New Dock
3   Malindi Restaurant
4   Ciné Afrique
5   Warere Guesthouse
6   Malindi Guesthouse
7   Malindi Sports Club (Dhow Office)
8   Malindi Police Station
9   Bwawani Hotel
10 Sea View Indian Restaurant
11 Ijumaa Mosque
12 Pyramid Hotel
13 Narrow Street Hotel
14 Peoples Bank of Zanzibar
15 Zanzibar Tourist Corporation
16 Peoples Palace
17 Kiponda Hotel
18 Maharouky Bicycle Hire
19 Floating Restaurant
20 Jamituri Gardens
21 House of Wonders
22 Arab Fort
23 Sama Tours
24 Spice Inn
25 Emerson's House
26 Market
27 Le Pecheur Bar
28 Yoghurt Shop
29 Post Office
30 St. Josephs Catholic Cathedral
31 Epicure Snack Bar
32 Dolphin Restaurant
33 UMCA Anglican Cathedral
34 Tippo Tip's House
35 Jasfa Tours
36 Africa House Hotel
37 Camlur's Restaurant
38 Flamingo Inn
39 Jamhuri Gardens
40 Peoples Gardens
41 National Museum

ZANZIBAR STONE TOWN

design was an indication of the owner's wealth and status. The use of studs probably originated in Persia or India, where they helped prevent doors being knocked down by war-elephants. In Zanzibar, studs were purely decorative.

The area outside the Stone Town used to be called Ng'ambo (*The Other Side*), and is now called Michenzani (*New City*). Attempts have been made to modernise it: at the centre of Michenzani are some ugly apartment blocks, built by East German engineers as part of an international aid scheme.

Walking is the easiest way to get around Zanzibar Town. Buses, pick-up vans (called *dala-dalas*) and taxis are available. You can also hire bikes and motor-scooters.

Where to stay

In the last few years, many new hotels of all grades have opened in Zanzibar Town. A small selection is listed below. Hotel rooms must be paid for in hard currency. Most prices include breakfast.

UPPER RANGE

Hotel Ya Bwawani   (PO Box 670, tel: 30200). On the northern edge of the Stone Town, this is supposedly the island's premier hotel. It's a shabby concrete block, lacking in style or atmosphere, and overpriced at $75 s/c double.

Emerson's House   (PO Box 4044, tel: 32153). This hotel in the heart of the Stone Town is tastefully decorated and has a stylish atmosphere. Good value. Doubles cost from $60 to $85.

Spice Inn   (PO Box 1029, tel: 30728). This older hotel has a feel of faded elegance. It is reasonable value at $30 a double or $45 s/c double.

MODERATE

Narrow Street Hotel   (PO Box 3784, tel: 32620). This small place is friendly and clean. $35 s/c double. Two annexes offer more basic doubles for $30 and $25.

Hotel Kiponda   (PO Box 3446, tel: 33052). This small quiet hotel near the sea, once a sultan's harem, has been renovated in local style. $20 double or $25 s/c double.

Malindi Guesthouse   (tel: 30165). Near the port, this is a popular place with a lot of character. $12/20 single/double, or $5 for a bed in a dormitory.

Flamingo Inn   In the centre of the Stone Town, this is another popular place. $14 double.

Garden Lodge   This new place near Victoria Gardens is spartan but clean. $14 double.

BUDGET

Pyramid Hotel   (PO Box 254, tel 33000). Near the sea and just behind the Ijumaa Mosque, this place is popular and clean. Rooms have mosquito nets and fans. $6/10 single/double.

Riverman Hotel   This new hotel behind the Empire Cinema is spotlessly clean and has good facilities. They can hire out bikes and scooters. From $7 per person.

Warere Guesthouse   Very near the port, this place is slightly drab but nevertheless popular. $10 double.

Mtoni Sunset Beach Hotel   This hotel, about 4km north of Zanzibar Town, is popular with budget travellers. Rooms start at $5 per person, but this is sometimes negotiable.

If you come into Zanzibar by boat, expect to be met by a group of hotel touts. Some are quite aggressive, but others are friendly and will find you a suitable hotel if you tell them what you want. It won't cost anything (the tout gets a commission from the hotel) and may save a lot of walking.

Where to eat

Emerson's House and the **Hotel Kiponda** both have good upper-range restaurants serving speciality Zanzibar and sea-food dishes. Meals cost between $5 and $10.

There are other restaurants catering mainly for tourists. The **Sea View Indian Restaurant** serves spicy snacks and good curries (including vegetarian) from about $2.50. The **Floating Restaurant** does basic meals from about $1.50. The **Dolphin Restaurant** serves mainly sea-food meals for around $2.50. At **Camlur's** Goan specialities such as fish and coconut curry start at about $4.

You can eat cheaply in the evening in the Malindi area, near the Ciné Afrique Cinema, where stalls sell cakes, chapatis, samosas and mandazi. In the nearby streets several simple eating houses, including the **Malindi Restaurant** and the **Passing Show Hotel**, cater mainly for locals.

On the sea-front, opposite the House of Wonders, is Jamituri Gardens, a gathering place for local people in the evenings, where stalls serve cheap snacks and drinks.

For a snack, **The Yoghurt Shop** sells tasty home-made yoghurts and milk drinks, and **Epicure** sells good salads and soups, herb teas, spices and many other delicacies, including 'Arabic pizzas'. Both are near Saint Joseph's Cathedral in the Baghani area.

Most tourist restaurants serve beer and many of the larger hotels have separate bars. The roof-top bar at the **Africa House Hotel** is popular at sunset. **La Pecheur Bar**, next to the Fisherman Restaurant, is the nearest thing in Zanzibar to a pub. It gets lively later in the evening.

Excursions

The Stone Town

You can spend many idle hours wandering through the fascinating labyrinth of narrow streets and alleyways of the old Stone Town. The following are some of the more interesting sights:

The market The market is worth a visit even if you don't want to buy anything. It's a vibrant place where you can buy anything from fish and bread to sewing machines and second-hand car spares.

The People's Palace Overlooking the sea on the western edge of the Stone Town, this large white building with castellated battlements was built in the late 1890s. It was the official residence of the Sultan of Zanzibar from 1911 until the 1964 revolution, after which it was renamed the People's Palace. It is now a government office and closed to the public. Photos are not allowed.

House of Wonders This square multi-storey building next to the People's Palace is surrounded by tiers of impressive balconies and topped by a clock tower. It was built as a ceremonial palace in 1883, and was the first building on Zanzibar to have electric lights. Local people called it *Beit el Ajaib*, meaning the House of Wonders. Until recently it was the CCM party headquarters. It is now closed, but you can see the huge carved doors and two old bronze cannons with Portuguese inscriptions from the outside.

The Arab Fort Next to the House of Wonders, this large brown building with castellated battlements was built by the Omani in the early 18th Century. It is open to visitors. You can reach the top of the battlements and go into some of the towers.

Tippu Tip's House Tippu Tip was an influential 19th-Century slave trader. He knew the African interior well and helped explorers such as Livingstone and Stanley with supplies and route-planning. The house where he lived is near the Africa House Hotel, behind the offices of Jasfa Tours. It is privately owned and closed to visitors, but the huge carved front door can be seen from the street.

Saint Joseph's Catholic Cathedral This large cathedral with prominent twin spires is in the Baghani part of town. It was built between 1896 and 1898 by French missionaries and local converts. There are now few Catholics on Zanzibar. The cathedral is rarely used and it is closed to the public.

The Anglican Cathedral The Cathedral of the Universities Mission in Central Africa (UMCA) is on the eastern side of the Stone Town. It was built over the slave market after it closed in 1873, and was completed in 1880. Tradition has it the altar stands on the site of the market's whipping block. Nothing of the slave market remains, though the cellar of the nearby St Monica's Guesthouse is reputed to be the remains of a pit where slaves were kept before being sold.

Sultan Barghash, who closed the slave market, is reputed to have asked Bishop Steere, leader of the mission, not to build the cathedral tower higher than the House of Wonders. When the Bishop agreed, the Sultan presented the cathedral with its clock.

The foundation of the UMCA was inspired by Livingstone: a window is dedicated to his memory and the church's crucifix is made from the tree under which his heart was buried in present-day Zambia. Several other missionaries are remembered on plaques around the cathedral wall, as are sailors who were killed fighting the slave trade and servicemen who died in action in East Africa during World War One.

The cathedral is open to visitors. You should show respect when inside and leave a donation if you can.

The National Museum The informative and well-organised museum, at the southern end of the Stone Town, has sections on archaeology, slavery, palaces, sultans, explorers, missionaries, traditional crafts, coins, and clove cultivation. In the annexe there is a library, and a natural history collection where dodo bones are exhibited. In the garden, a group of giant tortoises do their best to keep the grass short. The museum is open from 9.00am to 12.30am and 3.30pm to 6.00pm every day except Sunday. There is a small entrance charge. You may be asked to make an extra donation by the somewhat over-enthusiastic curator.

Near Zanzibar Town

Many travellers go on organised tours to the spice plantations. Known as spice-tours, these often include a visit to one of the island's ruins. Tour companies can arrange trips to other parts of the island, such as Jozani Forest Reserve, and boat trips to Chunguu Island. They can also help you with hotel, ship and flight reservations, car hire, and so on. Recommended companies include Jasfa Tours, near the Africa House Hotel (PO Box 4203, tel 30468), Dolphin Tours near the UMCA cathedral (PO Box 138, tel 33386), Sama Tours behind the fort, (PO Box 2276, tel 33543), and Sun and Fun Safaris in the Seaview Indian Restaurant (PO Box 666, tel 32132).

Spice tours can be arranged through independent guides, known locally as *papasi* after a kind of insect. They are cheaper than tour companies, but their tours are often shorter and do not include a proper guide, which will detract greatly from your enjoyment and understanding of what you see. *Papasi* are worth using for boat trips, however, or to arrange transport to the east coast. Some taxi drivers also organise spice tours. Recommended guides include Mr Mitu, who can be found near the Ciné Afrique, and Saleh Mreh, who can also organise special environmental tours.

Except for the islands, all the places listed below can be visited independently; by scooter or bike, or by a combination of foot and public transport. Maharouky Bicycle Hire (which is also a small grocery shop) between the market and the petrol station rents out bikes for $0.50 per hour or $4 per 24 hours. Nasor Aly Mussa's Scooter Service, near the UMCA cathedral, rents out motor scooters for around $20 per day.

Dala-dalas (pick-ups) carry passengers around town and to outlying suburbs. All routes start at the Darajani Bus Station on Creek Road. Route B goes past the Marahubi and Mtoni palaces to Bububu, from where you can walk to Fuji Beach, or the baths at Kidichi.

Marahubi Palace This palace, on the coast about 3km north of Zanzibar Town, was built in 1882 for the concubines of Sultan Barghash. At one time he kept around 100 women here. The palace was destroyed by fire in 1899; all that remains are the great pillars which supported the upper storey, and the Persian-style bath-house. You can also see the separate bathrooms for the women, the large bath used by the Sultan, and the original water tanks, now overgrown with lilies.

Mtoni Palace   The ruins of Mtoni Palace lie a short way north of Marahubi. Mtoni is the oldest palace on Zanzibar, built for Sultan Said in the 1840s. A book written by his daughter Salme describes the palace in the 1850s. At one end of the house was a large bath-house, at the other the quarters where Said lived with his principal wife. Gazelles and peacocks wandered around the large courtyard. Mtoni was abandoned before 1885. Only the main walls and roof remain. It was used as a warehouse in World War One; evidence of this alteration can still be seen.

Kidichi Persian Baths   These were built in 1850 for Said's wife, Binte Irich Mirza, the grand-daughter of the Shah of Persia, and are decorated with Persian-style stucco. You can enter the bath-house and see the bathing pool and toilets, but there is mould growing on much of the stucco. A colony of bats seems to have taken up residence. To get there from Bububu, a village on the main road north of Zanzibar Town, turn right into a dirt road and follow it for about 4km. The baths are the low white building on the right.

Kizimbani Persian Baths   These baths near Kidichi were also built in the Persian style for Said. They are not decorated inside. The plantations surrounding Kizimbani originally belonged to Saleh bin Haramil, the Arab trader who imported the first cloves to Zanzibar.

Mangapwani   Near this village, 20km north of Zanzibar Town, are a large natural cavern and a man-made slave cave. The natural coral cavern has a narrow entrance and a pool of fresh water at its lowest point. The Slave Cave, a square cell cut into the coral, was used to hold slaves after the trade was abolished in 1873. The natural cavern may also have been used to hide slaves, but this is not certain.

To get to Mangapwani village, take the main road to Chuini then follow the left fork towards Bumbwini for 7km. There are occasional buses to Mangapwani on Route 2.

At Mangapwani, a road forks left towards the coast. About 2km past the village this road ends and a small track branches off to the right. Follow this for 1km to reach the Slave Cave. About halfway between Mangapwani and the track to the Slave Cave, a narrow track to the left leads to the natural cavern.

Fuji Beach   This is the nearest swimming beach to Zanzibar Town. Nearby is a small cafe where the staff will look after your gear while you swim. Fuji is just past Bububu village.

Islands near Zanzibar Town

Several small islands lie near Zanzibar Town. Boat-trips arranged
with a tour company or independent guide cost from $20 to $60. To
cut the individual cost, get a group together.

Changuu Island   Changuu was originally owned by a wealthy Arab
who used it as a detention centre for disobedient slaves. It is also
known as Prison Island; a prison was built on it in 1893, but was
never used. A path circles the island (about an hour's easy stroll).
There is a small beach, a restaurant and a guest house. Masks and
flippers can be hired for snorkelling. The island is home to several
giant tortoises, probably brought from the Seychelles in the 18th
Century, which seem much of their time mating. This long and noisy
process is apparently successful: the tortoise population is said to
be growing. A fee of $1 per person must be paid in hard currency.

Chapwani Island   Chapwani, also called Grave Island, has held a
Christian cemetery since 1879. Most of the graves belong to British
sailors who were killed fighting Arab slave ships; others date from
World War One. There is a small beach.

Useful information

Zanzibar Tourist Corporation   ZTC is the state travel service. You
can make bookings for all **ZTC bungalows** at the main office in
Livingstone House (PO Box 216, tel 32344) on the northeast side of
town. The ZTC office on Creek Road, near Kenya Airways, sells good
maps of Zanzibar.

Banks and forex bureaux   The People's Bank of Zanzibar is near
the Fort. There are several forex bureaux in Zanzibar Town.

Post and Telephones   The main post office in the new part of town
has a post restante service. To make international phone calls, you
can also use the old post office on Kenyatta Road, in the Shangani
area.

Hospitals and Pharmacies   The main public hospital on Zanzibar
Island is at Mnazi Moja, on the south side of the Stone Town. Private
medical centres include Island Private Hospital, on Soko Muhogo
Street, tel 31837; Afya Medical Hospital, near the Zanzibar Hotel, tel
31228; and Mkunazini Hospital, near the market, tel 30076.

Air companies   The Air Tanzania office is on Vuga Road, near its junction with Creek Road. The Kenya Airways office is at the northern end of Creek Road. Air Zanzibar Ltd (PO Box 1784, tel 33098) charter flights throughout East Africa. If a plane is flying empty, spare seats are sold to the public. Seats on the newspaper-plane to Dar es Salaam are sold at Musoma Bookshop near the market and cost around $40.

Dhows The agent for dhows out of Zanzibar has an office in the Malindi Sports Club on Malawi Road, almost opposite the Police Station.

THE EAST COAST

This is where you will find the idyllic tropical beaches you dreamed about during those interminable bus rides on the mainland: clean white sand, lined with palms and lapped by the warm blue water of the Indian Ocean. Some travellers come here for a couple of days, just to relax after seeing the sights of Zanzibar Town, and end up staying for a couple of weeks. Visitors on tighter time restrictions always wish they could stay for longer...

The most popular stretch of coast is in the south, between Bwejuu and Makunduchi. There is plenty of accommodation here, and most hotels have restaurants. You can usually buy fish and vegetables in the villages, but supplies are limited; if you are self-catering, stock up in Zanzibar Town.

Getting there and away

The East Coast can be reached by rented car, scooter or bike. You can also go by bus: no 9 goes to Paje (and sometimes either Bwejuu or Jambiani) and no 10 goes to Makunduchi. Normally one bus leaves Zanzibar Town daily, in the market area. Buses are cheap but slow.

Several tour companies and some independent guides arrange minibuses to the popular East Coast beaches. There is normally at least one vehicle a day in each direction, costing between $3 and $5 per person each way. Unless you specify where you want to stay, minibus drivers prefer to take you to a hotel that gives them commission.

Where to stay

Half a dozen ZTC bungalows are dotted around Zanzibar Island. These used to be the only out-of-town accommodation and are simple, somewhat delapidated buildings, costing around $20 for the whole building. This includes the services of a caretaker. For information and reservations go to the ZTC office in Livingstone House in Zanzibar Town.

Paje

There are two guest houses in this village: the **Ufukwe** and **Amani**. Double rooms cost $5 per person, including breakfast.

Bwejuu

Bwejuu village is north of Paje. The clean and basic **ZTC bungalow** costs $20 if booked through the ZTC office, but you could try to make an arrangement with the caretaker if you only want one room.

Rooms in **Dere Guest House** cost $5 per person, including breakfast. Bungalows cost $15 for up to four people. Meals at the restaurant are good value at around $1.25.

Double rooms at the smarter **Palm Beach Hotel** cost $10 per person; beach bungalows cost $20 s/c double. The restaurant serves local meals for between $2.50 and $5. Advance orders are appreciated. The bar sells beer.

You can explore the offshore reef with snorkelling gear hired from the Dere Guesthouse (around $3 per day). You can also hire bikes (same price) from the hotel and cycle a few kilometres up the beach to a point where the reef can be more easily reached.

Jambiani

Jambiani is south of Paje, and spreads for several kilometres down the coast. The **Horizontal Inn** and **Manufaa Guesthouse** are both small family-run places where clean rooms cost $5 per person, including breakfast. Lunch and dinner cost $2 to $3, and must be ordered several hours in advance. The **ZTC bungalow**, in the usual style for the usual price, appears to be little-used.

About 2km further south, self-contained rooms at the smarter **Jambiani Beach Hotel** cost $10 per person. The restaurant serves local dishes for between $3 and $6. It has a bar.

A further 1km south, rooms at the friendly and clean **Shehe Guesthouse** cost $5 per person, including breakfast. A shop sells biscuits, sodas, and a few items of tinned food. The cafeteria serves fixed-menu lunch and dinner for around $3. Meals must be ordered several hours in advance.

Makunduchi

Makunduchi New Town is at the southern end of the island. Despite the grand title, it is only a large village, though it does have a bank and a post office. Two **ZTC bungalows** offer the usual facilities for the usual price. Rooms at the **Kigaeni Reef Lodge** cost $5 per person, including breakfast. You can also camp in the garden for $3. It has a basic restaurant. Fishing and snorkelling trips can be arranged.

Excursions

On the way to the East Coast beaches, you pass two places of interest: the Bi Khole Ruins and Jozani Forest. If you are in a group, you can arrange for a tourist minibus to stop on the way. Alternatively, these places can be reached as a day-trip from Zanzibar Town.

Bi Khole Ruins

The Bi Khole Ruins are about 6km south of the village of Tunguu, to the west of the main Zanzibar Town-east coast road. Khole was a daughter of Sultan Said (Bi is a title meaning Lady). The house was used up to the 1920s, but only the main walls now stand. The main road there passes through a splendid boulevard of gnarled old mango trees, supposedly planted for Khole. The track to the ruins branches off about halfway down this.

Jozani Forest Reserve

This remnant of the indigenous forest which once covered much of central Zanzibar is home to several rare mammals. Two endemic subspecies, Kirk's red colobus monkey and Zanzibar leopard, are found nowhere else; Ader's duiker is found only in Jozani and in one forest in Kenya. Unfortunately all these animals are shy and rarely seen, and Zanzibar leopard may even be extinct. You are more likely to see the common blue monkey. The entrance to Jozani is off the main road, a few kilometres south of Pete.

Kizimkazi Mosque

At the small settlement of Dimbani, near Kizimkazi village west of Makunduchi, are the remains of the oldest known mosque in East Africa. Kufic inscriptions date it to 1107 AD. Kizimkazi was then a large walled-city, traditionally founded by a king called Kizi. Little of the city remains, but the mosque has been rebuilt several times, most recently in about 1800.

The Kufic inscriptions, around the niche at the eastern end of the mosque (facing Mecca), are in the decorative floriate style. Similar inscriptions have been found in old buildings in Persia. The silver pillars on either side of the niche are decorated with pounded shells from Mafia Island. Two decorative clocks, which show Swahili time, were presented by local dignitaries. Recently-installed electrical sockets do not have a comparable degree of style or decoration.

To see inside the mosque, now protected by a corrugated iron roof, you must find the caretaker who lives nearby. It is respectful to cover any bare limbs and take off your shoes when you enter.

PEMBA

Pemba Island lies northeast of Zanzibar, and directly east of Tanga. It is smaller than Zanzibar and has a more undulating landscape. It is also more densely vegetated, both with natural forest and plantation; it now produces more cloves than Zanzibar does. Few tourists visit Pemba and facilities are limited. For many people, this is its main attraction.

During holidays, traditional bull fights are sometimes held on Pemba. The origins of this sport are uncertain; it may have been a Portuguese introduction. Pemba is a centre for traditional medicine and witchcraft. People seeking cures for spiritual or physical afflictions come from Zanzibar Island and the mainland — even as far away as Uganda and Zaire — to see Pemba's doctors.

The island's largest town is Chake Chake, north of which lies the main port, Wete. Mkoani is a smaller port in the southwest. There are banks and post offices in Chake Chake, Wete and Mkoani, but only the Chake Chake bank can change travellers cheques. The main hospital in is Chake Chake. There is a ZTC office next to the ZTC Hotel in Chake Chake.

Getting there and away

Air Tanzania flies between Zanzibar and Chake Chake a few times a week, but is notoriously unreliable. A charter company, Air Zanzibar, flies the same route. Spare seats cost around $35.

ZSC ships go between Zanzibar and Mkoani twice a week; they are cheap but unreliable. Dhows sometimes sail between Zanzibar and Mkoani, but there is no schedule; enquire at the Malindi Sports Club (see *Zanzibar Town*).

Dhows between Pemba and Tanga or Mombasa are irregular and

less than idyllic. Mapicha Travelling Agency on the main street in Wete knows about dhows to Tanga.

The Flying Horse and Sea Express are due to operate between Mombasa, Tanga, Pemba and Zanzibar in 1993.

Where to stay/eat

There is a **ZTC hotel** in each of Chake Chake, Wete and Mkoani. Identical in style (angular concrete), they are all run down but clean and cost $20 double, including breakfast.

Sharook Guest House in Wete is a simple family-run place near the bus station ($5 per person). The private guest house due to open in Mkoani in 1993 will cost about the same; contact Faizin Tours (see *Tour Companies* below) for details.

Meals at the ZTC hotels cost between $2 and $4. The **Standard Cafe** and **Naas Restaurant** in Chake Chake and the **Annuwar Restaurant** in Wete serve cheap, basic meals. There is a pleasant open-air cafe at the end of Wete's main street.

Excursions

Chake Chake is linked to Wete by bus and dala-dala number 6, and to Mkoani by number 3. These normally run in the morning.

You can sometimes hire bicycles through the receptionist at the ZTC Hotel in Chake Chake, or through Faizin Tours in Mkoani. A Mr Nassour, contactable through the ZTC Hotel in Chake Chake, rents out a Suzuki 4x4 and driver for about $20 per day (petrol is extra). If you want to visit Mesali Island or the Ras Mkumbuu Ruins by boat, he also rents out a motor boat for about $35 per day (including petrol and captain).

Faizin Tours in Mkoani (PO Box 70, Mkoani, tel 6028 or PO Box 702, Zanzibar Town, tel 32501) is a cooperative encouraging small-scale environmentally-sensitive tourism on Pemba. They can arrange trips to Mesali Island or the beach at Wambaa Bay.

Ras Mkumbuu Ruins These 11th-Century ruins on the end of the peninsula west of Chake Chake include the remains of a mosque and several pillar-tombs. The most enjoyable way to reach Ras Mkumbuu is by boat, combined with a visit to Mesali Island.

Mesali Island This small island west of Chake Chake is surrounded by a coral reef. Its idyllic beach is good for swimming, especially if you have a mask and snorkel. The notorious pirate Captain Kidd is reputed to have had a hideout here in the 17th Century.

Pujini Ruins This is about 10km southeast of Chake Chake. You can walk there and back in a day, but it is easier to travel by hired bike or car. The ruins are the remains of a 13th-Century Swahili town, locally-known as Mkame Ndume (*milker of men*) after a despotic king who forced the inhabitants to carry large stones for the town walls while shuffling on their buttocks. The overgrown remains of the walls and ditches can be seen, as can a walkway which joined the town to the shore, some wide stairways that presumably allowed access to the defensive ramparts, and the site of the town's well.

Appendix One

Communicating in Swahili

INTRODUCTION

Swahili, the official language of Tanzania, is a Bantu language which developed on the East African coast about 1,000 years ago and has since adopted several words from Arabic, Portuguese, Indian, German and English. It spread into the Tanzanian interior along with the 19th-Century slave caravans and is now the *lingua franca* in Tanzania and Kenya, and is also spoken in parts of Uganda, Malawi, Rwanda, Burundi, Zaire, Zambia and Mozambique.

Even if you are sticking to tourist areas, it is polite and can be useful to know a bit of Swahili. In Dar es Salaam, Zanzibar, Arusha, Moshi and the northern game reserves, you can get by with English well enough. If you travel in other parts of the country, you will need to understand some Swahili.

There are numerous Swahili-English dictionaries on the market, as well as phrasebooks and grammars. The most useful dictionary is D.V. Perrot's *Concise Swahili and English Dictionary* (Hodder and Stoughton, 1965) as it has two sections — one translating each way — as well as a basic grammar. Peter Wilson's *Simplified Swahili* (Longmans) is regarded as the best book for teaching yourself Swahili. Of the phrasebooks, Lonely Planet's is probably the best. It is best to buy a Swahili book before you arrive in Tanzania; they are difficult to get hold of once you are there.

For short-stay visitors, all these books have practical limitations. Wading through a phrasebook to find the expression you want can take ages, while trying to piece together a sentence from a dictionary is virtually impossible. In addition, most books available are in Kenyan Swahili, which often differs greatly from the purer version spoken in Tanzania.

The following introduction is not a substitute for a dictionary or phrasebook. It is not so much an introduction to Swahili as an introduction to communicating with Swahili speakers. Before researching this guide, my East African travels had mainly been in Kenya, Uganda and parts of Tanzania where English is relatively widely-spoken. We learnt the hard way how little English is spoken in most of Tanzania. I hope this section will help anyone in a similar position to get around a great deal more easily than we did at first.

Pronunciation

Vowel sounds are pronounced as follows:

a   like the a in *father*
e   like the e in *wet*
i   like the ee in *free*, but less drawn-out
o   somewhere between the o in *no* and the word *awe*
u   similar to the oo in *food*

The double vowel in words like *choo* or *saa* is pronounced like the single vowel, but drawn out for longer.

Consonants are in general pronounced as they are in English. *L* and *r* are often interchangeable, so that *Kalema* is just as often spelt or pronounced *Karema*. The same is true of *b* and *v*.

You will be better understood if you speak slowly and thus avoid the common English-speaking habit of clipping vowel sounds — listen to how Swahili-speakers pronounce their vowels. In most Swahili words there is a slight emphasis on the second last syllable.

Basic Grammar

Swahili is a simple language in so far as most words are built from a root word using prefixes. To go into all of the prefixes here would probably confuse people new to Swahili — and it would certainly stretch my knowledge of the language. They are covered in depth in most Swahili grammars and dictionaries. The following are some of the most important:

Pronouns

ni	me
u	you
tu	us
wa	they
a	he or she

Tenses

na	present
ta	future
li	past
ku	infinitive

Tenses (negative)

si	present
sita	future
siku	past
haku	negative infinitive

From a root word such as *taka* (want) you might build the following phrases:

Unataka soda	You want a soda
Tutataka soda	We will want a soda
Alitaka soda	He/she wanted a soda

In practice, *ni* and *tu* are often dropped from simple statements. It would be more normal to say *nataka soda* than *ninataka soda*.

In many situations there is no interrogative mode in Swahili; the difference between a question and a statement lies in the intonation.

Greetings

There are several common greetings in Swahili. Although allowances are made for tourists, it is rude to start talking to someone without first using one or other formal greeting.

The first greeting you will hear is *Jambo*. This is reserved for tourists, and a perfectly adequate greeting, but it is never used between Tanzanians (the more correct *Hujambo*, to which the reply is *Sijambo*, is used in some areas).

The most widely-used greeting is *Habari*, which more-or-less means *What news*. The polite reply is *Mzuri* (good). *Habari* is rarely used by Tanzanians on its own; you might well be asked *Habari ya safari*, *Habari ako* or *Habari gani* (very loosely, *How is your journey*, *How are you* and *How are things* respectively). *Mzuri* is the polite reply to any such request.

When we were in Tanzania, *Mambo* was a fashionable greeting, especially on the coast. Few tourists recognise this greeting; reply *Safi* and you've made a friend.

In Tanzanian society it is polite to greet elders with the expression *Shikamu*. To the best of my knowledge this means *I hold your feet*. In many parts of rural Tanzania, children will greet you in this way, often with their heads bowed and so quietly it sounds like *Sh..oo*. Don't misinterpret this by European standards (or other parts of Africa where *Mzungu give me shilling* is the phrase most likely to be offered up by children); most Tanzanian children are far too polite to swear at you. The polite answer is *Marahaba* (I'm delighted).

Another word often used in greeting in *Salama*, which means peace. When you enter a shop or hotel reception, you will often be greeted by a friendly *Karibu*. This means *Welcome*. *Asante sana* (thank you very much) seems an appropriate response.

If you want to enter someone's house, shout *Hodi!*. It basically means *Can I come in?* but would be used in the same situation as *Anyone home?* would in English. The normal response will be *Karibu* or *Hodi*.

It is respectful to address an old man as *Mzee*. *Bwana*, which means *Mister*, might be used as a polite form of address to a male who is equal or senior to you in age or rank, but who is not a *Mzee*. Older women can be addressed as *Mama*.

The following phrases will come in handy for small talk:

Where have you just come from?	*(U)natoka wapi?*
I have come from Moshi	*(Ni)natoka Moshi*
Where are you going?	*(U)nakwenda wapi?*
We are going to Arusha	*(Tu)nakwende Arusha*
What is your name?	*Jina lako nani?*
My name is Philip	*Jina langu ni Philip*
Do you speak English?	*Unasema KiEngereze?*
I speak a little Swahili	*Ninasema KiSwahili kidigo*
Sleep peacefully	*Kulala salama*
Bye for now	*Kwaheri sasa*
Have a safe journey	*Safari njema*
Come again (welcome again)	*Karibu tena*
I don't understand	*Sielewi*
Say that again	*Sema tena*

Counting

1	*moja*	40	*arobaini*
2	*mbili*	50	*hamsini*
3	*tatu*	60	*sitini*
4	*nne*	70	*sabani*
5	*tano*	80	*themanini*
6	*sita*	90	*tisini*
7	*saba*	100	*mia (moja)*
8	*nane*	150	*mia moja hamsini*
9	*tisa*	155	*mia moja hamsini na*
10	*kumi*		*tano*
11	*kumi na moja*	200	*mia mbili*
20	*ishirini*	1,000	*elfu (moja)* or *mia kumi*
30	*thelathini*		

Swahili time

Many travellers to Tanzania fail to come to grips with Swahili time. It is essential to be aware of it, especially if you are catching buses in remote areas. The Swahili clock starts at the equivalent of 6.00am, so that *saa moja asubuhi* (hour one in the morning) is 7.00am, *saa mbili jioni* (hour two in the evening) is 8.00pm etc. To ask the time in Swahili, say *Saa ngape?*.

Always check whether times are standard or Swahili. If you are told a bus leaves at nine, ask whether the person means *saa tatu* or *saa tisa*. Some English speakers will convert to standard time, others won't. This does not apply so much where people are used to tourists, but it's advisable to get in the habit of checking.

Day-to-day queries

The following covers such activities as shopping, finding a room etc. It's worth remembering most Swahili words for modern objects, or things for which there would not have been a pre-colonial word, are often similar to the English. Examples are *resiti* (receipt), *gari* (car), *polisi* (police), *posta* (post office) and — my favourite — *stesheni masta* (station master). In desperation, its always worth trying the English word with an *ee* sound on the end.

Shopping

The normal way of asking for something is *Ipo?*, which roughly means *Is there?*, so if you want a cold drink you would ask *Ipo soda baridi?*. The response will normally be *Ipo* or *Kuna* (there is) or *Hamna* or *Hakuna* (there isn't). Once you've established the shop has what you want, you might ask *Nataka koka mbili* (I want two cokes). To check the price, ask *Shillingi ngape?*. If your Swahili is limited, it is often simpler to ask for a brand name: *Omo* (washing powder) or *Blue Band* (margarine), for instance.

Accommodation

The Swahili for guest house is *nyumba ya wageni*. In my experience *gesti* works as well, if not better. If you are looking for something a bit more upmarket, bear in mind *hoteli* means restaurant. We found self-contained (*self-contendi*) to be a good key-word in communicating this need. To find out whether there is a vacant room, ask *Ipo chumba?*.

Getting around

The following expressions are useful for getting around:

Where is there a guest house?	*Ipo wapi gesti?*
Is there a bus to Moshi?	*Ipo basi kwenda Moshi?*
When does the bus depart?	*Basi ondoka saa ngapi?*

When will the vehicle arrive?   *Gari tafika saa ngapi?*
How far is it?   *Bale gani?*
I want to pay now   *Ninataka kulipa sasa*

Foodstuffs

Avocado	*Parachichi*	Meat	*Nyama*
Bananas	*Ndizi*	Milk	*Maziwa*
Bananas	*Matoke/*	Onions	*Vitungu*
(cooked)	*batoke*	Orange(s)	*(Ma)chungwa*
Beef	*(Nyama ya)*	Pawpaw	*Papai*
	ngombe	Pineapple	*Nanasi*
Bread (loaf)	*Mkate*	Potatoes	*Viazi*
Bread (slice)	*Tosti*	Rice (cooked	*Wali*
Coconuts	*Nazi*	plain	
Coffee	*Kahawa*	Rice (cooked	*Pilau*
Chicken	*Kuku*	Rice	*Mchele*
Egg(s)	*(Ma)yai*	(uncooked)	
Fish	*Samaki*	Salt	*Chumvi*
Food	*Chakula*	Sauce	*Mchuzi/supu*
Fruit(s)	*(Ma)tunda*	Sugar	*Sukari*
Goat	*(Nyama ya)*	Tea	*Chai (ya*
	mbuzi	(black/milky)	*rangi/maziwa*
Maize	*Ugali*	Vegetables	*Mbogo*
porridge		Water	*Maji*
Mango(es)	*(Ma)embe*		

An alphabetical list of useful words and phrases

Afternoon	*Alasiri*	No problem	*Hamna tatizo*
Again	*Tena*	Now	*Sasa*
And	*Na*	Only	*Tu*
Ask (I am	*Omba*	OK or fine	*Sawa*
asking for...)	*(ninaomba...)*	Passenger	*Abiria*
Big	*Kubwa*	Pay	*Kulipa*
Boat	*Meli*	Please	*Tafadhali*
Brother	*Kaka*	Person	*Mtu (watu)*
Bus	*Basi*	(people)	
Car (or any	*Gari*	Road/street	*Barabara/mtaa*
vehicle)		Shop	*Duka*
Child	*Mtoto (watoto)*	Sister	*Dada*
(children)		Sleep	*Kulala*
Cold	*Baridi*	Slowly	*Polepole*

Come here	Njoo	Small	Kidogo
Excuse me	Samahani	Soon	Bado kidogo
European(s)	Mzungu (wasungu)	Sorry	Polepole
		Station	Stesheni
Evening	Jioni	Stop	Simama
Far away	Mbale kubwa	Straight or	Moja kwa
Friend	Rafiki	direct	moja
Good (very good)	Mzuri (mzuri sana)	Thank you (very much)	Asante (sana)
Goodbye	Kwaheri	There is	Ipo/kuna
Here	Hapa	There are	Zipo
Hot	Moto	There is not	Hamna/hakuna
Later	Bado	Thief (thieves)	Mwizi (wawizi)
Like (I would like...)	Penda (ninapenda...)	Time	Saa
Many	Sana	Today	Leo
Me	Mimi	Toilet	Choo
Money	Pesa/shillingi	Tomorrow	Kesho
More	Ingine/tena	Want (I want...)	Taka (ninataka...)
Morning	Asubuhi	Where	(Ipo) wapi
Nearby	Karibu/mbale kidogo	Yes	Ndiyo
Night	Usiku	Yesterday	Jana
No	Hapana	You	Wewe

Useful conjunctions include *ya* (of) and *kwa* (to or by). Many expressions are created using these; for instance *stesheni ya basi* is a bus station and *barabara kwa Moshi* is the road to Moshi.

Days of the week

Monday	Jumatatu
Tuesday	Jumanne
Wednesday	Jumatano
Thursday	Alhamisi
Friday	Ijumaa
Saturday	Jumamosi
Sunday	Jumapili

African English

Although some Tanzanians speak a bit of English, few speak it fluently or grammatically. Africans who speak English tend to structure their sentences in a similar way to how they would in their own language: they speak English with Bantu grammar.

For a traveller, knowing how to communicate in African English is just as important as speaking a bit of Swahili, if not more so. It is noticeable that travellers who speak English as a second language often communicate with Africans more easily than first language English-speakers.

The following ground rules may help you to communicate with people who speak a limited amount of English:

• *Unasema KiEngereze?* (Do you speak English?). This small but important question may seem obvious. It isn't.

• Greet in Swahili then ask in English. It is advisable to go through the Swahili greetings (even *Jambo* will do) before you plough ahead and ask a question. Firstly, it is rude to do otherwise; secondly, most westerners feel uncomfortable asking a stranger a straight question. If you have already greeted the person, you'll feel less need to preface a question with phrases like *I'm terribly sorry* and *Would you mind telling me* which will confuse someone who speaks limited English.

• Speak slowly and clearly. There is no need, as some travellers do, to speak as if you are talking to a three-year old, just speak naturally.

• Phrase questions simply and with Swahili inflections. *This bus goes to Moshi?* is better than *Could you tell me whether this bus is going to Moshi?*; *You have a room?* is better than *is there a vacant room?*. If you are not understood, don't keep repeating the same question, find a different way of phrasing it.

• Listen to how people talk to you, and not only for their inflections. Some English words are in wide use; others are not. For instance *lodging* is more likely to be understood than *accommodation*.

• Make sure the person you are talking to understands you. Try to avoid asking questions that can be answered with a yes or no. People may well agree with you simply to be polite.

• Keep calm. No-one is at their best when they arrive at a crowded bus station after an all-day bus ride; it is easy to be short tempered when someone cannot understand you. Be patient and polite; it's you who doesn't speak the language.

Appendix Two

Further reading

History

The following are recommended as general introductions to African or East African history:

McEvedy, C. *Penguin Atlas of African History* (Penguin 1980)
Oliver, R. & Fage, J.D. *A Short History of Africa* (Penguin 1988, 6th edition)
Oliver, R. & Crowder, M. (eds) *Cambridge History of Africa* (Cambridge, 1982)
Iliffe, J. *A Modern History of Tanganyika* (Cambridge, 1979)
Maxon, R. *East Africa: An Introductory History* (Heinemann 1989)
Odhiambo, E. & Ouso, T. & Williams, J. *A History of East Africa* (Longmans, 1977)
Sutton, J. *A Thousand Years of East Africa* (British Institute in East Africa, 1990)

Oliver and Fage's *Short History* has a thorough and useful further reading section. The following books cover the era of European exploration and colonisation:

Moorehead, A. *The White Nile* (Hamish Hamilton; Penguin 1960)
Hibbert, C. *Africa Explored: Europeans in the Dark Continent* (Penguin 1982)
Packenham, T. *The Scramble for Africa* (Wiedenfield and Nicholson 1991).

Background to National Parks

For most visitors, the excellent series of booklets issued by Tanzania National Parks will be more than adequate. These are usually available from the National Parks Office in Arusha for $2.50, or from stalls in Arusha and Dar es Salaam for around $5. There are booklets for the Ngorongoro Conservation Area and Arusha,

Tarangire, Kilimanjaro, Serengeti, Lake Manyara, Ruaha, Mikumi and Gombe Stream National Parks. The Gombe Stream booklet is also useful if you are visiting Mahale Mountains.

If you are interested in the poaching problem in Tanzania, Nicholas Gordon's *Ivory Knights* (Chapmans 1991) makes compelling reading.

A number of field studies and photographic books cover individual national parks.

Gombe Stream
Goodall, J. *In the Shadow of Man* (Collins 1971)
Goodall, J. *Through a Window* (Wiedenfield and Nicholson 1990)

Mahale Mountains
Nishida, T. *The Chimpanzees of Mahale* (University of Tokyo, 1990).

Serengeti
Grzimek, B. *Serengeti Shall Not Die* (Collins, 1959)
Goodall, J. & Van Lawick, H. *Innocent killers* (Houghton Mifflin 1971)
Hanby, J. & Bygott, D. *Lions Share* (Collins 1981)
Schaller, G. *Serengeti: A Kingdom of Predators* (Collins 1973)
Iwago, M. *Serengeti* (Thomas and Hudson 1987)
Van Lawick, H. *Savage Paradise* (Collins 1977)
Van Lawick, H. *Among Predators and Prey* (Elm Tree 1986)

Lake Manyara
Douglas-Hamilton, I. *Amongst the Elephants* (Penguin 1978)
Matthiessen, P. and van Lawick, H. *Sand Rivers* (Aurum 1981)

Kilimanjaro
Reader, J. *Kilimanjaro* (Elm Tree Books 1982)
Savage, M. *The Walker's Guide and Map to Kilimanjaro*

The Rift Valley
Willock, C. *Africa's Rift Valley* (Time-Life International 1974)
Smith, A. *The Great Rift: Africa's Changing Valley* (BBC 1988).

Both of these are coffee-table in style, but have informative text. The latter is based on an excellent BBC three-part documentary.

Field Guides

The following will be adequate for most visitors' needs:

Dorst, J. and Dandelot, P. *A Field Guide to the Larger Mammals of Africa* (Collins 1970)
Blundell, M. *A Field Guide to the Wild Flowers of East Africa* (Collins, 1987)
Carcassan, R. *Handguide to the Butterflies of Africa* (Collins 1971)
Williams, J. and Arlott, N. *A Field Guide to the Birds of East Africa* (Collins, 1980)

The illustrations in Williams's bird guide are mediocre, they only cover half the species recorded in East Africa, and are biased towards species common in Kenya. Some additional species are described in the text, but European migrants are virtually ignored. If you are remotely serious about birds, supplement Williams with a guide to southern African birds. A few are available, of which Kenneth Newman's beautifully-illustrated *Birds of Southern Africa* (Southern Books, 1992 edition) is the most useful in the field and Gordon Maclean's *Roberts' Birds of Southern Africa* (John Voelcker Bird Fund, 6th edition 1993) has the most detailed behavioural information and gives continental distribution (Newman's only gives distribution within southern Africa).

Also useful, especially in southern Tanzania, is Kenneth Newman's *Birds of Malawi* (Southern Books, 1992). This illustrates all of the 60-odd birds found in Malawi but not in southern Africa. It also includes an annotated checklist of all birds found in Malawi, which should prove useful when trying to determine whether a particular bird species will be found in Tanzania. A European field guide will be useful for migrants, but the vast majority of those found in East Africa are in Newman's guide.

Almost without exception, the best African mammal field guides come from South Africa, but until recently none of these has covered species which are only found north of the Zambezi. The appearance of Chris and Tilde Stuart's *Southern, Central and East African mammals: A photographic Guide* (Struik 1993) is therefore highly welcome. It's remarkably lightweight but very thorough, with photographs, distribution maps and text covering 152 mammal species; definitely the book I'll take with me next time I visit East Africa. Rather less compact, but highly absorbing if you are interested in animal behaviour, is Richard Estes' *The Safari Companion* (Russel Friedman Books, South Africa; Chelsea Green, USA; Green Books, UK, 1992), which contains detailed behavioural studies of virtually all the large mammal species found in East and southern Africa.

When I was last there, a good range of South African-published field guides was available at most large bookshops in central London.

Travel Guides

Two other travel guides are available to Tanzania, both published in Africa. Neither have much practical information, but they are strong on background. I enjoyed Gratian Luhikula's *Tourist Guide to Tanzania* (Travel Promotion Services, Dar es Salaam 1991 edition) for its historical information, and would recommend it highly as a companion to this guide. *Spectrum Guide to Tanzania* (Camerapix 1992) is lavishly-illustrated and informative, but not really practical for backpackers. It would make a good memento.

David Else's *Guide to Zanzibar*, also published by Bradt Publications, expands greatly on the information about Zanzibar and Pemba he supplied for this book.

Fiction

Very little fiction has been written about Tanzania. William Boyd's *The Ice-cream War*, set in Tanzania during World War One, is a notable exception, and well worth reading before you go to Tanzania, especially if you plan to visit the Rufiji and Makonde regions. Although it has a fictional setting in West Africa, there are links between the same author's bestselling *Brazzaville Beach* and chimp behaviour first noted at Gombe Stream (I should add these similarities are limited to the chimps; the human characters are fictional).

Even less fiction has been written by Tanzanians: no-one I know (including people who have studied African literature) can name any Tanzanian writers. There are, however, a number of well-known Kenyan authors who write in English: try Ngugi wa Thiongo or Meja Mwenge.

Maps

A number of maps covering East Africa is available. The best is the Austrian-published Freytag-Berndt 1:2,000,000 map. Most European maps seem to get their accommodation information from the same source, and they show plenty of hotels which either never existed or closed years ago. The best map of Tanzania that I have seen is the 1:1,250,000 map produced by BP. This is generally available in Dar es Salaam and Nairobi, but don't bank on it. One major inaccuracy on this map is that Mlalo in the Usambara Mountains is shown in the wrong place (it should be where Mbangala is).

Town plans and 1:50,000 maps of most parts of the country can be bought from the Department of Lands and Surveys on Kivukoni Front in Dar es Salaam.

Bibliography of Tanzania

Darch, C. *Tanzania* (World Bibliographical Series; Clio Press 1988). This series lists and describes every book of importance on a given country. Invaluable to those with special interests or insatiable curiosity.

Further Travels in Africa and the Indian Ocean

Guide to Mauritius by Royston Ellis.
A complete guide to every aspect of Mauritius and its dependency, Rodrigues.

Guide to the Comoro Islands by Ian Thorpe.
Four seldom visited islands lying between Madagascar and Africa.

Guide to Madagascar by Hilary Bradt.
How and where to see the island's spectacular wildlife, rainforests and semi-desert. A complete guide for all budgets.

Guide to South Africa by Philip Briggs.
Budget travel and bird-watching, walks and game parks, beaches and cities, suggested itineraries.

Guide to Namibia by Chris McIntyre.
On and off the beaten track in this sparsely populated country.

No Frills Guide to Zimbabwe and Botswana by David Else.
A handy pocket-sized book full of hard information on where to stay, what to see, and how to get around.

Africa Handbooks: Zaire, Malawi, Senegal, Ivory Coast
Four pocket-sized guides to the less-visited countries of Africa.

Through Africa: the overlander's guide by Bob Swain and Paula Snyder.
Driving, motor-cycling, or mountain-biking through the continent. Preparations, routes, campsites, travellers' tales.

Backpacker's Africa - East and Southern by Hilary Bradt.
Hiking and backpacking off the beaten track with an emphasis on natural history. Covers Ethiopia, Eritrea, and Sudan and countries south.

Backpacker's Africa — West and Central by David Else.
Public transport and hitching, walking and exploring.

Camping Guide to Kenya by David Else.
Describes every official campsite in Kenya plus suggestions for camping wild in the mountains.

Guide to Zanzibar by David Else.
A detailed guide to the islands of Zanzibar and Pemba.

No Frills Guide to Mozambique by Bernhard Skrodzski
The first guide to this former Portuguese colony.

Guide to Uganda by Philip Briggs
All of the country plus gorilla watching in Zaire and Rwanda.

And then there's the rest of the world...
Send for a catalogue from Bradt Publications, 41 Nortoft Road, Chalfont St Peter, Bucks SL9 0LA, England. Tel/Fax: 0494 873478.

INDEX